ARISTOTLE'S ETHICS AND LEGAL RHETORIC

For Josh
who said he wanted a copy of my first book
even if he didn't read it

And for my parents

Aristotle's Ethics and Legal Rhetoric
An Analysis of Language Beliefs and the Law

FRANCES J. RANNEY
Wayne State University, USA

LONDON AND NEW YORK

First published 2005 by Ashgate Publishing

Published 2016 by Routledge
2 Park Square, Milton Park, Abingdon, Oxon OX14 4RN
711 Third Avenue, New York, NY 10017, USA

Routledge is an imprint of the Taylor & Francis Group, an informa business

Copyright © 2005 Frances J. Ranney

Frances J. Ranney has asserted her right under the Copyright, Designs and Patents Act, 1988, to be identified as the author of this work.

All rights reserved. No part of this book may be reprinted or reproduced or utilised in any form or by any electronic, mechanical, or other means, now known or hereafter invented, including photocopying and recording, or in any information storage or retrieval system, without permission in writing from the publishers.

Notice:
Product or corporate names may be trademarks or registered trademarks, and are used only for identification and explanation without intent to infringe.

British Library Cataloguing in Publication Data
Ranney, Frances J.
  Aristotle's Ethics and legal rhetoric : an analysis of
  language beliefs and the law. - (Law, justice and power
  series)
  1. Aristotle. Nichomachean ethics 2. Law - Language 3. Feminist
  jurisprudence 4. Rhetoric, Ancient
  I.Title
  340.1'4

Library of Congress Cataloging-in-Publication Data
Ranney, Frances J.
  Aristotle's ethics and legal rhetoric : an analysis of language beliefs and the
  law / by Frances J. Ranney.
      p. cm. -- (Law, justice, and power)
  Includes bibliographical references and index.
  ISBN 0-7546-2541-9
  1. Aristotle--Ethics. 2. Aristotle. Nicomachean ethics. I. Title. II. Series.

  B491.E7R36 2005
  340'.11--dc22
                                                                2005011819
Transfered to Digital Printing in 2011

ISBN 9780754625414 (hbk)
ISBN 9781138257139 (pbk)

Contents

Acknowledgments		*vii*
Notes		*ix*
1	Rhetoric, Law, Ethics, Feminism	1
2	The Things We Value: Theory, Practice, and Production	19
3	The Things We Say: The Speculations of Legal Science	53
4	The Things We Do: The Activities of the Legal Imagination	81
5	The Things We Make: The Productions of Legal Rhetoric	107
6	Erring for Justice	136
Appendix		*168*
Bibliography		*181*
Index		*193*

Acknowledgments

I wish I could say without drama that my son gave birth to me. This statement is true in a simple way whose expression eludes me. Both by choice and by the necessity of raising an incredibly smart, joyful, and inquisitive child I became the person who wrote—sometimes painfully, often slowly, and occasionally passionately—this book. That child is now an adult, but I have not forgotten either his precocious references to Aristotle as 'that Air-head guy' or his tipping me off, just a few years later, to the rhetoric match in *Rosencrantz and Guildenstern are Dead*. Because of him I know Björk and Nappy Roots; because he has faith in me and in this book I finally finished it. I am constantly inspired by his intelligence, his wit, and his *joie de vivre*.

I have been fortunate also to have had the support of the English Department and Wayne State University through the Josephine Nevins Keal Foundation, a University Research Grant, a Research and Inquiry Grant, and a Minority and Women's Grant that all provided necessary research, financial, and/or sabbatical support. My colleagues and friends at Wayne State University—Ellen Barton, Gwen Gorzelsky, Richard Marback, and Ruth Ray—provided feedback and support in forms professional, personal, and occasionally nutritional. The Law and Humanities Junior Scholars Workshop, especially through senior scholars Nomi Stolzenberg and Margaret Jane Radin, provided comments on an early draft of Chapter 2 that made the rest of this book possible.

Robert R. Johnson, my dissertation director and the person who 'made me' read Book VI of the *Nicomachean Ethics*, has been essential to my life scholarly and otherwise in more ways than I can count. His work is the impetus for everything I've managed to do in this book, and his personal example points the way for me as a scholar, mentor, and friend in the future. My parents, James F. and K. Alaire Ranney, 'understood' even when they didn't understand, and my siblings, Elaine Roy, Arthur Ranney, and Robert Ranney, provided services ranging from dog-sitting to dirges and professional inspiration; all made allowances during both good and difficult family times. Esme, a smiling face at Caribou Coffee, took an interest she didn't have to take and kept me going through the sheer necessity of explaining daily what I was doing. M. R. Williams provided red wine, dark chocolate, and angel hair. Robert E. Rich provided a professional perspective and legal advice along with nearly thirty years of friendship. Kenneth R Morris, intellectual colleague and friend, provided both 'outsider' perspective and continuous optimism for projects on-going and yet unborn. M. Ann Brady made graduate school possible and remains a warm and sustaining presence. Linda Muirhead provided intellectual curiosity and memorable meals. And Cynthia Parr Delaney, *ma chère petite*, LPQ will remember you always.

Notes

Citations to Aristotle's *Nicomachean Ethics* are to the Rackham translation unless otherwise noted.

For translations of ancient Greek terms I have used the seventh edition of the *Intermediate Greek Lexicon* by Liddell and Scott.

Chapter 1

Rhetoric, Law, Ethics, Feminism

> Our proper course with this subject as with others will be to present the various views about it, and then, after first reviewing the difficulties they involve, finally to establish all or, if not all, the greater part and the most important of the opinions generally held with respect to these states of mind; since if the discrepancies can be solved, and a residuum of correct opinion left standing, the true view will have been sufficiently established.
>
> Aristotle
> *Nicomachean Ethics*, Book VII

I still remember the day I first heard the words 'reasonable' and 'woman' together in a sentence. It was 1991 and, though I had recently resigned my position as an employee benefits paralegal at a large corporate law firm in Cincinnati, I had taken on the job of assembling a newsletter for its labor law department. The decision in *Ellison v. Brady* had just been published and the front page headline of the newsletter read 'Court Upholds Reasonable Woman Standard for Sexual Harassment Cases.'

Should I confess that I laughed? After twelve years of immersion in tax law and of invoking the 'reasonable man' as the standard for fiduciaries of pension plan trust funds, I found the combination of 'woman' with 'reason' odd. But it was also intriguing, and if only because I could easily imagine both the hilarity and the consternation in the halls of my old law firm at this turn of events, I found myself reading not only *Ellison v. Brady* but every sexual harassment case it cited, and the cases they cited, and Catherine A. MacKinnon's *Sexual Harassment of Working Women* and, eventually, everything I could find on feminist jurisprudence and the 'Reasonable Woman' herself. It made for an interesting and chaotic graduate school year, the first in my PhD program. Of such serendipitous and dissonant moments are scholarly careers born, or such is my fond belief.

It was only upon leaving the 'practice' of law (for paralegals manifestly do not practice law, or don't admit to it) that I found the luxury I needed to think theoretically about what I had been doing during those years. It is one of the arguments of this book that both activities, both practice and theory, are knowledge-making activities that are valuable for what they can contribute to our understanding of legal and ethical problems. But this book also argues for a third way of knowing, the productive, that mediates between those two and calls into question not only the gap we tend to believe exists between them but the 'bridge' we attempt to build as we conceive of practice as the simple enactment of theory—

wrongly, as Stanley Fish is fond of pointing out (*There's No Such Thing as Free Speech* 347-8). This third way of knowing is described, as are theory and practice, in great detail in Aristotle's *Nicomachean Ethics*; Aristotle called it *poiesis* and the method it employed—what he called a 'habit of mind'—*techné*, or 'art.' The art the ancient Greeks used to practice law was called rhetoric and it is precisely here, in the conjunction of law and rhetoric that my (para) professional and academic careers mirror, that I focus my attention in this book.

If rhetoric has had a long and troubled history—and it has—its relationship with law has been even more troubled. From their early intimate association, where to practice law meant to employ rhetoric, law and rhetoric are now barely on speaking terms. When, why, and how the rupture in the law-rhetoric relationship came about is a matter of dispute and interpretation ranging from the conclusion of legal scholars Linda Levine and Kurt M. Saunders, that it was prompted by Peter Ramus's excision of logic from rhetoric (110) to the position expressed by Gerald Wetlaufer and seconded by Austin Sarat and Thomas R. Kearns, that law's 'rhetoricity' has become a source of a fair amount of twentieth- (and now twenty-first-) century professional anxiety (Sarat and Kearns 1). Certainly the law-rhetoric rupture is associated with the rise of science in the seventeenth century, more than two thousand years after the 'invention' of both law and rhetoric in Athens. But science could not have replaced rhetoric in law's affections if the relationship were not already troubled, and indeed it was. From its early pre-eminence both in Athens and later in Rome rhetoric had slipped, and slipped badly. Indispensable at a time when democracy was born and grew up, both for the making of laws and for their adjudication in litigious societies, rhetoric became dangerous and potentially subversive as empires began to take the place of democracies. Rhetoric, it appears, fell before Rome, fell with the head of Cicero, its greatest rhetorician. In retrospect, the implications for rhetoric could not have been clearer if Cicero's tongue had been cut out, nailed to a pike, and paraded about town—as, of course, it was.

Janet M. Atwill's study of the fate of rhetoric in the liberal arts argues that rhetoric had already undergone a gradual transformation whose beginnings are apparent in Aristotle and begin to become obvious in Quintilian, a century after Cicero's death. This transformation of rhetoric, 'from an art of social and political intervention into the curricular content of a humanist education' meant that rhetoric would become institutionalized as a school subject (*Rhetoric Reclaimed* 32) and taught continuously throughout the medieval period and the Renaissance—it would be difficult, in fact, to find a century during which rhetoric was not an essential school subject prior to the twentieth. Rather than disappear after Rome, rhetoric moved away from politics and into other spheres, including (due to the influence of Augustine) that of the early Catholic Church, where it was transformed into the arts of preaching and of letter writing (Bizzell and Herzberg 377). It survived, then, primarily as the study of eloquence, or of literary 'style,' and primarily at the pre-university level as an essential member of the *trivium* along with grammar and logic. It remained associated with law through the canonical letters that promulgated church law, and was taught to aspiring church and secular lawyers at the first university established at Bologna in the medieval period (Clark 678). For this period of its history, however, rhetoric remained primarily the occupation of schoolboys and only rarely made it to the universities.

Here again law and rhetoric are linked, for though civil law fit easily into the curriculum of universities on the European continent, the English common law tradition from which our own legal system is descended had problems achieving the kind of stature required for admission to the British university. That, in fact, became one important reason for law's fascination with science and grew out of the educational motivations behind Sir William Blackstone's promulgation of 'legal science' in his eighteenth-century *Commentaries on the Laws of England* (Currie 348, Lemmings 226). Christopher Columbus Langdell, persuaded by the *Commentaries* and by his own instruction at Harvard's law school, also used science as a lever to get legal instruction consistently out of apprenticeships and law offices and into the universities in the late nineteenth and early twentieth centuries. It was an ingenious combination of persuasion and necessity that led Langdell to claim, first, that law was a science; secondly, that it was a specifically empirical science and, thirdly, that the data to be observed by this empirical science were contained in judicial cases—and thus in 'the ultimate sources of all legal knowledge,' the printed books that only a university could provide (quoted in Harno 58-9).

In case there were any lingering doubts about law's theoretical and thus 'scientifical' status (to parrot Blackstone) Langdell maintained that the purpose of law school was not to teach the basics of law practice—not to teach law students to churn out legal products—but instead to teach a process, a method of inquiry and a way of thinking, 'like a lawyer.' Through what came to be known as the Langdellian or case-study method, law students were to infer from their readings of judicial opinions the basic premises, or Blackstonian 'principles,' of legal science. This turn away from product in favor of process allowed the case method to accomplish several interesting feats in one fell swoop. First, it made legal study plausibly 'scientific' by focusing on empirical data through an arguably inductive method. Second, legal study became respectably theoretical, thereby rejecting the memorization of legal rules and pleading forms in favor of a search for a system of underlying legal principles. Third, that theoretical nature in turn rendered law worthy of university study as an undertaking that was, fourth and completing the circle, explicitly and unabashedly impractical. Through this apparently master stroke Langdell and his case method succeeded in relatively short order, 'definitely and firmly implant[ing] the teaching of law in the universities' (Harno 59).

Residence in the university did not, obviously, settle the question of law's nature or even of how it might best be taught. Langdell and his method were both controversial, the method because its claim to 'science' was highly questionable by the standards of the time (and even more so by today's) and the man because of a rather unusual character that led to perceptions such as that of his contemporary Jerome Frank, that Langdell was a bizarre individual with an 'obsessive and almost exclusive interest in books' (quoted in Chase 330). Substantial and sometimes scathing criticism both in his time and ours has made of Langdell a caricature, says educational scholar Bruce A. Kimball (302), who notes that only recently has scholarship taken a close look at primary sources to counteract the now conventional wisdom that Langdell himself could be given little credit for developing the pedagogical method that bears his name (for one account of this conventional wisdom see Chase 332). But Langdellian case method remains a factor to be dealt with in both legal education and legal scholarship; Kimball notes that 'hundreds, if not thousands, of publications have discussed him and his work, in no small part because Langdell is identified with the modern paradigm of legal education' (329). Scholarship that advocates movement 'beyond the case method' or 'beyond Langdell,' for example (Moskovitz; Torres and Harwood) affirms that Langdell was 'arguably the most influential figure in the history of legal education in the United States,' the figure, in fact, who 'shaped the modern law school' (Kimball 277). The method was not an unequivocal triumph, of course; alternatives to the Langdellian Harvard model were proposed throughout the twentieth century and continue to influence the law school curriculum today. Clinical legal education, for example, which Richard J. Wilson claims is 'one of the most significant and successful pedagogical developments since Langdell's case method' (421), grew out of the psychoanalytical approach that Frank proposed in the decade of the 1930s to replace Langdell's 'narrow professional' model (McManis 598). Still other models were proposed at Columbia and Yale to accommodate critiques put forward by legal realism (Currie 536, Reed 360-2). These 'functional' models survive in courses based on what is sometimes called 'law and' jurisprudence—or, by its critics, 'law and whatever.'

Among these last are, of course, the movements to pair law with literature, with economics, and with feminism. I have chosen to investigate work by scholars associated with these movements in my own work because the conflict between 'legal art' and 'legal science' presented by the literary and economic perspectives, respectively, beings into high relief the long absence of rhetoric from legal studies—while feminist critiques of both perspectives invite, if only implicitly, renewed interest in its presence. My place in this debate is complicated by at least two factors, however; first by my position as an outsider (or at the very best as a para-insider) and second by my variant definitions of the key terms involved. In the struggle between art and science I take the part of art, but of an art that is specifically non-literary and geared not toward the interpretation of text but toward its production—an art that is rhetorical in a classical, Aristotelian sense. But even though I side with art, I have considerable interest in the legal science offered by the Law and Economics movement, the formulation of which bears an uncanny resemblance to science in the classical sense, in which 'science' is understood as a discursive inquiry into a discursive culture. Again, my definition is Aristotelian. Ultimately, these definitions depart from both 'literature' and 'economics' in their current senses, for neither modern concept is thinkable in the classical terms I employ. Nevertheless, the literary and economic perspectives on legal thought are essential to my project because of the questions they raise about the nature of law and of legal analysis, and because the answers they suggest (and feminist responses to those answers) have significant implications not only for our understanding of law but for our understanding of rhetoric as well.

Because of rhetoric's longstanding interest in the nature and functions of language, I have chosen to demonstrate that latter claim through an examination of prevailing, characteristic approaches to the role of language in economic, literary, and feminist analyses of the theory and practice of law. Those characteristic approaches are illustrated, I will claim, by the work of major figures in each movement—Richard Posner, James Boyd White, and Robin West, respectively. In these figures rests an enormous influence on the choice of significant issues in the fields of economic, literary, and feminist legal analysis, as each is alternately lauded, criticized, cited, repudiated, and elaborated upon—extensively. However, I choose these figures not in order to provide a comprehensive analysis of each movement, which is not my goal. Instead, I see in the work of Posner, White, and West beliefs about language that are characteristic of the disciplines they bring to bear on legal scholarship. While these beliefs are not diametrically opposed, they do offer widely variant responses to the limitations and possibilities presented to legal theory and practice by the alternately alarming and liberating capacities of law's language. The market-based theory espoused by Posner holds language to a standard of certainty and clarity that attempts to make of it a mere tool, albeit one that requires significant honing; that view of language is contested by the literary and rhetorically-based theory of White, which recognizes the ambiguity of language without relinquishing belief in our ability to become more conscious users of it and, thereby, to exercise some control over its consequences.

To the analysis of Posner and White I bring to bear the feminist perspectives on law offered not only by West but also by classical scholar Martha C. Nussbaum. Within legal studies the feminist response to both Law and Economics and Law and Literature has been mixed, determined in large part by the language theory that grounds the work of various scholars. In Nussbaum's work we find a moderate feminism that, recognizing with Aristotle the contribution language makes to ethical reasoning, sees in both economic and literary approaches to legal analysis the potential for important ethical insights (*Poetic Justice* 82). In constitutional law scholar West's work we find a far more radical feminism; however, where Nussbaum's language theory openly acknowledges and even embraces the role that language could play in constructing Aristotle's theories of knowledge—and attributes to him that same perspective—West mistrusts or even fears the propensity of language to lead to consequences unintended by its speakers. Recognizing what White also admits, that 'not everything can be said in this language' that is law (*Heracles' Bow* 241), West urges scholarship to go beyond— or behind—the verbal (*Caring for Justice* 192).

I thus focus my attention not only on the contributions each approach to legal analysis may make to a rhetorical understanding of legal thought and language, but also to its limitations, and on reservations grounded in the feminist apprehension— in both senses of that term—of the language theory inherent in each movement. What feminism has apprehended, in other words—that legal language (in the more radical formulations, that language itself) is inherently 'male'—also creates apprehension regarding the implications for women of both the economic and literary approaches to law. My goal is to extend the response of feminist legal scholarship as I offer a specifically rhetorical slant on language generally and on legal language in particular, a perspective that considers not only how women have been shaped by legal discourse but how women and men may shape the discourse themselves. While I hope that one effect of such analysis may be to ease the apprehension regarding language that is common in feminist legal scholarship, I expect that it will also complicate the undue optimism of some rhetorical scholarship through its recognition that words literally, visibly, and immediately 'matter' in law.

Through my feminist, rhetorical perspective I hope to explain, contest, or replace not only the responses to the issues that literature and economics identify in legal studies, but the invention, identification, and framing of the issues themselves. At the deepest level these issues center on the certainty of law, the meaning and effects of legal texts, and the potential of those texts and of law itself to serve the demands of justice. Justice is also at issue, not only in terms of how it may best be served (or whether it can be served) by law but also in terms of its definition, indeed of its very relevance to the theories and practices of law and legal method. The core argument of this book on that issue, and on which all other of its arguments rest, is simply this: because law must work with and through language—White has said that law literally is a language (*Heracles' Bow* 78)—the various beliefs about justice and law's relationship to it that are maintained by the literary, economic, and feminist movements are evidenced and founded in— indeed, sometimes founder in—their characteristic beliefs about the nature of language and its relationships to knowledge, truth, and reality.

This is an argument to which I return in each of the chapters that follow, and that is synthesized and fully argued in the last. But before providing a preview of that argument and the chapters through which it develops, it is time to take a step back from this work's basic argument to the values that inform the method through which I support it. Why, one might ask, would a scholar with feminist sympathies rely on Aristotle as a theoretical basis? As Cynthia A. Freeland points out in the introduction to *Feminist Interpretations of Aristotle*, the feminist literature on Aristotle has generally been negative, with feminists finding 'much to disparage and little to salvage' from his work (1). Indeed, recent feminist rhetorical work has turned to the Sophists as an alternative to Aristotle, and for compelling reasons. Susan C. Jarratt provides a comprehensive and persuasive analysis of those reasons, including the parallels between the interests (often considered 'faults') of the Sophists and characteristics traditionally linked to the female. For Plato, she notes, 'the sophists signified opinion as opposed to Truth, the materiality of the body...vs. soul, practical knowledge vs. science, the temporal vs. the eternal.... This cluster of terms,' she says, is 'coincident on many counts with the cultural stereotype of the "feminine" operating in the West for centuries' ('The First Sophists and Feminism' 29). One can hardly argue with this analysis, and I have no intentions to do so.

However, I also have no intention to argue one alternative thesis, that 'Aristotle was a feminist,' as Linda R. Hirschman provocatively declares at the outset of 'The Book of "A"' (971). Like Nussbaum, who responds to Hirschman's thesis in

'Aristotle, Feminism and Needs for Functioning' I do agree that Aristotle's method can support feminist method (Hirschman 972). Where Hirschman sees parallels between his discursive method in the *Nicomachean Ethics* and feminist consciousness-raising (977) Nussbaum sees an 'allegedly conservative ethical methodology' that in fact is compatible with feminist goals. In actuality, she says, it 'prompts a sweeping and highly critical scrutiny of all existing regimes and their schemes of distribution' ('Aristotle, Feminism, and Needs for Functioning' 1021), an assessment that inspires Nussbaum's own interests in extending feminist research to the needs of women (and men) in countries where necessities such as food and shelter are lacking or unevenly distributed.

Both Nussbaum and Hirschman, in slightly different ways and to different purposes, note Aristotle's interest in the life of a community and the relationship of individuals to that community. Hirschman argues that Aristotle's interest in the social body is compatible with the feminist understanding of the personal as political (986) and contends that his 'ideal of the good life for citizens may be the best source of substantive answers about politics and the political community...which feminism, like any normative theory, must ultimately produce' (972). Nussbaum extends that argument with a deeper understanding of its complexities and contradictions but ultimately supports Hirschman's conclusion. What Aristotle understood, Nussbaum says, is that each human being 'is, and is necessarily, a "this" and "one in number."' (1023). Further, he saw both political and ethical consequences of this view; his 'fundamental respect for choice' (1027) both allows him to account realistically for human functioning and flourishing, and to counter the potential for postmodern ethical relativism (1024) with a particularism that does not neglect the role of community in shaping an individual life.

Despite the misogyny that Hirschman and Nussbaum acknowledge in Aristotle's corpus, both conclude that, to quote Nussbaum, 'contemporary feminism does indeed have a great deal to learn from Aristotle' (1019). Here even Posner, who also responded to Hirschman, agrees. Doubtful of the 'feminist' claim, he maintains that Aristotle's thought nevertheless 'is not a seamless web so that if you pull out one thread the whole thing unravels.' One could, in other words, throw out his misogynistic biology 'without jeopardizing what he has to say about reasoning in the face of uncertainty' ('Ms. Aristotle' 1017). Nussbaum concurs not only with this sentiment—'we may proceed to appropriate other elements of his thought,' she says, 'without fear that they are logically interdependent with his political and biological misogyny' (1021)—she also makes overt Posner's more implicit reference to Aristotle's *Rhetoric*. It is 'above all' in this work about reasoning in the face of uncertainty, she says, that Aristotle offers 'a subtle defense and justification of many emotions, as playing a crucial role in the rational and virtuous response to many of life's events' (1022). An Aristotelian consciousness of such circumstances lends contingency, says Nussbaum, its 'ethical relevance' (1025). Carol Poster questions the assumed primacy of Aristotle's *Rhetoric* both historically and today, pointing out that his recognition of the emotions and the private sphere as valid materials and locations for rhetorical performance are still grounded in his beliefs in the superior worth of logical appeals in the public sphere (338-9). Poster concludes on this basis that 'feminist rhetoric can stand on its own' but, while I sympathize with that position, I must disagree with her assumption that it can do so 'without authoritative male antecedents' (344). Feminist rhetoric cannot and does not operate outside its contexts, and must acknowledge the tradition out of which it grows even as it struggles to depart from it. Thus feminists cannot ignore the answers Aristotle developed through his relentless pursuit of 'the woman question' (Hirschman 979-80), even if we don't like them. Indeed, many non-feminist scholars don't like those answers either. But unlike Jasper Neel, who contends that with Aristotle's thought we inevitably import intonations of slavery, sexism, and elitism (14-26), Hirschman, Nussbaum, Posner—and I—agree that Aristotelian method does not make Aristotle's own conclusions inevitable.

I will return to my reliance on Aristotle in this overtly feminist work in order to extend that argument. But first, a few words of explanation as to why I rely on Aristotle's ethical system for the structure of a rhetorical work. After all, centuries of scholarship—beginning most notably with Plato's *Gorgias*—have strictly opposed rhetoric to ethics. This, in fact, is Posner's position on the question; noting that when Aristotle begins to discuss rhetorical performances we move into an 'amoral' world, he concludes that the rhetorical function of invention 'is just the sort of thing that troubles people about rhetoric' (*Overcoming Law* 512). In economic terms, he explains, rhetoric comes into play as a function of 'information costs,' so that even if it is truly amoral, neither a good nor a bad thing, it is certainly 'an indispensable thing' when more certain knowledge is unavailable (524). Unfortunately, as Posner explains, rhetoric's ethical valence is entirely dependent upon that of those who wield it; though it may be used to 'make truth sound like truth' it can also make falsehood sound like truth, or vice-versa (529). Thus Posner echoes Plato more truly than Aristotle, particularly the charge in the *Gorgias* that rhetoric leads not to truth but to belief that itself may be true or false (454 d-e).

While Posner's manner of discussing the issue is unique, the issue itself clearly is not. Aristotle himself may be seen as responding to Plato in the very passage of the *Rhetoric* where he considers the question of the relationship of rhetoric to truth and justice. Socrates summarily dismisses the claim advanced by Gorgias, that as its function in the law courts rhetoric took as its concern matters of 'right and wrong' (*Gorgias* 454 a-b). But Aristotle maintains that 'rhetoric is useful because the true and the just are naturally superior to their opposites' (*Rhetoric* I.I.12). Precisely what this passage implies is a subject of debate; William M. A. Grimaldi maintains that in this passage Aristotle clearly connects rhetoric with truth by showing that 'it is through the instrumentality of the art that truth and justice are able to realize themselves in the decisions of men' (173). In making his own argument, however, Grimaldi must provide an alternative translation of the passage that completes Aristotle's statement about the relationship of rhetoric to truth and justice, a passage that reads in the Rhys translation 'so that if the decisions of judges are not what they ought to be, the defeat must be due to the speakers themselves'—or, in the Freese translation, 'they must owe their defeat to their own advocates.' Both translations suggest that rhetoric is, indeed, a neutral tool that may be used well or badly.

Both Atwill and Barbara Warnick have taken issue with Grimaldi's re-translation of this passage and the argument it therefore advances, for similar reasons. Grimaldi can only make his argument for the intimate connection of rhetoric with truth by linking Aristotle's method to subjects that, Warnick says, are 'quite different from those Aristotle intended,' based on those he used as examples in his own text (300). Atwill agrees that it is Grimaldi's desire to make of rhetoric a much closer cousin of philosophy than Aristotle intended that informs what she sees as a flawed argument. She also questions his desire to similarly link rhetoric with ethics ('Instituting the Art of Rhetoric' 106); contending that Aristotle himself saw rhetoric and ethics as distinct, she claims that 'there is good reason for rescuing rhetoric' from the imperative of ethics, to aim at Aristotle's 'good life' (*Rhetoric Reclaimed* 163). Here Atwill provocatively disagrees with a great deal of contemporary scholarship on rhetoric that quite consciously intends to rescue rhetoric for ethics. And despite my agreement with that latter scholarship, among which prominently figure various feminist perspectives on rhetoric, I must also agree with Atwill's assessment that Aristotle's 'greatest contribution to rhetoric may have been his willingness to allow' its 'two failures'—to deny its identity with either philosophy or ethics and thus allow rhetoric an identity of its own (164). But before I explain what may appear to be a triple paradox—my use of Aristotle's ethical thought to agree with contradictory positions regarding the place of rhetoric within it—let me turn to the various arguments advanced, against Atwill's, for the inherently ethical nature of rhetoric. To do so I provide in the next section a short historical and disciplinary survey of the rhetorical methods and definitions upon which I rely. Maintaining that any methodology inevitably (if implicitly) expresses an ethic, I recognize that the feminist perspective informing my work encourages a definition of rhetoric that itself leads to my methodological choices. Though Aristotle's thought is often seen as inimical to feminist interests, I conclude with a definition of rhetoric that, drawing upon Aristotle's *Nicomachean Ethics*, resolves some of the contradictions not only between Aristotle and feminism, but between feminism and rhetoric itself.

Rhetorical Criticism and Analysis: Toward Productive Feminism

In 1973 feminist communication scholar Karlyn Kohrs Campbell chose as her label for the rhetoric of women's liberation, as it was then more likely to be called, the oxymoron. She could do so, however, only because of the prevailing definition of rhetoric at that time, a definition that had held sway for centuries without absorbing the influence of alternative voices. That definition becomes evident as she explains precisely why the rhetoric used by women in the 1960s and 1970s was, as she puts it, 'anti-rhetorical' (78). It is, she says, 'a genre without a rhetor, a rhetoric in search of an audience, that transforms traditional argumentation into confrontation' (86). In its quest to 'violate the reality structure' (81, quoting the Female Liberation Movement), the rhetoric of the women's liberation movement intentionally flouts the expectations of an audience and calls its deeply held values into question.

Here, in a nutshell, are not only most of the elements of the traditional definition of rhetoric growing out of Aristotle's work (stated, of course, in the negative); here, too, are all the reasons for the continuing struggle of feminist rhetoricians to define an alternative practice for themselves. Traditionally understood as the 'art of persuasion,' a definition that I will soon suggest is not strictly Aristotle's, 'rhetoric' had evolved into a term that reflected a practice closely centered on the figure of a speaker-leader who, drawing upon the time-honored beliefs of his culture, would move an audience to consensus and often action through persuasion (as rhetoric's friends generously maintain) or flattery and manipulation (as its enemies often charge). Campbell's observation of the practices of feminist consciousness-raising groups suggested that the expert leader did not exist in that practice; furthermore, while one might argue that the goal of the group was to uncover an alternative set of values from among the group, those values were usually set against the values of the larger culture in which the group existed. If the consciousness-raising group could be seen as an audience, it could not be seen in the traditional sense as existing to be persuaded. And while the larger culture within which that group existed might need to be persuaded, even coerced, it had not at that time formed itself as an audience for the rhetoric offered by 'women's liberation.'

Though times have indeed changed, they have not changed so much that prevailing definitions of rhetoric have become entirely congenial to the interests of feminists. Nor has the larger culture changed sufficiently to suggest that feminist rhetoricians may no longer be needed, as 'feminist backlash' has taken root and flourished (Faludi). Concurrently, elements of the traditional definition of 'rhetoric' have, in some cases, migrated in a direction hospitable to feminist interests but in others remained problematically located. In the discussion that follows I call upon definitions of rhetoric that exist across fields and across eras; recognizing that one's definition often becomes apparent in the assumptions of one's methodology, I draw heavily on scholarship in the discipline of Communication, where methodological assumptions are subject to far more explicit research than they have been to date in my home field of English or in legal rhetorical studies.

I begin with a purposely very broad definition of rhetoric; comparing it to typical definitions from the field of Communication, I then move to a discussion of the dominant mode of rhetorical analysis in that field, a method that goes by the name of 'criticism.' Having established the definitional terms that are common to criticism and forms of rhetorical analysis in other fields, I then move to describe various analytical projects and the moves made by feminist rhetoricians—myself finally included—to work in a field long dominated (as what field has not traditionally been?) by so-called 'male' modes of thinking, speaking, and knowing. I conclude with a narrowed definition of rhetoric that is nominally my 'own,' though it grows directly out of the Aristotelian and a growing body of research on the nature of what Aristotle called *techné*, the 'art' that determined his view of rhetoric.

Let me begin, then, with a broad definition of rhetoric *as a perspective on language that is conscious of itself as such*. In this broad definition I rely not on Aristotle, who would hardly have thought in such terms, but on current disciplinary scholarship that uniformly insists on two key elements—language and consciousness. Because I characterize it as a perspective it is clear, I hope, that rhetoric is not synonymous with language, but is intimately concerned with its uses. This element of my definition is consistent with frequent references in all kinds of rhetorical scholarship to rhetoric's keen interest in the use of symbols. Charles Bazerman's contribution to a collection of work by scholars primarily from the field of English argues that the question of 'how symbols are used as a medium of social exchange' (3) is one of rhetoric's two primary concerns ('an orientation toward practice' is the other); a primarily Communication-based collection begins with a definition of rhetoric as 'the human effort to induce co-operation through the use of symbols' (Brock, Scott, and Chesebro 15). Another Communication-based work begins by explaining that 'rhetoric is the human use of symbols to communicate' (Foss, Foss, and Trapp 1). All three of these definitions reiterate the interest in language as the use of symbols; all also articulate the 'consciousness' of my definition by way of references to the human use of such symbols in a social undertaking of some kind. All three also extend my definition, however, through the addition of an element of intent. One engages in rhetorical activity, according to these definitions, in order to effect an exchange, possibly persuasive or co-operative in nature, or more simply to 'communicate' (itself a complex activity). All of those definitions refine my own and simultaneously both expand and contract it through the addition of a purposive element that is exercised within a context of constraints. We become conscious of ourselves as users of language, in other words, because we have a goal in mind; that goal, however, is mitigated by the necessity of the co-operation of others within a social unit of some kind.

The foregoing definitions assume that 'rhetoric' is something that all humans do, and do consciously. But the everyday consciousness of humans who intend to persuade others or engage in almost any kind of social exchange is different from the activity in which professional (academic) rhetoricians engage. That activity involves a somewhat rarified form of consciousness, a meta-consciousness that my own definition recognizes. In the field of Communication that activity is generally called 'criticism;' in the Brock collection, the frame of mind in which it is undertaken is called 'the critical impulse' (10). As an attitude interested in human intentions and their social products, the critical impulse undertakes to evaluate the rhetorical activity of a chosen text 'with knowledge and propriety,' providing good reasons for its judgments and directing those judgments themselves toward a social end; criticism, they say, 'seeks to change the human condition' (13).

Given that ambitious goal, it is important to attend to the ways in which criticism itself may be judged, and Brock et al. indeed provide a good accounting of this somewhat knotty problem. Working within the tradition that understands rhetoric as the art of persuasion, earlier Communication scholarship had endorsed rhetorical success as the standard by which critical activity could be judged; in evoking this standard such work attempted, at least in part, to distinguish itself from the literary criticism that was perhaps more familiar in academic settings, then as now. Herbert Wicheln, for example, had claimed in 1925 that while literary critics focused on 'the permanent value that they find in the work under consideration,' rhetoricians were concerned neither with permanence nor with beauty, but with 'effect' (quoted in Brock et al. 24). The criterion of effectiveness, however, can become 'embarrassing,' as Brock and his colleagues admit (17), lending fuel to the frequent argument that rhetoric is amoral or even immoral. They therefore attempt to settle on the alternative of 'good practice,' but this alternative brings with it a separate set of hazards, most notably the circularity inherent when 'the appeal to good practice helps to establish principle and the appeal to principle helps to determine good practice' (19). Writing from the disciplinary location of English, Carolyn R. Miller notes that the reliance on 'good reasons' risks the 'vicious circle that has made for rhetoric so many enemies;' a good reason, she explains, 'is a reason that will be accepted as a good reason' ('Rhetoric and the Community' 85). In other words good practice is communally determined—and the community, sometimes lapsing theoretically into simply 'the gathering of the similar' (Bellah, quoted in Miller 83) is in turn identified through its 'good' practices. Maintaining that 'circularity is inevitably part of building a tradition,' Brock et al. point to 'exciting' recent work suggesting the potential of 'an intrinsically rhetorical ethic,' but conclude that they 'cannot argue the questions raised by such a potentiality here' (19).

Such questions continue to excite the attention of scholars eager to demonstrate that rhetoric, as the arena of one's earnest professional effort, is not as inherently unethical as the tradition of centuries has suggested. Work by Ernesto Grassi and Richard Weaver, both more properly philosophers than rhetoricians, has served as source and inspiration for some such efforts, including mine. The individual situation that provides rhetoric with its focus is not as Platonists maintain, says Grassi, 'the accidental, the futile, and unimportant, but quite to the contrary' (*Renaissance Humanism* 81); it is in the individual case that human beings answer the social and thus ethical demands put to them. Because the 'rational principles' of philosophy, in their attempts at universality, attempt to exclude that individual case they miss the ethical mark; rhetoric, operating in 'the here and now,' places matters 'before our eyes.' Rhetoric thus 'discovers the meaning of beings in the context of the historical situation' (81). Weaver's work similarly emphasizes the ethical dimensions of the concrete situations of human beings. Aware of rhetoric's intimate connection to culture and community, he maintains that it is 'a loss of historical consciousness' (*Visions of Order* 55) that leads some to insist that we should do without it. In fact, such insistence is 'a fast road to social subversion' because it is only through rhetoric that the propositions of dialectic may be related to 'the existential world in which facts are regarded with sympathy and are treated with…historical understanding and appreciation' (56-7).

The inescapable humanness of rhetoric, then, supplies it with an ethical dimension that we ignore to our loss and at our peril. But given that ethical element, how should one proceed to act in one's role as a rhetorician? It is no small question, and one that has occupied a great deal of disciplinary energy since Aristotle first considered how rhetoric and its method might be distinguished from philosophy and its method, dialectic. The strong similarities between the two disciplines and their methods led Aristotle to conclude in the first sentence of his *Rhetoric* that rhetorical method was a 'counterpart,' or 'offshoot,' of dialectic, depending upon the translation; ever since, rhetoric has struggled to distinguish itself from a number of counterparts generally considered more distinguished. In both rhetorical criticism, as it is called in Communication, and analysis, as it is more generically called in English and legal research, we find a great deal of energy devoted either to imitating or distinguishing rhetorical method from its currently more privileged counterpart, the interpretive method of literary analysis. Walter R. Fisher's formulation of rhetorical criticism provides a useful demonstration of the former strategy, yoking its evaluative claims to a 'narrative paradigm' that provides standards by which texts (his analysis uses overtly persuasive speeches from Plato's *Gorgias*) may be judged. The evaluative element of this critical method judges texts on the basis of their adherence to principles of what Fisher calls 'narrative rationality,' principles that he says may be inferred from the values texts express, their rhetorical appeals, and the good reasons they provide to support them—the foregoing offset against any problems that these elements may create, whether singly or in combination. Without conceding the inherent circularity of 'good reasons' or the standards by which values may be judged, Fisher concludes that texts that exhibit narrative probability and fidelity satisfy the test of narrative rationality (252).

I will devote considerable effort to a discussion in later chapters of the ways in which the approach to rhetoric typical of legal studies similarly imitates literary analysis rather than classical rhetorical method. Certainly, work such as White's grows out of the literary tradition; just as certainly, his position that legal language is part of 'an entire social and dramatic system,' that the legal imagination 'creates a world' ('Imagining the Law' 38) is consistent with the assertion that rhetorical criticism seeks to change the human condition. But so is the position of Peter Goodrich, who claims to see in legal rhetorical scholarship a nearly universal assumption of rhetoric's value to law as 'resident in its capacity to produce agreement.' To this assumption Goodrich counters that rhetoric 'cannot plausibly be viewed as anything other than a return to a fundamentally antithetic dispute' as to the character of law, conducted as it is through language, 'the sign of plurality and confusion' (100). White sees rhetoric as facilitating a 'culture of argument' that brings speakers together through a consensus built on 'acts of hope' conducted through its language, as his book by that title asserts; Goodrich sees it as inducing an inevitably antagonistic culture built through the indeterminacies of the very same medium.

Whether optimistic or pessimistic at base, these conclusions do share an investment in understanding the ethical capacity of rhetoric and rhetorical method in the facilitation or inhibition of social exchange. But their shared investment in an essentially literary method ultimately determines and limits its return, as any method will. As scholars seek and find meaning through interpretation of the texts that create and define their field, those texts jointly constitute a 'given'—they literally 'give' the field and its practitioners and scholars their identity as interpreters or critics. Even when the texts themselves are not strictly literary, as is often the case in rhetorical criticism, the circularity of disciplinarily determined 'good reasons' engenders frustration in critics and interpreters committed to changing the conditions within which they work. For example, in her more recent work Campbell, with Kathleen Hall Jamieson, has turned to the analysis of non-literary genres as such, looking for recurrent rhetorical forms in such texts as eulogies and papal encyclicals. Understanding a genre as 'composed of a constellation of recognizable forms bound together by an internal dynamic' (336) Campbell and Jamieson argue against a deductive method that assumes the existence of a genre and then infers generic features from an exemplary text; such a model not only tends toward simplistic classification and evaluation, but also is inherently circular as critics measure the model by its own standards (337). Their inductive method, examining a collection of texts to determine whether a genre indeed exists (332), understands the text as an 'act' and, through its attempt to re-create its 'symbolic context,' seeks to understand 'the ways in which rhetoric is shaped by prior rhetoric, by verbal conventions in a culture, and by past formulations of ideas and issues' (342).

Taking a turn away from the literary text, then, does not necessarily constitute a turn away from literary analysis, as Campbell and Jamieson's reliance on Northrop Frye's genre theory attests (333). Inductive genre analysis improves upon the deductive version through its frank acknowledgment of the constraints of past rhetoric upon current rhetorical action; nevertheless, the primary purpose of genre analysis remains working with the text in question in a manner largely that of the literary critic. What I find significant, however, are the allegiances, particularly Campbell's, to feminist perspectives that are not foregrounded in this genre work but are evident in her more overtly feminist analyses ('Inventing Women;' 'Gender and Genre;' 'Hearing Women's Voices'). While it is not only feminists who are willing to confront the necessarily circular nature of their work, the feminist emphasis on changing the world, if not 'the human condition,' requires this confrontation. In feminist rhetorical study, then, the question is particularly explicit and acute. Richard Leo Enos, a rhetorical scholar in the field of English, alludes to that question when he chides the tendency of his colleagues to be satisfied with their role as 'stay-at-home textual commentators who,' he adds, are 'akin to the new critics of the previous generation of literary scholars' (68). Enos links the need for what he calls 'fieldwork' specifically to the imperative to develop a history of women in rhetoric, urging the field to 'dilate the range of primary sources to include non-literary evidence' (69), particularly of archaeological artifacts such as pictures and inscriptions on ancient pottery that provide evidence of the literary activities of women. However, once such artifacts are discovered (with the aid of such tools as a working knowledge of ancient and modern Greek and the physical stamina necessary to ward off angry dogs, bees, and the occasional revolution) the job of the rhetorical scholar is to reconstruct the artifact's context, analyze it as discourse, and display (publish) one's findings (77)—again, much like the literary critic. Enos suggests that the rhetorical scholar literally read the artifact as one would any other 'text.'

All of these scholars suggest worthy work and contribute substantially to the body of rhetorical theory. But as Jeanne Fahnestock and Marie Secor suggest in a collection devoted primarily to linguistic methods of discourse analysis, rhetoric 'developed in antiquity as a heuristic rather than a hermeneutic art.' Thus classical rhetoric is neither interpretive nor analytical, but 'a theory—or at least a list of things to try—to construct an effective speech' (178). The problem with such an understanding of rhetoric—which, in its emphasis on the production rather than on the interpretation of texts, approaches my own—is that it is very difficult to discover such productive processes in extant texts. The attempt to do so, in fact, constitutes the 'intentional fallacy' that has become anathema in literary criticism—and rightly so, because one cannot safely assume that textual elements (even if 'correctly' interpreted by the critic) are directly representative of authorial intention. Nevertheless, attention to the productive processes of rhetoric is crucial to feminist research projects such as those urged by Carol Mattingly, for example. In 'Telling Evidence' she makes the familiar call for attention to non-literary texts (in this case, of newspaper accounts of first-wave feminist speeches). Based on a valuable analysis of the prevailing rhetorical conditions for female speakers—conditions that included a primary focus not on their words but upon their dress and their manner—Mattingly calls for feminist efforts in 'reading it slant, imagining it differently, or looking for patterns that define better ways for regarding evidence' (107). This call issues from her survey of the work of other feminists who attempt to bypass the masculine tradition. Whether deliberately contextualizing fragmentary information as does Cheryl Glenn with respect to Aspasia of Miletus, or making 'speculative leaps' as Jarratt characterizes her own feminist rhetorical method (quoted in Mattingly 104), both scholars provide clues leading to an inventive and productive method that bears traces of Aristotle's classical definition of rhetoric.

What Mattingly, Glenn, and Jarratt offer most visibly is a set of methods intended to help us understand texts created by women, whether in antiquity or in the more recent past; they also help us to 'add' to the rhetorical canon texts not previously considered worthy of analysis or sufficiently complete to warrant scholarly conclusions. But while none of these three suggest so explicitly, their methods can also help us to construct our own 'effective speeches,' to intervene in a prior rhetoric, to test the verbal conventions of our culture in order to alter past formulations of ideas and issues. I have borrowed here from Campbell and Jamieson's description of the goals of their inductive genre analysis in order to point to both the limitations and possibilities of each method I have discussed in this brief survey. We cannot necessarily infer from the features of a text, however valid our analysis, the processes that created it or the intention that fueled that process. What we may be able to infer, however, is a set of resources by which to respond to the exigencies of our own situations as creators, not just readers, of texts. We have now circled back to Aristotle, on whose definition of rhetoric I base my own, narrower definition. For Aristotle rhetoric is not simply the art of persuasion—it is, he says, the art of discovering 'in each case the available means of persuasion' (*Rhetoric* I.I.12-14). Having assembled the first and still most exhaustive compendium of such means, he then offers a set of strategies for textual production—a heuristic, not a hermeneutic. We need not adopt Aristotle's strategies wholesale in order to divert our thinking from the literary hermeneutic that has preoccupied rhetoricians for centuries—though we may usefully consider the more nuanced of the strategies he provides. And if we include in our repertoire the Aristotelian ethical system of which rhetoric, as a *techné,* was an essential component, we have both an ethical definition of rhetoric's place in human exchanges and a heuristic for our own rhetorical method.

In the epigraph to this chapter, Aristotle describes his method; it is, he says, to 'present the various views' about his subject and, through a review of the difficulties they involve, to 'preserve the greater part and the most important of the opinions' held by those who investigate what he called the 'frames' or 'habits' of mind through which human beings aspire to 'truth' (*Nicomachean Ethics* VII.1.5). In fact, it is his ethical method that feminists are most likely to see as promising for their scholarship (Freeland 1, Groenhout 171); this despite the many ways in which other aspects of this thought rely upon an essentialism that justifies the subordinate role of women in social structures then and now (Groenhout 179). And while some feminists continue to object to the hierarchical nature of his ethics, Groenhout believes that its incorporation of the role of emotions to ethical reasoning and its recognition of 'the self as situated, particular, and enmeshed in social relationships' offer a needed corrective to the failings of some feminist thinking, especially the feminist ethic of care that is often criticized for its reliance on essentialized portraits of women and enforcement of 'the very traits that traditionally have been used to justify the relegation of women to a private domestic sphere' (173).

Particularly relevant to my decision to rely upon Aristotle is that he proposes to conduct his ethical investigations through *phainomena*, literally 'the things we say' about ourselves, to the extent that we say them most consistently. It is thus that Aristotle 'saves the appearances,' says Nussbaum (*Fragility of Goodness* 242), preserving cultural wisdom as an insufficient truth that will nevertheless have to do. The habits of mind that Aristotle surveys in the *Nicomachean Ethics* and that he calls *theoria, phronesis,* and *techné* (translated, somewhat awkwardly, as theory, practical wisdom, and art) operate in realms of knowledge he calls *epistemé, praxis,* and *poiesis*. Through science, practice, and production, as these latter terms may themselves be translated, human beings aspire toward truth—more comfortably for us, perhaps, knowledge—which itself changes as it is approached from each habit of mind. Chapter 2 provides a detailed discussion of each habit of mind as a way of explaining how the structure Aristotle provides serves as a heuristic for my method in this work. Here it is important to say simply that rhetoric, as a *techné* and thus as one example of a habit of mind essential to Aristotle's ethical system, lives in a productive realm that will 'bring into existence a thing which may either exist or not' (*Nicomachean Ethics* VI.iii.4). Thus Aristotle's understanding of rhetoric preserves for it a place in his ethical system without turning it into 'ethics' itself—in which case it would, indeed, need to be 'rescued,' as Atwill has said. As a *techné* rhetoric focuses not on its own reproduction, as does *phronesis* (practical wisdom, the method of ethics) nor even on the production of an artifact (though an artifact may result from rhetorical method) but on the use of that artifact by those for whom it is intended. Rhetoric thus escapes some, though not all, of the circularity inherent in Aristotle's distinctly ethical method. With this understanding of its relationship to, not identity with, ethical method, I offer a narrowed definition of rhetoric as *a conscious perspective on language that sees it as a means not of interpretation but of the production of a broad range of 'texts,'* from the literal speech, story, or argument to the social conditions wrought by the legal turn of phrase. Rhetoric understood thus does, indeed, carry the potential to change the human condition, for better or for worse.

I follow Aristotle's method in succeeding chapters in which I examine the things we say, do, and make as we talk about law from the perspectives of economics, literature, and rhetoric. Though I speak about all three disciplines, my method in each chapter is rhetorical in a number of senses drawn from the preceding review. Following Grassi, I place each discourse in the here and now through 'the individual case'—here, a sexual harassment case for which Judge Posner has written the judicial opinion. This individual case is not (as Grassi points out) accidental, futile, or unimportant, but an exemplar of the concrete situations in which we find ourselves as human beings and to which we must respond. Thus, though in Chapters 3 and 4 my rhetorical method is critical and analytical, 'reading' the case from the perspectives of economic and literary theory, it follows Aristotle in its attempt to cull from some of the most important opinions available a 'true view' from what is 'left standing.' I depart from the critical or analytical method that has been the subject of my own critique in this chapter as I move to Chapter 5 and a demonstration of one method of rhetorical productivity. Though I first read the opinion rhetorically rather than from the perspectives of economics and literature, I proceed to produce an alternative opinion through a rhetorical heuristic called *stasis*, a method of invention used even before Cicero to develop legal arguments intended to define the issue at the heart of a dispute. In literally reproducing the opinion I make visible and central an issue that Posner purports to dismiss—the curious legal phenomenon of 'welcome harassment.'

A few words about that case, then, before we proceed. It is *Carr v. Allison Gas Turbine Division*, a suit filed against General Motors by a female tinsmith named Mary Carr and decided by the Seventh Circuit Court of Appeals in 1994. I first analyzed this case in 1998 as a part of some early work on judicial rhetoric ('What's a Reasonable Woman to Do?') and returned to it in a more extensive analysis centered on Posner's rhetoric in particular ('Posner on Legal Texts'). In an unusually happy coincidence, Nussbaum has also paid published attention to *Carr* (*Poetic Justice* 104-11) in a manner that enriches my own understanding of the case, despite my disagreement with her conclusions regarding it. I chose it for my earlier work because Posner is the first (and only) justice of whom I am aware to have discovered 'welcome harassment,' at least in writing. Its existence, as he points out in *Carr*, is implied in the judicial precedent requiring plaintiffs to show that they have been subjected to its logical counterpart, *un*welcome harassment. I choose it for this current work not in order to theorize sexual harassment itself, which was the goal of my earlier work and has been accomplished admirably by others, first (and again recently) by MacKinnon (*Sexual Harassment of Working Women*; *Directions in Sexual Harassment Law*) and in work by such scholars as Mia Cahill (*The Social Construction of Sexual Harassment Law*), Augustus B. Cochran (*Sexual Harassment and the Law*), and Anna-Maria Marshall (*Confronting Sexual Harassment*). Instead, I choose this case for this work because it clearly illustrates the effects of one's beliefs about language on one's beliefs about law. Because 'welcome harassment' is an oxymoron, Judge Posner tells us, it must be dismissed. Where language strays from the strictly logical, his language theory holds, we must not trust it; because of its seeming irrationality, then, 'welcome harassment' cannot really exist (*Carr* 1008).

My language theory holds not only that it can, but that it does. Furthermore, I maintain that it matters. In the chapters that follow I hope to demonstrate this provisional truth and, in the final chapter, show how a purposely 'errant' relationship to our language can alter the realities that this particular oxymoron constructs. Through my use of Aristotle to accomplish that purpose I hope to put forward a case that is theoretical, practical, and productive. I thus use Aristotle's ethical structure rhetorically, as a heuristic for thinking about the construction of human nature, male and female, through the language of law. As to whether law may be science, literature, or rhetoric, I do not know; I suspect it is all three, and more. As a rhetorician, I am inclined to believe that how we see law is a product of how we see our language and how comfortable we are with that vision. But that is to get ahead of myself. Instead, allow me to quote the closing line of Aristotle's *Nicomachean Ethics*; turning to his students after 643 pages of analysis, he suggests to them simply, 'let us then begin our discussion.'

Chapter 2

The Things We Value: Theory, Practice, and Production

> Let it be assumed that the states by virtue of which the soul possesses truth by way of affirmation or denial are five in number, i.e. art, scientific knowledge, practical wisdom, philosophic wisdom, intuitive reason...
>
> Aristotle
> *Nicomachean Ethics*, Book VI

In this passage from the *Nicomachean Ethics*, Aristotle begins to provide a sketch of the human soul, or *psyche*. He goes on to tell us that it is composed of two parts, the *logos* and *alogos* ('rational' and 'irrational,' in both the Rackham and Ross translations). The five qualities that he enumerates here are aspects of the rational part of the soul, and thus constitute what Rackham translates as the virtues of the intellect, the Greek *arête* that may also be translated as 'excellence.' The preceding translations are all, of course, necessarily inadequate. What the qualities of *logos* and *alogos* suggest is not really whether the half in question is rational or irrational in modern terms; instead, as one of many alternative translations of *logos* suggests, Aristotle is concerned about the extent to which we may provide an *account* of the operation of these parts of our nature. Indeed, it is one of the tasks of the *Ethics* to do just that—to provide an account of the half of the *psyche* that is susceptible to his method, the 'rational' half.

The presumption of the *Ethics*, stated explicitly in Book VI and assumed throughout the entire account, is that the rational half of the soul is characterized by a constant craving and striving toward what Aristotle calls truth (*aleitheia*). We humans conduct this striving through the five means that Aristotle has named *sophia* (wisdom), *nous* (mind, intelligence, or intuition), *epistemé* (science or knowledge), *praxis* (practice), and *poiesis* (production). While his energies in the *Ethics* are devoted primarily to discussing only the latter three, and among them primarily *praxis*, all five are essential elements of Aristotle's ethical thought. They are also intimately interconnected; *sophia*, Aristotle explains, is a combination of *epistemé* and *nous* (VI.vii.3). As for *praxis* and *poiesis*, they are so closely related that it is only with great difficulty and, according to much current scholarship, little success that he distinguishes them. Particularly in the case of rhetoric we have an example of Aristotle's tendency to combine elements of *praxis* and *poiesis*. George A. Kennedy, in the introduction to his recent translation of the *Rhetoric*, notes the organizational scheme of the *Nicomachean Ethics* and acknowledges that most scholars attribute to Aristotle the view that rhetoric is a productive art and thus *poiesis* rather than *praxis*, but goes on to claim that 'what [Aristotle] actually says is that it is a mixture,' partly a 'method' and partly a 'practical art' (12). Here we must note Kennedy's own mixture of art and practice, a conflation that is hardly unique and that arises from Aristotle's own inconsistencies. Joseph Dunne, for example, claims that 'phronesis and techne are two modes of what we would call *practical*, as distinct from theoretical knowledge' and notes that Aristotle distinguishes them only when he 'is being strict in his usage' (237, emphasis in original). Eugene Garver's philosophic treatment of the *Rhetoric* similarly notes the division Aristotle creates between *phronesis* and *techné*; unlike Kennedy and Dunne he follows those divisions quite strictly in order to conclude that Aristotle was consciously constructing through the *Rhetoric* an 'art of civic character.' In the process, however, Garver associates rhetoric explicitly with *phronesis* and deliberation, rather than *techné*, despite Aristotle's explicit definition of rhetoric (in Book I) as the latter. The tension between *techné* and *phronesis* that, one review of Dunne's work points out, is 'legible in Aristotle's ethical writings' demonstrates that the two are unavoidably entangled (Gaonker 509).

Even if Aristotle is not entirely successful in creating the distinctions he intends, and it is clear he is not, the method through which he conducts the attempt is significant. He founds his distinctions on the basis of three variables—the context in which each faculty comes into play, the habit of mind that characterizes each, and the end of the activity in which each faculty engages. Within this contextual and teleological system it is with *poiesis* that Aristotle is most innovative, attempting a significant departure from the thought of his teacher Plato. It is also in this realm, and particularly through the habit of mind that he called *techné*, or 'art,' that he clearly exposes what are now seen as the traditional conflicts between theory and practice. These latter two are, respectively, the habit of mind of *episteme* and the faculty whose habit of mind Aristotle called *phronesis*, or practical wisdom.

It should already be apparent that the structure Aristotle erects in the *Ethics* is both complex in its original and complicated by intervening centuries of literal and metaphorical translation. Through *poiesis*, Aristotle developed and argued for a type of knowledge that mediated between the certainty he attributed to *episteme* and the uncertainty associated with cultural practices. Insisting on distinctions that Plato had not recognized between *episteme* and (through *techné*) *poiesis*, he succeeded in creating only blurry distinctions between *poiesis* and *praxis*. One tradition of scholarship has attempted to build on Aristotle's thought in order to clarify those distinctions—Janet M. Atwill's work on the potential of *techné* to transform our understanding of the liberal arts is an example from specifically (and classically) rhetorical studies (*Rhetoric Reclaimed*), as is Robert R. Johnson's use of *techné* to create a rhetorical approach to technical communication (*User-Centered Technology*). David Roochnik's study of Plato's use of *techné* (*Of Art and Wisdom*) and Peter Caws's distinction of *techné* from *praxis* to elucidate the role of knowledge in technology provide examples from the perspective of philosophy ('*Praxis* and *Techne*'), while David P. Haney uses the *techné-phronesis* distinction in his study of aesthetics ('Aesthetics and Ethics'). Another tradition takes advantage of the vagaries of Aristotle's distinctions for its own ethical purposes; in classical rhetorical studies and technical communication, both Carolyn R. Miller and Dale L. Sullivan use the ambiguity of Aristotle's classification of rhetoric in order to ally it with *praxis*, in both cases to argue for the ethical valence of rhetoric ('What's Practical about Technical Writing,' 'Political-Ethical Implications of Defining Technical Communication as a Practice').

The latter arguments take their impetus from a modern tendency to short-change *techné*, ignoring its essential role in Aristotle's ethics while recognizing the obvious ethical role of *phronesis*. The modern tendency to reduce *techné* to 'technology' encourages us to think of both as enterprises driven by unthinking knack (Young, Johnson) and a bare ethic of 'technical' expediency (Katz). In so doing, however, we not only ignore significant differences between the ancient understanding of *techné* and our own understanding of technology, as philosopher Carl Mitcham points out (131)—we also create an unnecessarily impoverished version of a set of activities that in Aristotle's understanding were intricately involved in and contributed to the ethical life of a culture. In short, we have excised *poiesis*, known to us pejoratively through our vernacular understanding of 'production,' not only from ethics but also from the rational half of the human psyche as Aristotle described it. The result is a de-humanized concept of modern 'production' that, besides its tendency to contribute to unfounded beliefs in the 'neutrality' of our technologies, as Martin Heidegger pointed out ('The Question Concerning Technology' 4), is inconsistent with Aristotle's individual thought and the ancient approach more generally to the material world (Mitcham 133).

In this chapter I extend the work begun by Atwill, Johnson, Roochnik, Dunne and others as I look at each of the three faculties to which Aristotle devotes significant attention in the *Ethics*. My aim is not only to elucidate all three faculties, but to argue for the value of bringing *techné* back into the realm of knowledge and ethics that Aristotle created for it. Approaching each such faculty as a 'method' in modern terms I argue, in keeping with my discussion in Chapter 1, that each faculty is inspired by an ethic that animates it—in Aristotelian terms, is characterized by a particular 'habit of mind.' These means and habits, methods and ethics, I connect to existing trends in legal scholarship—particularly, the Law and Economics, Law and Literature, and Law and Rhetoric 'movements.' I argue that Law and Economics, claimed by many as a 'scientific' approach to the study of law, is descended from classical *episteme* and its characteristic habit of mind, the *theoria* that may be variously translated as theory, observation, or speculation. Tracing the conceptual development of a more generally understood 'legal science' from William Blackstone through Christopher Columbus Langdell and then on to Richard Posner, I link the developing understandings of such a science and claims for its value to other values—those expressed most recently, in Posner's work, by an ethic of detachment. I then turn to *praxis* and what I see as its descendant, Law and Literature. Promoted by some nearly as an antidote to economics, the literary approach to law, under the rubric of 'legal art,' exhibits an ethic of cultural immersion that is also characteristic of *phronesis*, the habit of mind Aristotle linked to *praxis*. Here I begin with claims linking the modern Law and Literature movement to early Greek rhetorical practices (through the figures of the Sophists) before turning to the work of James Boyd White and other key figures in the movement. Finally, I turn to a much smaller recent body of scholarship in the nexus of law and rhetoric. Not properly a 'movement' of the magnitude of Law and Economics, or even of the much smaller Law and Literature of which it is more realistically seen as one branch, scholarship in the conjunction of law and rhetoric would do well, I argue, to distinguish itself from both larger movements by relying on the faculty of *poiesis* and the habit of mind of *techné*, 'art' in its ancient, non-literary sense. Were such scholarship to do so, I maintain, it would bypass some of the circularity inherent in the cultural immersion of *phronesis* as it simultaneously refocuses its attention from the interpretation of text to its creation through the value of use.

A note before I begin that discussion, however: I am aware that in assigning Law and Economics to Aristotle's realm of *epistemé* I am going against the grain of scholarship that links Law and Economics to pragmatism and, through the pragmatism developed in the thought of Heidegger, Hans-Georg Gadamer, William James, Richard Rorty, and others, to 'practical reasoning' and thus back to Aristotelian *phronesis*. Thomas F. Cotter provides a thorough discussion of this pedigree in order to argue that certain varieties of legal pragmatism could draw on it to soften some of the more troubling aspects of economic analysis—by mediating, for example, between what he calls 'the competing goals of efficiency and egalitarianism' (2140). Despite the promise of such potential, I have chosen in this work to study Law and Economics as an instance of *epistemé* because its claim to 'science' is far less problematic in Aristotelian terms than it is in our own. When 'science' becomes *epistemé* its grounding in discursive phenomena requires far less justification than it would in less classical terms; in other words, the specifically *social* science of economics may be as plausibly connected to Aristotelian *epistemé* as to *phronesis*, and without the necessity of amending the classical term by bringing it forward through an extensive body of modern thought that includes, in Cotter's account, utilitarianism, American pragmatism and neo-pragmatism, and postmodern continental philosophy (2072).

I am also aware that Law and Literature scholars, given the economic claim to *phronesis* through pragmatism and practical reasoning, may well resist the attribution I make here of literary analysis to *praxis*. However, it will presently become clear that in linking the literary habit of mind to *phronesis* I am quite specifically not linking Law and Literature to the pragmatism described and claimed by Law and Economics. As a rhetorician rather than as either a philosopher or a legal scholar, I am far less interested in discussing legal theory in its 'own' terms than I am in using the heuristic provided by Aristotle in the *Nicomachean Ethics* to question those very terms. Further, it is not my goal to investigate the entire western philosophic tradition of modern pragmatism or, for that matter, literary theory. Instead, it is my goal to re-characterize trends in legal thought, at least temporarily, to suggest an alternative that neither Economics nor Literature contemplates—that rhetoric, understood as an example of Aristotelian *techné*, provides at the very least a valuable supplement—in stronger terms, a viable alternative—to the perspectives of both.

The Value(s) of Speculation: Claiming Detachment

It is neither accidental nor necessary that the word *episteme* should come down to our time translated as both 'knowledge' and 'science.' While I believe the latter translation betrays cultural biases that, through the centuries, literally came to equate developing meanings of science with knowledge itself, I take advantage of such biases in order to question law's self-designation as 'legal science.' Further, by linking Law and Economics to *episteme* and thus to the habit of mind of *theoria*, I do not mean to suggest that it alone among the approaches I discuss here is 'theoretical' in modern terms. Instead, I simply take economic approaches at their word as they look at law through the lens of 'social science.' While the definition of science has changed in many particulars through the centuries and most recently through its increasing application to social phenomena, the vestiges of Platonic and Aristotelian *episteme* that appear in claims made for a specifically legal science can make significant contributions to our appreciation of the advantages and limitations the tradition of *episteme* brings to legal thought.

In his understanding of *episteme*, as in many other matters, Aristotle was heavily influenced by his teacher, Plato. But in 'following' him both chronologically and philosophically, Aristotle used Plato's work not so much as a model as a point of departure for his own thought. David Roochnik's extensive accounting of the function of both *episteme* and *techné* in Plato's work explains that, for Plato, *episteme* was knowledge 'of something'—in other words, knowledge of a specific and focused subject matter (112, 114). But this seemingly clear conception of *episteme* was complicated by Plato's tendency to use the words *episteme* and *techné* as near synonyms (90 fn1). Nussbaum tells us that there was, in fact, no systematic distinction between the two terms prior to Plato's time and that even Aristotle, who clearly attempts to distinguish them in the *Ethics*, occasionally uses them nearly interchangeably (*Fragility of Goodness* 94). Whether represented in the Platonic dialogues as *episteme* or *techné*, however, this specific knowledge of a limited subject matter was put forward by Plato as 'real' knowledge and, as such, contrasted with *doxa*, or opinion (Dunne 237). The certain knowledge of *episteme* was the recovery of what the soul, according to Plato, already knew (Atwill *Rhetoric Reclaimed* 134). Its subject matter, Plato insisted, was so precise and delimited as to be literally measurable (Detienne and Vernant 315). Indeed, as Nussbaum and many others tell us, Plato was so enamored of measurement that he saw it as a model for moral knowledge (*Fragility of Goodness* 90).

Plato's widely presumed search for an *episteme* of morality is contested by Roochnik, who argues at book length against what he calls this 'standard account'

(3-12). That account is provided and itself argued at length by Nussbaum in an analysis of the Socratic dialogue *Protagoras* which, she says, tells us that Plato wanted to assimilate practical reasoning to counting, weighing, or measuring in order to create 'scientific precision and control' in the face of the multiplicity—and thus confusion—of values being promoted by his contemporaries (*Fragility of Goodness* 90, 93). In Nussbaum's version of Plato's position, *episteme* is a universal kind of knowledge that, precisely because of that universality, can predict, control, and explain the objects of its study with precision (95-98). Nussbaum tells us that measurement itself is an *episteme* for Plato, who sees in the choice of a standard unit of measurement the possibility to render all choices commensurable so that moral or practical reasoning might be made instrumental, might consist merely of decisions about how to maximize the production of that standard unit (108-9). In the *Protagoras* Socrates suggests, uncharacteristically, that this measure might be pleasure. Nussbaum argues, in the face of the inadequacy of this measure to Plato's consistent moral project, that he uses pleasure simply as a placeholder, as a way of making his argument intelligible to his readers (110). Roochnik, however, argues that on this point Nussbaum 'is dead wrong' (228), that the failure of the Socratic dialogues to identify a *techné* of any given virtue, or of virtue itself, indicates Plato believed *techné* (and by extension, given Plato's usage, *episteme*) to be an inadequate model for moral knowledge (208-11).

Whatever Plato's actual position on this question may have been, with Aristotle we find the ambition to develop an *episteme* of moral knowledge dropped in favor of revising and refining distinctions among more, and more specialized, types of knowledge. This project resulted in Aristotle's claim for a moral knowledge (the 'practical reasoning' to which Nussbaum refers, called by Aristotle *phronesis*) that was separate from *episteme*; this project necessitated another, a not entirely successful attempt to overcome the near-interchangeability we see in Plato of *episteme* and *techné*. Aristotle distinguished these three major types of knowledge, what he called *dunameis* or 'faculties,' on a number of bases, including the realms in which they operated, their characteristic habits of mind, and their methods of investigation. Following Plato's emphasis on the role of the soul in knowledge, Aristotle defines *episteme* as one, but only one, of several ways by which the soul may aspire to truth. It was also a means by which human beings might aspire to the first principles that grounded all knowledge, if exercised properly with both intelligence (*nous*) and wisdom (*sophia*). Also like Plato, Aristotle assumes for *episteme* a separation between the knower and what is known, a 'habit of mind' he calls *theoria* and that may be translated not only as theory but also as observation or speculation. But where Plato, depending upon whom we believe, had given *episteme* a role in human moral life, Aristotle claims that it is instead knowledge of 'the most exalted objects' (*Nicomachean Ethics* VI.vii.3)—of the sun, stars, and planets, as Rackham tells us in the notes to this comment. Aristotle thus preserves the universality, certainty, and necessity of *episteme* and links the divinity of its objects of knowledge to those who study them (VI.i.5). Thus he maintains only a limited role for *episteme* in moral life and that only for a select few, because the posture of observation that Aristotle assumes for those who pursue this kind of knowledge requires a certain degree of detachment from everyday life. As he notes in both the *Ethics* and the *Metaphysics*, it is only after all the necessities of life have been provided for that we have the luxury—the detachment from everyday life—required for the pursuit of *epistemé*, of knowledge for its own sake (X.vii.4, I.II.11).

By the seventeenth century, the time of Francis Bacon and the 'New Science,' the translation of *episteme* into 'science' was complete. It is not surprising, then, that as science increasingly became the standard for knowledge, legal scholars would attempt to align the knowledge of law with that of science. Thus Sir William Blackstone undertook to provide an extensive and comprehensive statement, in his mid-eighteenth century *Commentaries on the Laws of England*, of a new and explicitly legal science. In undertaking this task Blackstone was faced with a particularly vexing problem, because the legal system for which he wished to claim the values of science was perceived even by his contemporaries as especially chaotic and certainly not 'divine' in Aristotle's sense. But he was also presented with an extraordinary opportunity: as the Vinerian Professor of Law at Oxford from 1753 until 1766, he was the first to lecture on English common law at the university level. Up to this time the common law tradition had been transmitted informally through apprenticeships or other types of association with practitioners and, of course, through the written judicial decisions that were its basis. But precisely because of this basis in practice, the common law tradition lacked the prestige of other more obviously theoretical pursuits; further, because its obvious complexity was not easily amenable to formulation as a compendium of black-letter rules, it was not apparent that the law could easily be taught by university professors or learned by their students. Indeed, prior to Blackstone no one had been able to effectively argue that this apparently formless and unwieldy mass had a coherent theoretical base that could be taught at all, whether in the universities or elsewhere.

Blackstone's *Commentaries*, based on the Oxford lectures, thus provide an implicit and extended argument for the presence of law in the university curriculum. The *Commentaries* do much more, however; while the stated goal of the Vinerian professorship was to improve the quality of legal education, an unstated but related goal was the redemption of the legal profession itself, whose numbers were declining in tandem with the reputation of the Inns of Court that were, prior to Blackstone and for some time thereafter, the primary training grounds for would-be barristers. In part, that declining reputation was based on the location of the Inns in a disreputable quarter of London, 'abounding with …pleasure grounds and fleshpots' that, worried parents presumed with some justification, would distract law students from their studies (Lemmings 236). But contributing to parental reluctance was the serious decline in the quality of the studies itself; the 'gentlemanly training' that had from the late Middle Ages into the sixteenth century included lectures and Moot Court exercises had gradually degenerated into a purely social initiation that, by Blackstone's time, allowed young men to 'eat their way to the bar'—to complete their training literally by eating a specified number of meals at one of the Inns (McManis 602, Lemmings 230). The lack of manuscripts or student notes after 1700 serves as evidence that there was little to no substantive legal education at the Inns by Blackstone's time (Lemmings 229). These educational problems combined with growing dissatisfaction with the legal system itself—with nuisance suits, high legal fees, and the uncertainty of legal outcomes—to increase the use of legislation, rather than litigation, to redress legal problems. English barristers, says Lemmings, had finally become 'not so much unpopular as irrelevant' (217).

Blackstone thus found himself working toward multiple and conflicting goals; this 'thoughtful conservative' (Boorstin 11) needed to improve legal education, reduce failures at the Bar, and bolster the profession, all while preserving a common law system that seemed to be at the root of the educational and professional malaise. Claiming scientific status for law was a way Blackstone could accomplish all of his goals, drawing on the contemporary prestige of science to bring legal studies into the university while using the body of accumulated common law decisions as the source from which the necessary scientific 'first principles' could be drawn. As Daniel J. Boorstin has pointed out in his extensive study of the *Commentaries*, wrapping law in the mantle of science allowed Blackstone to command respect for law while simultaneously discouraging doubt about its validity (6); the 'mysterious science of the law,' says Boorstin, allowed Blackstone to attribute the seeming chaos of the common law system to its distinctive excellence—its ability to accurately mirror and provide for the complexity of the cultural system it supported and to exactly match every possible injury to an effective remedy (Boorstin 101). That cultural system was itself a mirror of the nature of 'man' whose selfishness, reformulated by Blackstone as self-love, had been ordained by God and was regulated by the phenomenon of social organizing in general, and of English society in particular. Human disorder, it would now appear, was in perfect alignment with divine order, and the English common law as close to Natural Law as possible (Boorstin 51-53). Though legal science was clearly not itself divine, it was, Blackstone argued, derived from and thus included the study of things divine, universal, and certain.

Current responses to Blackstone are mixed. Lemmings claims that he was successful only in coating law with 'a thin veneer of intellectual respectability and rhetorical glamour' (215). Most scholarship acknowledges his enormous historical influence, and much of it agrees that he had his greatest successes, somewhat inadvertently, on the American continent, where by 1790 as many copies of his *Commentaries* had been sold as had in England. The *Commentaries* became a sort of 'do-it-yourself guide' (Boorstin xiii) for law study in the United States, ironically extending the era during which law could be studied outside a university setting. Eventually, of course, the *Commentaries* made their way into organized law schools in the United States, beginning with the private, proprietary schools before appearing in institutions on the order of the University of Virginia.

It was nearly a century after Blackstone that Langdell would play an important but somewhat ambiguous role in the furtherance of legal science through the development at Harvard Law School of the case-method pedagogy that bears his name. In a move similar to Blackstone's, Langdell assumed that the law was based on a limited number of foundational principles that could be inferred through the reading of judge-made case law. This method he promoted as inductive and therefore scientific, going so far as to claim that the judicial opinion served as the scientific 'specimen' in much the same way that natural specimens served the botanist or zoologist (Reed 344). The similarity to Blackstone's thought is not likely to be coincidental; there is evidence that law professors were lecturing on the *Commentaries* at Harvard as late as 1855 (Harno 51) and, therefore, some likelihood that Langdell, who attended Harvard from 1851 to 1854, would have attended such lectures. He left Harvard without graduating but the lack of a formal degree, which was not at all unusual at the time, did not interfere with his professional ambitions; from his departure in 1854 until his return to Harvard as the Dane Professor of Law in 1870, Langdell practiced law in New York City. What he actually did during his sixteen years of legal practice, however, is the subject of some controversy. Once again we have what may be called a 'standard account,' as much research maintains that he spent most of his time in the law library (Reed 343) and that he was, as Bruce A. Kimball summarizes the usual account, 'a rather pathetic figure: a self-absorbed, reclusive, though successful, grind who failed miserably as a lawyer, ultimately fearing to leave his garret office and engage other attorneys in court' (279). Kimball counters this portrait with one culled from extensive research into neglected primary sources that show, he says, that Langdell was successful as a lawyer both in arguing cases in court and in pioneering the creation of the technical written brief (278); that he was a far more prolific writer than is generally acknowledged (281); and that his role in developing the Langdellian case method was far more significant than the standard account (see, for example, Chase 332) is willing to concede (Kimball 288-301).

What Kimball hopes to question is a paradox obvious in scholarship on Langdell, that 'the received disparaging view has developed and persisted despite the enormous influence of Langdell and his model of legal education' (329). That influence has indeed been enormous, as Langdell's efforts at reform in legal education had sweeping influence both in his time and ours—in his capacity first as a law professor and then, just a few months later, Dean of the Harvard Law School, he instituted admission requirements for law study, created a sequenced and graded curriculum with annual examinations and, most significantly for a discussion of 'legal science,' the inductive case-method pedagogy (277). Like Blackstone, then, Langdell clearly had pedagogical and professional goals, attempting to move law securely into the realm of the university by way of appeals to a systematic procedure that not only could be successfully taught but that was also plausibly scientific by the standards of his time. To do so, and absent the necessity Blackstone had faced to align English law with natural law, Langdell aligned its American cousin with the natural sciences. While this alignment placed legal science even more openly in the human realm, Langdell's model circumvented the otherwise inevitable chaos of law's human location through its insistence that legal science was nearly as natural and thus as reliable as such sciences as zoology or botany. With the appellate decision serving as a legal 'specimen', the certainty of nature could substitute for the certainty of the divine; meanwhile, the law library, serving as the lawyer's 'laboratory' (Reed 344), provided the order previously supplied by God and the universe.

The supposed empiricism of Langdellian case-method pedagogy was questionable even in his time, and is more so in ours. Its critics argue that, at best, its proponents could claim that the necessity to classify, distinguish, and reason through analogy turned law students into 'scientific technicians' (Reed 356). Yet despite the blistering criticism he suffered then as now Langdell had in large part succeeded, for under his influence law moved securely into the universities, where Langdellian pedagogy rapidly became the standard model of instruction. His success, however, appears to be based not only in the scientific claims he put forward for law, but also on the genius of one very practical claim. Explaining the history and rationale behind the development of the case method in an address to the Harvard Law School Association in 1886 Langdell said his purpose had been 'to establish at least two things: first, that law is a science; secondly, that all the available materials of that science are contained in printed books.' While Langdell's conclusion was simply that 'if law be not a science, a university will best consult its own dignity in declining to teach it' (quoted in Reed 344) a less arguable conclusion was available. If law were a science, and if it were the legal case that provided law with both its specimen and the data from which its principles could be drawn, then law not only could be but, given the scarcity of printed books, could only be taught in a university.

By 1921, then, the Harvard model had become the primary teaching model throughout U.S. law schools (Currie 332). Though few law professors have been pure case-method teachers since at least 1953 (Harno 69), it remains the official standard for American Bar Association accreditation (Reed 343, 375). It has not gone unchallenged, however, and it has suffered from the insults both of detractors and of educational reformers. From its inception the Harvard model was criticized as too narrowly 'professional' or 'technical,' based as it was on the belief that law could be studied in isolation from other disciplines and without the contribution of non-legal theories (McManis 652). The purely legal realm that Langdell claimed for law placed it 'in a strait mold which was for years to dissociate it from the living context of the world about it' (Harno 59). This mode quickly came to be deemed insufficient in light of the development of 'social' sciences, and reactions against the perceived narrow professional model at Harvard took center stage at various law schools during every decade of the first half of the twentieth century. A functionalist model developed at Columbia in the 1920s to draw on social studies, and the clinical model developed by Jerome Frank in the 1930s, drawing on psychoanalytical models for student-provided legal services for indigent clients, contested the Langdellian faith in law as an autonomous discipline. Noting that Langdell had at least briefly succeeded in making his belief in the autonomy of law 'an academic faith,' Posner argues that the supports for this faith have by now 'been kicked away' by the movement toward contextualized legal studies (*Problems of Jurisprudence* 424, 428). The influence of the reactions against Langdellian autonomy is in fact still felt in what is often called the 'law and' movement in today's legal academy, the proliferation of courses not only in Law and Economics but also in Law and Literature, Law and Feminism, and others.

It was in the 1960s, and in the wake of just such sociological or functional approaches to legal study, that legal analysis came to be pursued within the order and structure that could be provided by economics. As a major element in that movement and the most prolific and audible voice in support of the economic analysis of law, Posner's work has echoed the arguments of both Blackstone and Langdell, claiming that a descriptive economic theory of law can 'enabl[e] the jumble of common law rules and doctrines to be arranged in a coherent system' and simplify legal education 'by exposing students to the clean and simple economic structure beneath the particolored garb of legal doctrine' (*Problems of Jurisprudence* 373, 362). But Posner contends that the 'prestige, authority, and (underlying these) the achievements of the natural sciences' has worked against a Langdellian faith in law's disciplinary autonomy (432-3). What economics, as a social science, brings to legal analysis is not only a systematic structure but a context—a realm that Posner's economic analyses of such disparate and seemingly non-economic subjects as literature and sexuality (among many others) would seem to claim is virtually unlimited. The subject matter of science, limited by Aristotelian *episteme* to the divine, extended by Blackstone's legal science to human nature in accord with the divine, and restricted by Langdell to law itself as a quasi-natural science, becomes in Posner's work all human behavior, a subject matter decidedly less than divine. But the move to what Aristotle saw as an inherently uncertain and unpredictable realm, that of the human, does not for Posner mean that certainty has been lost. For the order of the universe Posner substitutes a universalized human, the construct of Economic Man whose rationality Posner has likened to that of a 'pigeon or a rat' (*Problems of Jurisprudence* 382). This 'coldly calculating, rational, alert, well-informed' individual differs 'in some unspecified degree from real types,' Viner explains (61); however, like other economic analytical constructs, Economic Man is assumed sufficient to serve the interests of theory and is routinely, if implicitly, used to ground economic speculation.

Economic analysis would thus seem to build on the accomplishment Posner has told us he sees in Blackstone's work, the placement of law within a social context, paired with the use of theory to illuminate the operations of its legal system ('Blackstone and Bentham' 586). But the relationship of all three of these legal scientists to the contexts they seek to explain and regularize is somewhat ambiguous. The posture of detached speculation that Aristotle required of *episteme* has become difficult to achieve; the more specialized and the less divine the subject matter of *episteme* has become, the more immersion in that subject matter seems both necessary and inevitable, with the results Aristotle would have expected—each scholar develops an increasing 'affinity' (VI.i.5) with the objects of his study. Blackstone, as we have seen, was thoroughly committed not just to explaining but to preserving the English common law system in which he was immersed; Langdell, whatever we may assume is the truth about his personal role in the development of the case method, was certainly immersed in and committed to his 'legal specimens.' And Posner is unquestionably immersed in the culture and thought of both law and economics, however detached he may be from the contexts of everyday living by virtue of the economic abstractions upon which his analysis relies. Indeed such abstraction, Posner has argued, is neither a flaw nor a limitation of economic analysis. It is simply a characteristic of all science, economic science included, which of necessity abstracts from its data in order to avoid choking on a 'superfluity of detail' (Cohen quoted in *Problems of Jurisprudence* 366).

I do not mean to suggest by this account that the immersion of these legal scientists in the contexts within which they work detracts from the value of their observations. Aristotle, in fact, noted that 'we see men of experience [*empeiras*] succeeding more than those who have theory without experience' in undertakings intended to culminate in effects in the human realm (*Metaphysics* I.I.7). As *empeiras* becomes 'empiricism' and, eventually, experience, so does science become 'modern' and knowledge become 'useful.' But we must be mindful that such usefulness is in direct contrast to the value of *episteme*, which Aristotle had claimed was *achreistos*. Translated literally as 'useless,' *achreistos* could also mean outside the realm of *ta chreimata* or 'valuable things,' and the exchange they enabled in their role as 'money.' Thus, even though Posner insists on the usefulness of economic analysis in every possible realm of human activity, he does not venture as far as we might think from the Aristotelian ideal. For just as Aristotle insisted that observation was useless, so Posner insists that his own is 'value neutral,' or value-free. Whatever its investment in the realm of human activity and options, Posner's work not only maintains its distance from the values it observes; as we will see in Chapter 3, he insists that judges refrain from attempts to evaluate the rightness of the current distribution of wealth, pointing out that somewhat coincidentally their collective decisions meet the requirements of wealth maximization, what he calls a 'genuine social value,' that focuses on exchange in the service of efficiency (*Problems of Jurisprudence* 360).

As we move from Aristotelian *episteme* to Posnerian legal science, then, we see a gradual transformation of the meaning and value of knowledge and the methods by which it is presumed to be attainable; nevertheless, the contours of *episteme* linger and are recognizable. The detached contemplation of divine objects had been made possible for Aristotle's time by the provision of all daily needs; it was through *schole*, a word that may be translated as both 'school' and 'luxury,' that those who pursued *episteme* could remove 'scholarly' interest from human activity and maintain, as Aristotle did, that they pursued knowledge strictly for its own sake. As translations of *episteme* evolved from 'knowledge' to 'science,' reflecting later beliefs that true knowledge simply was scientific, the objects of contemplation became more earthly than heavenly but remained natural phenomena and objects rather than human nature or behavior. In the desire to maintain distance from the objects of knowledge, *empeiras* became Baconian empiricism and the goal of observation reversed Aristotle's: scientists attempted not to become like the objects of their contemplation but to avoid the possibility that those objects might become like them—contaminated—through the activity of observation.

Blackstone's attempt to harness the cachet of science for law maintains the claim of detachment by constructing the body of English common law as a mirror of British society, rather than as an outgrowth of it. Through his perception of the God-given rightness of that society, he derives the position that the law is also natural and right; he thus also, though perhaps inadvertently, resurrects the Aristotelian connection of 'science' to the divine as he claims to find in the unwieldy mass of the mysteriously divine common law a set of foundational legal principles. Langdell makes a similar move, inferring supposedly foundational legal principles from Anglo-American case law and using that 'inductive' method as the basis for legal pedagogy. Avoiding Blackstone's invocation of God, natural law, and British (or American) society, he also avoids Blackstone's particular version of circularity; his experience is not of the human social arrangements that give rise to legal disputes but of the written cases that are abstracted from and thus several steps removed from them. As Langdell averts potential contamination in either direction, however, he pays a price that Posner recognizes, the price of removal from the real world of legal practice for which he has been criticized, rightly or wrongly, for over a century.

Rejecting the decontextualization inherent in Langdell's method, Posner prefers to emulate Blackstone's placement of law within a real social context. He is not, however, interested in perpetuating Blackstone's metaphysics; through the social science of economics he focuses on the accumulated data of human choices and thus turns away from 'nature' or even 'human nature' toward what he represents as human behavior. From this accumulated data he derives not foundational principles of law but something more like maxims from which predictors of future human behavior may be inferred. The detachment that Posner achieves is thus twofold: through his contention that neither the data nor the predictions of economic legal analysis need be verified through direct observation of or testing against actual human behavior, he achieves an experience that is highly abstracted; through his refusal to evaluate the ethical or moral implications of human actions he achieves an assumed value neutrality for economic social science that is nearly a parody of Aristotle's claim for the 'uselessness' of *epistemé*. Ironically, then, he maintains the detachment Aristotle attributed to *epistemé* while simultaneously claiming an immersion in human behavior that, I will argue in Chapter 3, is disingenuous. Meanwhile, his rejection of the metaphysics of Blackstone cannot be characterized as a rejection of the 'divine' in Aristotelian terms, for his reliance on an admittedly questionable model of human behavior in the form of Economic Man invokes a universality for the human realm that Aristotle reserved for *epistemé*.

The trajectory may therefore be summarized as follows: As *epistemé* becomes first science, then social science, so *empeiras* becomes empiricism and then the highly abstracted 'experience' of economic data. The hope that the human may draw closer to and become like the divine through contemplation of heavenly bodies eventually changes to fear that those heavenly and earthly bodies may become contaminated by the human—until, finally, values become 'neutral' and the human becomes a parody not of the divine, but of itself. Whether the concern is divinity or universality, the derivation of knowledge through observation and speculation, or the necessity and possibility of detachment—and despite the differing understandings of these elements from Aristotle to Posner—the very questions that Aristotle identified with *epistemé* provide direction for the energies of legal science.

The Values of (Literary) Practice: Embracing Immersion

While the Law and Literature movement may not have originated in direct response to the development of social scientific and, specifically, economic perspectives on the nature and study of law, it is fair to say that its proponents offer literary method and perspectives as an alternative to the 'scientific.' In arguments that pervade the legal literature regarding the nature of law as art or science it is nearly always Law and Economics that is presumed as the 'science' and Law and Literature that is presumed as the 'art' in that opposition. Although I will argue, in the next section, that the literary tradition is not 'art' in the Aristotelian terms I am using, I will not question that attribution here. Instead, I will show that the opposition of the economic and literary perspectives on law is parallel to the opposition of *epistemé* to *praxis* as those terms are developed in the *Nicomachean Ethics*, and that the nature of that opposition lies in the methodological values assumed by their relative detachment from and immersion in the world of human activity. Countering the refusal of Law and Economics, particularly through Posner, to evaluate human 'preferences' in relationship to each other, Law and Literature insists upon the primacy of human values and the role of culture in creating, enabling, and restricting them.

The literary embrace of communitarianism, and along with it of an egalitarian vision, makes of Law and Literature a self-proclaimed subversive or sometimes radical movement. It is not possible, however, to paint the entire movement with the radical or subversive brush; while the literary work of the Critical Legal Studies movement may generally make such a claim, much literary work is content to celebrate the values of literature that itself either celebrates or questions the values of law. Rather than attempt to characterize the movement as a whole, then, my purpose is to examine in detail the work of scholars whose sometimes competing, sometimes compatible visions focus on the nature of a community and of 'the good' as defined by that community. In this group I necessarily place Posner, whose *Law and Literature* was at one time among the texts most frequently used in law school 'law and literature' classes (Gemmette) and whose literary theory is clearly derived from the assumptions of his economic theory. Beginning with the nature of Law and Literature as a humanities-based approach to legal theory, I question claims that it derives its pedigree directly from ancient thought before moving to discuss the perspectives of legal and literary scholar James Boyd White, constitutional scholar Robin West, and classical philosopher Martha C. Nussbaum, with references to Posner's work in order to highlight their divergences from his economic literary model. Characterizing their work as an example of the habit of mind Aristotle called *phronesis*, I conclude that it carries all the advantages and disadvantages of the classical term, bringing to legal studies a perspective based in values that, acknowledged as such, cannot support all the liberatory, revolutionary, or radical claims made for them.

White's work is particularly useful for highlighting the nature of literary analysis as animated by *phronesis*, in large part because he and Aristotle are in remarkable agreement concerning the effects of activity, what each also calls 'practices,' on human character. As he argues for the value of literary activity, White echoes Aristotle's insight that the quality of our character depends directly on the quality of our actions, repeatedly connecting individual character to what he sees as law's most significant activity, its language. In calling language an activity White is purposely literal; language, he says, is not merely a system of communication but a 'practice,' an 'act,' a 'gesture' (*Justice as Translation* xiii-xiv, 245). And largely because law is itself, at least for White, 'in a full sense a language' (*Heracles' Bow* 78) law, too, is an activity, 'something we do with words' (49). It is for these reasons that White advises students that their task in law school is not to learn a system of rules but, in working through the material of law, to 'fashion a character' for themselves through their experiences (*Heracles' Bow* 59). The 'literary position' that makes the life of the lawyer itself 'literary' is 'a way of giving attention to experience' (ix) that, we are to presume, is ultimately responsible for the benefits White wishes to claim for literary values.

White's purpose is not, however, to make explicit the connection to Aristotelian thought that will soon occupy us. It is, instead, to argue against the economic view that law is a policy science in favor of White's own position, and that of most Law and Literature scholarship, that law is more properly understood as one of the humanities (xii). Certainly, White is not alone in arguing for the benefit of literary values to legal study; nor is he alone in attributing these benefits to literature's own character as a member of the humanities. Indeed, in a great deal of Law and Literature scholarship, literature seems to function nearly as a metonymic stand-in for what is perhaps more accurately seen as its larger milieu. And while literature now often functions as a quintessential representative of the collection of studies we call the humanities, such was not always the case. Scholarship in law and other fields generally traces the humanities tradition to medieval times and a curriculum that took on standard form in that period as the *trivium* (the 'primary' education originally composed of rhetoric, grammar, and logic) followed by the *quadrivium* (a 'secondary' education in arithmetic, geometry, astronomy, and music). This plan of education, further elaborated by Italian humanists in the fourteenth century (Bizzell and Herzberg 466), has recognizable roots in the Roman educational system as well and constitutes 'in rudimentary form,' as Bernard Knox tells us, 'all our liberal arts' (86).

Michael Pantazakos ventures farther back than most to search for—and, he claims, find—the roots of the humanities tradition in Aristotle's time and before, in the itinerant scholars known as the Sophists. Relying on W. K. C. Guthrie's work in rhetorical history to identify the Sophists as the very first humanists, Pantazakos argues for similarities between the sophistic agenda and that of today's Law and Literature movement. Characterizing the work of the Sophists as 'the study of literature for moral edification and political empowerment, the formulation of reasoned hermeneutical methodologies, [and] the zeal to awaken the communal conscience to persons shut out from social interaction and equality' (46) Pantazakos largely succeeds not only in establishing similarities but also in arguing for one presumed consequence, that these similar agendas have led to perceptions of the Sophists and today's literary jurisprudes, indeed, even literature itself, as Nussbaum notes, as 'subversive' (Pantazakos 46, Nussbaum *Poetic Justice* 1).

But Pantazakos's use of the Sophists as 'the immediate precursor of our modern law and literature proponents' (46) is problematic. First, the sophistic 'humanism' he claims focused on empowering otherwise marginal groups supported a system that, however much it expanded a political franchise beyond what had existed in Athens prior to the sophistic movement, is marked by the same faults that Pantazakos says require us to reject the era that much other Law and Literature scholarship claims as a model and starting point for humanistic legal values. The Antebellum United States, frequently offered as a Golden Age when 'every educated man possessed a thorough background in the Great Books of literature' was rife with race and gender-based persecution (36), a condition that works against its 'Golden Age' status for a movement marked by its concern for community and egalitarianism. While it is indeed true that the rights of citizens and the reach of citizenship itself expanded greatly during the Athenian democratic movement, and that the Sophists both responded to and facilitated that expansion, it is also true (as Pantazakos indeed notes) that Athenian democracy was extremely limited, supported by a 'culture of racial and gender discrimination [that] also influenced later societies' (51) including, quite obviously, the Antebellum United States. Those persons formerly 'shut out from social interaction and equality' in Athens were an otherwise privileged group that did not, ironically, include the Sophists themselves, most of whom were not Athenians, but foreigners (Knox 90, Jarratt 'The First Sophists and Feminism' 27); Athenian citizenry, though it may no longer have been restricted to an 'aristocracy' based strictly on the accidents of birth, simply created a new aristocracy justified by the accidents of property, and of course only males of certain bloodlines could qualify (Knox 12).

But even though the democratic claim is questionable, Guthrie himself does provide a more useful and less politically problematic argument for sophism as the prototype for humanism. The sophistic recourse to human values was, he explains, part of a larger rejection of what we would today call 'science'—the world presented to ancient Athens by its physicists, particularly through their theory of the existence of invisible particles called 'atoms.' The sophistic 'revolt of common sense' (63) prefigures the current revolt against the 'common sense' of our age in the resort to literature to counter the power of social scientific approaches, especially economics, to law and legal study. Indeed, one reason Pantazakos rejects the Antebellum United States as the birth of the fusion of law and literature is the birth of its fraternal twin, 'legal science,' as the dominant educational paradigm in U.S. law schools during that very same period (36). Just as today's resort to literature attempts to counter the world and human nature as economists present both, the Sophists countered the world as ancient physicists presented it, and the loss of faith in the possibility of absolute knowledge that accompanied it (Knox 66), with an increased faith in both the possibilities for and limitations of human knowledge. Finding its credo in Protagoras's famous dictum, that 'man is the measure of all things' (68) the sophistic agenda strongly resembles those strands of Law and Literature scholarship that draw from postmodern or deconstructive thought. There is, further, at least a kinship between the humanistic elements of sophistic thought and those of the literary scholarship I examine here—particularly if Pantazakos is correct in his assessment that sophistic thought was focused on values that 'bring a human community together' (Pantazakos 45).

Nevertheless, and for my purposes quite significantly, the equation of the humanities with literature, if sought through the phenomenon of the Sophists, is questioned by their own 'disciplinary' identity. The Sophists were, or claimed to be, 'interpreters of poetry' (Pantazakos 44, Knox 94) but they also claimed much more—Knox notes that as a group they covered an array of subjects that, like our later liberal arts, ranged from arithmetic to grammar to history. However, it was the art of rhetoric that was not only 'the core' (Knox 91) of their teaching, but their unique invention. The role they conceived for the literature of their time was as a source of cultural materials and values that their rhetorical practice itself, rather than a broad 'humanistic agenda' (Pantazakos 45) questioned. This relationship led to a further relationship, that of rhetoric and culture to 'the good,' that parallels but is less intimate than the relationship Aristotle conceived for the relationship of the good to *praxis*.

In fact, the connection of *praxis* to 'the good' is absolutely essential to Aristotle's thought. We can infer that connection from his occasional use early in the *Nicomachean Ethics* of an alternative term, *energeia*, also translatable as 'practice' but often in generic or negative senses. Though Dunne, in his exhaustive exploration of *phronesis* in *Back to the Rough Ground*, claims that *praxis* 'seems to be co-extensive with *energeia*' (248) Aristotle (whose usage, as often noted by both his detractors and his admirers, is not entirely consistent) makes available a subtle distinction between the two words that cannot be adequately rendered by one-word English equivalents. When, speaking generically, he explains that happiness is 'a form of activity' (*Nicomachean Ethics* I.x.3) he uses *energeia*, as he does when he also explains that the character of our 'activities' (which could conceivably be either positive or negative) controls the quality of our dispositions (II.i.8). To these generic senses of activity he also adds the quality of roteness implied by one sense of our word 'practice,' so that when he says we acquire virtues by 'having actually practiced them' (II.i.4) or that the virtues are 'exercised' through our 'activities' (III.iv.7) he once again uses *energeia*. And finally, when there is a chance that our activities may be destructive or distinctly non-virtuous, he also uses *energeia*, as when he provides as examples of 'actions' that affect our character such negative activities as negligence, drunkenness, and injustice (III.v.10) and notes that the virtues can be both created and destroyed by the same 'actions' (II.ii.8). But when Aristotle makes a claim for the necessary goodness of our actions he is far more likely to use some form of *praxis* rather than the alternative *energeia*, for example when he wishes to establish a link to 'noble actions' (I.ix.9) or voluntary choice (III.i.6).

White, Nussbaum, and West all argue, much like Aristotle, for a direct connection between literary values and the individual and social good, arguments that vary in the extent of their recognition of their own problematic nature. It is upon this basis that all three make the roster of what Posner calls an 'edifying school' of literary criticism that, he says, provides little more than 'didactic' and 'moralizing' criticism (*Law and Literature* 75, 308). West's early work maintains it is literature's 'humanizing' function that justifies its existence in the legal curriculum; asking and answering her own questions about why lawyers should read literature, she ultimately concludes that 'it makes us more moral. It makes us better people' (*Narrative, Authority and Law* 263). Nussbaum maintains that the very form of the novel fosters empathy for others on the part of the reader (*Poetic Justice* 2), thus arguing for an ethical 'fancy' by which judges may, if they judge well, imagine themselves into the situations of the parties before them; she fares better than either West or White with Posner, who accepts her argument that literature can increase our awareness of 'injustice and of moral issues generally' on the basis of what he calls her 'concrete' approach to literary texts (*Law and Literature* 316).

But Law and Literature scholarship generally, in Posner's view, fails to produce anything more useful than 'exhortation[s] to the judge and lawyer to be more sensitive, candid, empathetic, imaginative, and humane' (299). This failure could hardly be a fault of literature from a perspective such as Posner's, where to use literature for moral or practical legal purposes is both to misuse literature and to misunderstand law. 'The difference between a poet and a law professor,' Posner explains, 'is that we do not ask the poet to show us how to get from where we are to where in his imaginative vision he wants us to be' (204). This statement encourages the interpretation that we do, however, ask for such direction from the law professor; indeed, this chief advocate of the law and economics movement has already noted that 'economic analysis of law…brims over with proposals for reforming the institutions of the law' (182). In sharp contrast White's work, according to Posner, provides 'little in the way of proposals for improving the law's treatment of sensitive issues' (299). West's work, despite her attention to such issues, is no better: her use of literary texts to argue against his economic theory provides evidence 'entirely from fiction,' says Posner, 'her own and Kafka's' ('Ethical Significance of Free Choice' 1432). In the final analysis for Posner, 'writers of imaginative literature are rarely practical people with practical lessons to impart' (*Law and Literature* 316). For Posner, then, literary studies of law fail an all-important 'practical' test.

The question of literature's ability to deliver 'the goods' is of genuine concern, and I will return to that question at the end of this section. However, a larger concern is how those goods are to be defined, and by whom. White and Nussbaum—with Aristotle and Posner—place great faith in the role of individual agency in performing that function and—without Aristotle or Posner—the role of literature in extending agency to otherwise disempowered groups. Both Nussbaum and White construe individual agency as a function of judgment, whether it functions literally as legal decision-making or more figuratively as a response to legal or literary texts, and use literature to evaluate that function ethically (*Poetic Justice* 62-3; *Acts of Hope* 277). Drawing on Adam Smith's 'judicious spectator' for her model, Nussbaum calls for a concerned but unbiased judicial standpoint, one that is empathetic by way of its vivid imagination but that goes beyond empathy as it exercises judgment through proper, rational emotions. Surveying the legal scene with detachment, the judicious spectator is presumably able to provide a 'true view' of events that 'filters out' the commitments of personal situation (*Poetic Justice* 74). For White the hallmark of ethical judgment is the creation of a judicial voice that, like the ideal texts envisioned by New Critical method, reconciles opposing elements and creates a coherent text by 'comprehending the contraries' with which it has been presented (*Heracles' Bow* 114-17). For both Nussbaum and White, then, the self in whom authority vests is largely institutional, an ideal individual created by its professional role. Posner, because of his economic orientation generally the odd man out in this group, tends to see the individual and individual agency as consisting of a nexus of preferences or tastes that the individual will—and should—pursue autonomously (*Problems of Jurisprudence* 389). Posner's economic theory, as we have seen, constructs 'the good' as a purportedly value-neutral construct, simply an accumulation of choices whose ethical or moral basis it is not the task of law to evaluate (*Sex and Reason* 85). The parallel in his literary theory is his understanding of 'good' literature as that which survives the 'test of time' (*Law and Literature* 14-15), a sort of cultural taste-test that establishes which works will remain in the established canon over a period reaching to several eras.

West is generally sympathetic to the project of Nussbaum, which she describes as 'one of the most heartening and inspiring, as well as inspired, projects on the legal academic horizon' (*Caring for Justice* 189). She is, however, outraged by Posner's proposed model of agency and skeptical of White's. Locating agency in individual preferences, as Posner does, assumes a degree of individual autonomy and understanding of one's options that West believes does not reflect the constrained situation of many or most of us; his 'profoundly illiberal' position refuses to engage in what she believes are key moral practices and ultimately ignores 'the experiences of the silenced [which as such are] not likely to be reflected in the choices of "market actors"' ('Sex, Reason, and a Taste for the Absurd' 2417, 2445). As for White's faith in law's institutions, West sees his 'resurrection' of 'the early nineteenth century "man of letters"' as utterly compromised by its exclusionary historical legacy (*Caring for Justice* 182, 186). Seeing in Nussbaum 'the most promising attempt to further [White's] reconstructive project' (188) West proposes an alternative to White and Posner that, like Nussbaum's 'judicious spectator,' draws upon her faith in the possibility of the separation of individuals from their political commitments. In West's model, however, agency is located not in the institutional construct of the judicious spectator but in what she calls 'the animalistic self,' a 'natural, ahistorical' self whose 'natural human needs' (*Narrative, Authority and Law* 165-6) are presumably prior to individual political commitments and should accordingly inform legal activism and decision-making.

Both West and White attempt, in markedly different ways, to overcome what they see as flaws of 'typical' literary approaches to legal studies. For West, the flaw lies in a blindness to law's nature as an imperative, rather than interpretive, act (91). White's faith in institutional figures, she says, 'obscures the fact that law is a product of power' (paraphrased in *Acts of Hope* 182), thus thwarting its own interest in fostering the agency of disempowered groups. The lack of attention to the coercive power of legal texts that characterizes work such as White's, she concludes, lends support to the presumed morality of existing power (*Narrative, Authority and Law* 95). Conceding the connection between law and power, White argues that points such as West's, while valid 'in a sense,' also 'greatly overstate' that connection (*Heracles' Bow* 238). His own work is intended to correct the error he believes more typical of literary studies, its attempt to subvert authority, by developing an art by which 'good and bad forms of this phenomenon [authority] are to be distinguished' (*Acts of Hope* xiii). Nevertheless, it is clear that the power White does recognize is culturally conferred upon an individual by the institutional roles our legal system provides; further, it is also true that such an individual is, if not silenced in the manner of West's disempowered groups, still significantly constrained by professional legal culture in numerous ways. If, as White maintains, culture is 'a form of life and language' (*Justice as Translation* 46) then law's provision of a 'comprehensibly organized method' or a 'set of materials' from which to speak (*Heracles' Bow* 35) is also the provision of a culture. There is, then, 'a cultural inheritance which constitutes "us"' (103) as 'we,' individually and collectively, 'become the languages we use' (*Justice as Translation* 49). This dependence of the self upon its culture and language is, as White concedes, a 'radically problematic fact of our moral life' (*Heracles' Bow* 86), a situation that creates our 'habits of mind, of perception, and of feeling' (*Justice as Translation* 25).

Once again White is in remarkable accord with Aristotle, both on the level of the issues involved and that of his very vocabulary. But Aristotle is far more comfortable than White with the implications of this understanding for the formation of the 'quality of mind' (*Nicomachean Ethics* VI.viii.1) he called *phronesis*. If, as White recognizes, it is impossible for individual character to be formed in isolation, outside the bounds of a culture, for Aristotle that constraint is an unproblematic good. What White calls culture Aristotle calls deliberation, the distinctly human function of a citizen, or *politeis*, a political animal who must learn that function through immersion in the language and culture of the *polis*. The noble actions Aristotle claims for *phronesis* are enabled by what he understands as voluntary acts of will, despite what we, with West, may consider to be significant constraints on individual choice. In fact, Aristotle concedes that individual choices are not necessarily voluntary acts, that the two terms are not synonymous. Through his use of the Greek term *phainetai*, also translated as 'appears,' Aristotle recognizes that choices are only 'manifestly' voluntary (*Nicomachean Ethics* III.ii.2); as we might now say, our choices are often constrained by circumstance.

Again, for Aristotle the reality of cultural constraints on choice is less problematic than it may be for White. For even when choices only appear to be voluntary, Aristotle maintains that the origin of such choices so understood remains in the individual agent. 'Man,' he says, 'is origin of his actions,' significantly described here not as *energeia*, but as *praxis* (III.iii.15). Both the ethical cast Aristotle provides and what Nussbaum calls an 'anthropocentric' focus (*Fragility of Goodness* 291) that Dunne also sees as growing out of the centrality of the human agent (Dunne 263) make of *praxis* a fitting model for the ethical imperatives addressed by White, Nussbaum, and West. Further, the deliberative character of *praxis* clearly distinguishes it from contemplation or speculation, the habit of mind characteristic not only of Aristotelian *theoria* but arguably also of the detached perspective Posner claims for economic legal analysis. Just as Aristotle reminds us that we do not deliberate about things that cannot change, or about things that are not within our power to influence (*Nicomachean Ethics* VI.v.3), so Posner has argued for the simple, value-neutral observation of a human nature seen in economic terms as inevitable. Such things as these we may presumably only contemplate or observe, but practical deliberation—and literary legal studies along with it—purposely trains its focus on strictly human affairs, on matters that both Aristotle and most literary legal scholarship understand as highly changeable and uncertain.

Despite his recognition of the uncertainty of human affairs, Aristotle remained convinced that *praxis* attends to such things as are 'in our control and attainable by action' (*Nicomachean Ethics* III.iii.7) and that, consequently, 'man is the author of his actions' (III.v.6). But Aristotle must struggle to convince today's readers that the agent endowed with culturally conferred 'practical wisdom' is, of necessity, good when he does good actions 'from choice and for the sake of the acts themselves' (VI.xii.7). For who is authorized to decide whether an action is 'good'? Who, this group of Law and Literature scholars might well ask, deliberates as to the good, and how? One answer Aristotle suggests is frustratingly vague: one deliberates about good practice (*eupraxia*) through good deliberation (*euboulia*). Another answer he provides is frustratingly explicit: good practice is learned through *empeiras*, experience. Both of these answers are frustrating because they are circular; good deliberation is deliberation about 'what is good for human beings' (VI.v.6), and what is good for human beings is learned through experience, at least in part through the experience of such deliberation. Thus it truly is 'a hard task to be good,' as Aristotle explains in Book II, and though for him that task is hard because it requires the agent to identify and aim for the middle ground in activities that are not easily measured (II.ix.4), to more recent ways of thinking it is hard because there seems to be no way to step back from our activities and achieve any perspective from which to measure them at all.

Moreover, the examples Aristotle provides to illustrate the activities of *phronesis* in contrast to those of *theoria* are of limited persuasive power today. If we know as a general principle that 'light meat' is wholesome, he says, it is our practical knowledge that chicken is a light meat that leads us to eat it (VI.vii.7). This example is enlightening for several reasons, including the knowledge that humankind has understood for at least twenty-five hundred years that we should be eating chicken rather than beef. But this is a rather unproblematic good, as Dunne also notes, because it is based in what he calls 'technical as distinct from phronetic reasoning' (310): we have what we consider to be unproblematic information about the wholesome qualities of chicken that come to us from the realm of science. It is the job of *phronesis*, Dunne reminds us, to deal with more problematic situations where such guidance is not easily available—such as, he says, those questions of justice faced by a legal code (311).

There is yet another serious problem brought to light in Aristotle's chicken example, for practical reasoning as focused by Aristotle on means has had nothing to say about the ultimate end of eating chicken, that (presumably) of good health. Indeed, Aristotle specifically exempts *phronesis* from considering the question of good health, explaining that doctors do not deliberate about health—it is the assumed and unquestioned good at which doctors aim, as is persuasion for orators and good government for statesmen. And should such ends seem initially unproblematic, consider the manner in which Aristotle elaborates on this argument: it is not just doctors, or orators, or statesmen, but all 'professionals' who do not deliberate about the ends of their professions, but 'take some end for granted, and consider how and by what means it can be achieved...most easily and best.' Deliberation in *praxis*, in other and very explicit words, is 'not about ends, but about means' (III.iii.11). If Law and Literature scholarship is to achieve the ethical ends that White, Nussbaum, and West wish to claim for it, should not its focus be precisely opposite that claimed for *phronesis* by Aristotle? In other words, does the focus of literary scholarship on the 'activities' of language preclude a simultaneous focus on their results?

We have now encountered two problems considered most vexing by scholarship in Aristotelian ethics—the circularity and instrumentality of *praxis* and *phronesis* as Aristotle presents them. Both Nussbaum and Dunne take on these questions, and both conclude that *phronesis* is neither strictly instrumental nor viciously circular, though their methods differ substantially. Nussbaum begins by noting the problems inherent in translating Aristotle's phrase, *ta pros to telos*, as simple 'means,' rather than the more adequate translations she suggests, as '"what is *towards* the end,"—or, "what *pertains* to the end"' (*Fragility of Goodness* 297, emphasis in original). This more supple translation, she suggests, allows us to understand that while practical deliberation may be about some large end that is not currently in question (good health, in the chicken example) it is permissible within that deliberation not only to discuss the means but also to ask for some further specification of the end, about 'what is to *count* as the end' (297, emphasis in original). Practical deliberation, she concludes, provides no single standard or universal end; any given end can be a constituent in some larger end not currently up for discussion (297).

Coming at the question from a different angle, Dunne begins by noting that Aristotle employs the terms 'we say' (*legomena*) or 'it seems' (*phainetai*) when he makes his instrumentalist claims for *phronesis* (269). Where Nussbaum finds in these terms Aristotle's wholehearted and intentional support of the common wisdom (*Fragility of Goodness* 240-3), Dunne claims Aristotle uses these terms to report his 'considerable respect' for such wisdom without necessarily endorsing it (269). In support of this position Dunne distinguishes means that are 'external,' and thus directed toward an end separate from the means (a traditional understanding of the concept) from those means that are 'component' or *entelechia*, in which case the means include their own end (270). *Praxis*, he says, is *entelechia*, both is and contains its own end (262); *phronesis*, which both is and leads to an ability to deliberate well—both arises from and leads to good action—is also *entelechia*. Practical wisdom does not stand 'outside or above' our lives (Dunne 268) but, agrees Nussbaum, is 'immersed human reasoning' (Nussbaum 'Skepticism about Practical Reason in Literature and the Law' 743); as such, it simply does not provide the kind of knowledge that we may separate from a situation, systematize, and apply from any point outside the situation that calls for it. Indeed, we only know the situation calls for it because we are in the situation, says Dunne (268). Dunne concludes that practical reasoning is not really instrumental, in other words, not because certain ends may be contained within larger ends as Nussbaum explains, but because *praxis* and *phronesis* are simultaneously both the process and its end.

His strenuous attempt to save Aristotle from an instrumental mindset that Dunne acknowledges Aristotle himself found perfectly comfortable (269) therefore succeeds, if it does, only by highlighting the second feature of *praxis* and *phronesis* that is anathema to modern minds, their obvious circularity. Aristotle's account of practical reasoning unabashedly makes its every component lead through another and inevitably back to itself. The end of *praxis*, he says, is *eupraxia*, or good practice (*Nicomachean Ethics* VI.v.4) because 'a thing done is an end in itself' (VI.ii.5); while we are presumably the authors of our actions (III.v.6, using a form of *praxis*) it is those actions that determine the character, or disposition, from which our actions may arise (III.v.10-12). *Phronesis*, we are to understand, both guides action and arises from good action (Dunne 290). Though its function is to tell us what is good, it is actually of no use in helping us to become virtuous, says Aristotle, for 'knowing about [virtues] does not make us any more capable of doing them' (VI.xii.1). We cannot have the knowledge to help us become good unless we already are good, says Dunne (290); *phronesis* is therefore of no use either to the virtuous, who do not need it, or the non-virtuous, who do not have it.

There is no easy way out of this circle, and quite possibly no way out at all. Nussbaum discounts the attempt put forward by John Rawls, who claims that the abilities of a good judge are not ethical commitments, which presumably would arise from *phronesis*, but supposedly value-neutral abilities such as imagination, empathy, and factual knowledge. The obvious problem with this attempt is, as Nussbaum points out, that those abilities are not value-neutral; further, she explains, if we wish to remain with the Aristotelian paradigm, a simple enumeration of intellectual abilities (as she characterizes imagination and empathy) is simply insufficient (*Fragility of Goodness* 311). Aristotelian *phronesis* is both intellectual and moral, based in Aristotle's 'reverence...for the shared conventions of which character, through moral education, is the internalization' (310). And that morality is 'unrelentingly' located in the 'first-person agent' (Dunne 314) who serves as the standard of choice in any attempt we make to identify the good, defined by Aristotle as whatever the 'prudent man,' possessed of *phronesis*, would determine it to be (*Nicomachean Ethics* II.vi.15). Dunne therefore attempts to find an alternative way out of the circle by understanding *phronesis* as 'a perfected form of experience' (305). Not simply a systematized accumulation of past experience, *phronesis* is a dynamic orientation or attentiveness that tests past experience against a current situation in order to either confirm or revise its wisdom. *Phronesis* is thus the process through which experience becomes 'aware of itself' (289) and thereby 'self-correcting' (292).

What Dunne is suggesting seems to be a limited space between *phronesis* and the experience that both creates and is created by it, a very slightly detached perspective on itself. Certainly it is not the purportedly objective detachment often claimed for the theoretical perspective of *epistemé*, or science, which Nussbaum says would make of practical reason the stance of 'some sort of Martian social scientist' ('Skepticism about Practical Reason in Literature and the Law' 743). Perhaps aware of the irony in the implicit complaint that Aristotle is insufficiently linear for our tastes both Dunne and Nussbaum conclude that the circle of *praxis* and *phronesis* is not 'vicious,' (Dunne 279) that '[c]ircularity by itself need not dismay us' (Nussbaum *Fragility of Goodness* 313). What matters, according to Nussbaum, is that Aristotle has significantly complicated and expanded the circle by developing a concept of knowledge that can be brought to bear on concrete questions (313). *Phronesis* does not seek universal norms because we do not need them; the 'principles of adjudication and pictures of practical reason' we already have are sufficient to resolve our disagreements ('Skepticism about Practical Reason in Literature and the Law' 743). We need to imagine, with Aristotle, an account of 'immersed human reasoning' that adopts not the detached posture of the social scientist assumed by economics or of the 'playful figure' imagined by deconstructivist strains of Law and Literature, but the perspective of 'a figure who is...deeply immersed in the human issues at stake.' What we need, Nussbaum concludes, is 'an involved reader' (743).

White, too, has turned to law's literary nature to escape or at least complicate the circle of what he calls culture and what Aristotle calls deliberation leading to *phronesis*. Maintaining that we are made by our culture and language, White adds the claim that a literary approach to texts allows us to remake both as well (*Heracles' Bow* 87; *Justice as Translation* 23). But if literature can do all that has now been claimed for it—if it can make us better people, develop our capacity to empathize, facilitate some perspective on ourselves and our culture, and provide ethical standards for judgment—it remains to be seen what specific properties of literature enable all these capacities. In Chapter 4 I consider this question at length, weighing the assumptions of the scholarship against the demands of *phronesis* and the contention of literary and legal critic Stanley Fish that we are unable to occupy a space outside our disciplines from which to judge them. This contention is one that White, at least, acknowledges but that he optimistically assumes is not fatal to his project—though we cannot 'get outside' our discourse, he admits, we can become more conscious users of it (*Justice as Translation* 20). What White does not address, however, is the process through which we become 'users' in the productive rather than literary sense of that term—how we become writers rather than readers. White's claim that his conception of reading is also a conception of writing (*Heracles' Bow* 77) is plausible in the abstract sense in which he makes the claim, that a text is always remade through the response of each reader who engages with it. Those abstractly remade texts, however, exist at first in isolation, in the mind (or heart) of the solitary reader. If those remade texts do eventually become concrete through writers responding to those readings—a highly plausible assumption—White nevertheless does not investigate the concrete processes through which that remaking occurs. It is to that question—to the nature and operation of the processes through which texts come into existence, processes generally mystified into invisibility—to which I now turn.

The Value(s) of Production: De-Limiting Use

When we move from *praxis* to *poiesis* we undergo what is in some respects a subtle transition. Certainly, the distinctions between these two realms, characterized by Aristotle respectively as 'doing' and 'making,' can be difficult to maintain; early in the *Ethics* Aristotle says simply, and rather unhelpfully, that 'making is different from doing' (VI.iv.2) and refers his students to other of his discourses for a fuller discussion. As we will soon see, Aristotle does provide some grounds for making this subtle distinction in the *Ethics* itself, though with some difficulty. Fortunately, other distinctions between the two faculties are not so difficult to perceive and maintain. It is clear, for example, that for Aristotle *poiesis* is unlike *praxis* because it is concerned with the production of some artifact and, further, that whether the artifact is as concrete as shoes or as abstract as their fit, the end of the productive process lies not in its own activity (as is the case with *praxis*) but in the use of the artifact it creates. Still, Aristotle does tend to explain what *poiesis* is in large part by explaining what it is not, by contrasting it to both *epistemé* and *praxis*. As he pursues that method he is not, unfortunately, entirely consistent in his vocabulary, in his distinctions among the concepts themselves, or in the habits of mind he associates with them. Nevertheless, the elements of the triad of *epistemé*, *praxis*, and *poiesis* are 'some of the most stable concepts in the corpus,' says Atwill (*Rhetoric Reclaimed* 168) and as such their distinctions merit our attention. Further, some of the confusion Aristotle creates can be attributed to the differing purposes of the differing works in which he discusses these three concepts.

In the *Nicomachean Ethics*, for example, Aristotle's primary focus is on *praxis* and its related 'habit of mind,' *phronesis*. His frequent recourse in this work to *techné*, the habit of mind of *poiesis*, is therefore intended in part to present his contemporaries with both a comparison and a contrast to a more familiar example than those abstractions can provide; excellence in *techné* becomes the more visible counterpart of the less visible *phronesis*. Book II of the *Ethics* provides multiple examples of this strategy on Aristotle's part. Because 'good craftsmen look to the mean as they work,' for example, and given that 'virtue, like nature, is more accurate and better than any form of art,' it then follows for Aristotle that virtue, too, 'has the quality of hitting the mean' (II.vi.8-9). For Aristotle, then, *techné* and *phronesis* are alike in significant ways: both are, he tells us, means to 'the good,' although in *techné* we are led to presume that the good is defined not by human character, as is *phronesis*, but by the usefulness of an art or of its product (*Metaphysics* I.I.14; *Rhetoric* I.I.12-14; Mitcham 89).

Both *techné* and *phronesis* are also active in the realm of human experience and are jointly distinguished from *episteme* on that basis; however, their relationships to experience are significantly different. While humans learn both *phronesis* and *techné* through that medium, Aristotle says, in *phronesis* 'experience' is 'doing,' an activity driven by cultural immersion, especially the activity of a quasi-political deliberation regarding 'things that are good and bad for human beings' (*Nicomachean Ethics* VI.v.4) or human communities. Because in *techné* 'doing' is transformed into 'making,' deliberation changes accordingly; *techné* draws upon or uses deliberation rather than being constituted by it, as *phronesis* appears to be. Furthermore the type of deliberation necessary depends upon the type of *techné* involved, for the arts of gymnastics and music, for example, differ greatly from other more concrete and determinate arts such as house-building (Dunne 254). Rather than being driven by culture and politics, the deliberation characteristic of *techné* is developed through experience with various materials and directed at acting upon them in order to accomplish a pre-thought-out goal toward which 'making,' with greater or lesser assurance of success, is directed. Here again, however, *techné* may serve to illuminate the less visible *phronesis*; because the outcomes of both are determined by the cultural experience or productive process, respectively, through which they are generated, those outcomes are to some degree uncertain. Aristotle puts the point with respect to *techné* this way: while it is true that we can only learn the art of harping by the experience of harping, it is also true that 'both the good harpers and the bad ones are produced by harping' (*Nicomachean Ethics* II.i.6). The same holds, he continues, for 'the virtues. It is by taking part in transactions with our fellow-men that some of us become just and others unjust' (II.i.7). For Aristotle, then, *techné* is a useful analogy for *phronesis* because of its link to a good achieved through experience.

But the analogy should not be taken too far. *Techné*'s production of results 'separable' from the agent differs substantially from the production of *phronesis*, which implies not so much control over one's material circumstances as the reverse—the agent in *phronesis*, the person possessed of practical wisdom, 'becomes and discovers "who" he [sic] is' through actions that take place in a network of relationships with other agents (Dunne 263). Because the cultural material of *phronesis* is a given, then, *praxis* makes available a choice of actions within a culturally acceptable range, a condition that requires the agent to be 'in a certain condition when he does them,' and to make those choices 'from a fixed and permanent disposition of character' that is culturally supported (*Nicomachean Ethics* II.iv.3). This condition is not required of *techné* which, according to Aristotle, requires not a culturally sanctioned attitude but 'the mere qualification of knowledge' (II.iv.3), including a familiarity with both its materials and the forms toward which they are to be directed. But we must not assume that its differences from *phronesis* occur because ancient *techné* is roughly equivalent to modern technology, as may be tempting to assume (Mitcham 117); rather than a lock-step and invariable process leading to the mass production of invariable products, *techné* is a 'habit of mind' in an individual maker that permits varying degrees of control over one's materials and circumstances, resulting in products of correspondingly variable quality. The distinctions between *techné* and *phronesis* on the basis of their outcomes cause Dunne to ask two questions; first, whether Aristotle's treatment of *phronesis* 'does little justice to the role of knowledge in *praxis*' (263; see discussion of this question in Chapter 4) and second, whether the analytical abilities that Aristotle attributes to *techné* make of it an abstract, nearly theoretical kind of knowledge with little regard for the experiential base provided by its materials. What Dunne calls a 'mentalist' *techné* (346) is, he concludes, 'virtually coincident with rationality itself' and thus 'remains so close to [theory]' as to be, for Dunne at least, barely distinguishable from *episteme* (249-51).

To the extent *techné* begins to look more like the ability to reason about production and less like the ability to actually produce, it does begin to seem very similar to what Aristotle has claimed is *episteme*. In the *Nicomachean Ethics,* apparently minimizing the role of experience in *techné* in favor of 'the mere qualification of knowledge' (II.iv.3) Aristotle seems also to have minimized the role of the materials of *techné*, neglecting their ability to provide valuable feedback to the maker (Dunne 315, 323). His use of the verb *technazein* in *Ethics* VI.iv.4 to mean 'to *contemplate* [emphasis added] how a thing is to be brought into being' is further evidence for Dunne that Aristotle conceives of *techné* as a nearly theoretical faculty that he has already allocated to *episteme* (317). This perspective on *techné* is particularly visible, Dunne tells us, in the *Metaphysics* (252). Once again, however, we do well to note that Aristotle's primary purpose is not the explication of *techné* but its use in the explication of something else—in the *Metaphysics,* the nature of *episteme* understood somewhat generically as knowledge itself. His claims for *techné* in Book 1 of the *Metaphysics*—that *techné* is a knowledge of universals, even that *techné* 'is' *episteme* (I.I.12)—certainly do little at first to establish clear distinctions between the two concepts. But it is clear that Aristotle's purpose in the section in question is not so much to demonstrate the extent to which *techné* is like *episteme* as it is to show how both differ from 'mere experience,' which can provide only the knowledge of particulars that serves what he calls 'practical purposes' (*Metaphysics* I.I.7-10). In other significant ways, as he immediately goes on to explain, *techné* is quite distinct from *episteme*, including in the manner in which *techné* acquires the knowledge of universals that he claims for it. For while the 'wise man' who possesses an *episteme* (I.II.1) knows particulars only 'in a sense' because the universal logically 'comprises' the particulars (I.II.4) those possessed of a *techné* will know the particulars by virtue of the very experience from which *epistemé*, as *epistemé*, is detached.

This argument can be made clearer if we turn to a work where Aristotle is not using the concept of *techné* as a comparison or contrast to *praxis* or *epistemé* but where he is focusing on a particular *techné* itself. By necessity we therefore turn to his *Technes Rhetorikes* or 'art' of rhetoric. In turning to the *Rhetoric* we also turn, once again by necessity, away from the more concrete *technai* such as architecture or cobbling toward an art whose activities are performative and that may then issue in correspondingly abstract products. While we may easily conceive of 'texts' as concrete products, the speeches in the Athenian political assembly and law courts would have been committed to memory and rarely to writing. And if we see the product of either an oral performance or a concrete text as existing primarily in its effect on its audience, it is clear that we have gone a long way from the production of houses or shoes. Thus, according to Aristotle the *techné* of rhetoric has many affinities with the more abstract versions of both *epistemé* and *praxis*—in fact, he says that it is an 'offshoot' of both dialectic, the method designed to lead to the more certain knowledge of philosophy, and ethics (or politics), the latter two realms most firmly associated with *praxis* (*Rhetoric* I.II.7). Despite such close linkages that leave us with 'plenty of reason to be confused' about rhetoric's relationship with politics and thus its position in the triad of *epistemé*, *praxis*, and *poiesis* (Atwill 189 fn33) the work Aristotle intends for the *Rhetoric* seems clearly intended to distinguish this third term from the other two in order to tell us what a *techné* is, rather than what it is not.

Aristotle's purposes in writing the *Rhetoric* are complex and multifold, but most commentary on the work notes his intent to differentiate himself from predecessors with distinctly different views on the value and uses of this *techné*— not only from the Sophists, whose prior works on rhetoric he found inadequate, but also from his teacher Plato who, in calling it 'flattery' and mere 'habit,' had claimed (through Socrates) that rhetoric was not a *techné* at all (*Gorgias* 463b). The middle line that Aristotle creates and walks in his own rhetoric is based on his addition of rhetorical 'proofs,' more reliable than the emotional proofs on which he claims the Sophists rely while simultaneously less precise than the syllogistic proofs he associated with logic and, through dialectic, philosophy. Aristotle thus requires less precision of rhetoric, as *techné*, than Plato wished to demand of all *technai*, including rhetoric (Roochnik 186, 198). As an art focused on the production of speeches in the legal, political, and ceremonial assemblies central to Athenian culture, rhetoric must have seemed to both Aristotle and his contemporaries to be similar to *phronesis* in significant ways. In relying on universal statements systematically generated from that cultural experience, and by subjecting them to probabilistic assessment, rhetoric took on a flavor that approached that of *epistemé*. Yet Aristotle succeeds in giving a character to rhetoric that invokes both without becoming either.

Aristotle begins to carve out a space between *epistemé* and *praxis* by firmly and explicitly identifying rhetoric as a *techné*, declaring at the outset that rhetoric's methodical examination of argumentation and of the means to its success is a task that 'all would at once admit to be the function of an art [*techné*]' (*Rhetoric* I.I.1). Noting that its link to ethics can cause rhetoric to occasionally 'assume the character of politics,' he proceeds to distinguish it from *praxis* and *phronesis* by invoking and extending the earlier description of *techné* in the *Nicomachean Ethics*; thus, like any *techné*, rhetoric must work with the material it is given—in this case, from 'common subjects of deliberation' (I.II.11). With those subjects of deliberation as its material, rhetoric is thus distinguished from deliberation itself because it is a process of invention, a means to 'discover the possible means of persuasion in reference to any subject whatever' (I.II.1). And lest we assume, like Dunne, that its analytical function makes rhetoric take on a purely speculative or theoretical function, he proceeds to differentiate it from *episteme*, insisting that it is 'useful' (I.I.12-14). That such usefulness is due in large part to its general application is evident from Aristotle's related claims, that to the extent that his contemporaries attempt to turn rhetoric into *episteme* (which, he has earlier explained in *Nicomachean Ethics* section VI.vii.5, is 'useless') they destroy its real nature (*Rhetoric* I.IV.6). Over and over again Aristotle explains that rhetoric, while systematic, cannot be reduced to a particular science because it deals with matters of general interest and within general cognizance, because it is not applied to any particular class of things but to any subject whatsoever (I.I.14, I.II.1, I.II.7). Rhetoric is therefore like any other *techné*, Aristotle maintains, in that it deals with generalities rather than with particulars; the rhetorician will not consider what should seem probable to Socrates or Callias as individuals, but 'that which seems probable to this or that class of persons' (*Rhetoric* I.II.11). Rhetoric therefore attempts not to convince individuals but to convince groups of individuals as representative of categories based on what we would today call the 'demographics' of age, gender, or economic situation, among other factors.

Rhetorical categories, then, are general and have universalizing properties that seem to veer dangerously close to the universal knowledge Aristotle confines within the limits of *episteme*. But probable statements about carefully delimited circumstances based on the generalizing assumptions that for Aristotle were characteristic of rhetoric differ significantly from the demonstrable universal knowledge that he claimed for *episteme*. Moreover, the generalizing properties of rhetorical categories have been derived from experience with the particulars in a way that the universal knowledge of *episteme* has not. Here Aristotle is particularly clear: rhetoric, he says, is like *episteme* in that it attempts to provide a sort of demonstration using proofs. The deductive reasoning used in rhetoric, however, differs from the deductive reasoning, the syllogism, used in *episteme*. Rhetoric's method of deductive proof is the enthymeme (*Rhetoric* I.II.8), a sort of truncated syllogism with its major premise omitted. It is enough in rhetoric, for example, to say simply that Socrates, being a man, is mortal; the major premise (in this case, that all men are mortal) is left unstated precisely because the audience can be counted upon to provide it (I.II.13). The universal propositions of rhetoric thus, we may assume, 'comprise' the particular not simply as a matter of abstract logic, but very concretely: it is knowledge of and experience with the particular—even 'the particulars' themselves in the form of the audience—that literally produces those propositions.

So far I have concentrated on the ways in which Aristotle distinguishes *techné* from *praxis* and *epistemé* separately. But there is one significant point on which he distinguishes it from both simultaneously, and that is in his identification of the end of *techné*. To understand the significance of this distinction, it is first necessary to understand the relationship of the 'end,' what is often translated as the 'final' cause, to the remaining three of Aristotle's four causes. The distinctions among these four—the formal, material, efficient, and final causes—is central to Aristotle's thought not only in the *Metaphysics*, where he discusses them at length, but throughout the whole of Aristotle's work. It was a way for Aristotle to distinguish himself from the prior philosophical tradition and, most significantly, from Plato (Tredennick xxviii); it was also the means whereby he accounted for what he saw as one of his major contributions, an explanation of the processes of generation (Dunne 328). It would appear Aristotle was not, however, entirely successful in either of these undertakings. According to Tredennick, the four causes eventually collapse into two, the 'form' and 'matter' that also preoccupied Plato (xxviii, xxx); according to Dunne, generation is actually 'squeezed out of his conceptual scheme' (328). Fortunately, it is not necessary for Aristotle to have succeeded in either of these ambitions for us to use his thinking about causality in order to understand *techné* as the 'habit of mind' of *poiesis* and thus as distinct in important and substantive ways from *epistemé* and *praxis*. It is through the four causes as Aristotle distinguishes them that we can see how a formal cause such as the rhetorical heuristic of *stasis*, that I will demonstrate in Chapter 5, differs from its end, or final cause—and, further, how Aristotle's occasional equation of an 'end' to a 'limit' invokes not the sense of limitations, as we might see it, but of a tool with the potential to contribute to the undoing of such limitations.

What then, is the nature of the four causes, and how does Aristotle attempt to distinguish among them? Heidegger, who discusses the causes primarily in order to distinguish *poiesis* and thus *techné* from modern 'technology,' explains that our modern sense of causality is far more restricted than is that of the ancient Greeks, reducing the efficient cause to the modern notion of 'efficiency' (7) in order to focus on what is not only the most visible cause but also the closest, temporally, to what we consider to be the 'end' of production, a physical product. But the Greek 'cause,' or *aition*, means not a 'goal,' says Heidegger, but 'that to which something is indebted,' so that the four causes are 'ways, all belonging at once to each other, of being responsible for something else' (7). They are intended by Aristotle to provide, again with *techné* as his consistent concrete example (Mitcham 120), an analogy to enhance our understanding of natural generation, of 'change for a purpose' (Atwill 85). This move on Aristotle's part is useful because where art and nature most clearly differ, for Aristotle as for us, is in the nature of the efficient cause; natural products have in themselves the source of their own motion, while in art that source of motion is an external 'maker' (85).

It is admittedly difficult both for Aristotle and for us to distinguish between form and matter. Heidegger tells us that the cooperative relationships the ancient attitude assumes among form, matter, and the 'efficiency' of the maker distinguishes the 'bringing forth' of *poiesis* and *techné* from the 'challenging forth' of modern technological processes (10-14). Today, he suggests, we force form onto or into matter in a way the ancient maker would not. Mitcham, too, sees this distinction: in ancient Greek thought, he explains, matter was not inert or lifeless as we tend to assume today (Mitcham 131) but more or less receptive to—in Aristotle's thought even expressing a 'desire' or 'reaching out' for—appropriate form (122). It is for this reason that *techné* can serve Aristotle as a means to distinguish form and matter in ways far more visible than would be possible in reference to natural processes; *techné*, Aristotle says, imitates nature as it unites form and matter 'in a particular something' (Mitcham 122). But in *techné* and in nature both, form and matter can only be distinguished, not separated; they 'never exist apart' (Tredennick xxvii) but are merged in final products whether natural, such as a tree, or artificial, such as a brick house or bronze sphere (*Metaphysics* VII.VII.10-12). Thus *techné* allows Aristotle to distinguish form from matter by temporarily separating them through the example of *techné*, but only analytically. The example allows him to explain (in the *Physics*) that a 'producing *techné*,' such as architecture, will know the matter of a product (the materials leading to construction of a house) while a 'using *techné*,' such as that possessed by those who live in the house, will know the form (quoted in Atwill *Rhetoric Reclaimed* 88).

Note, however, that the house, the product of *techné*, is not the 'end' of the process as we might assume, but the form, the substantiation of matter. The 'form' is usually called by Aristotle the *eidos* or pattern, and thus the idea or visualization of the product in the mind of the maker, though he sometimes calls it the *logos* or 'formula,' and thus the rational account the maker is able to provide of the product's generation (*Metaphysics* III.IV.6, IV.V.21; I.III.1). It is this distinction between form and end rather than that between form and matter (luckily, given the difficulties of the latter) that is most useful for understanding the nature and significance of rhetoric, a *techné* designed to infuse form into (or derive it from) the nebulous matter of language. And it is here that we return to the idea with which we began our discussion regarding the four causes, with the distinctions among ends that allow Aristotle to, finally and definitively, differentiate *poiesis* from *epistemé* and *praxis*.

In the explanation provided in the *Nicomachean Ethics*, Aristotle's theory holds that both *epistemé* and *praxis* are circular activities with what we might call internal ends. The end of *epistemé* is itself, the pursuit of knowledge for its own sake (*Metaphysics* I.II.6-10); as for *praxis*, because 'a thing done is an end in itself' (*Nicomachean Ethics* VI.ii.5) 'doing well [*eupraxis*] is in itself the end' (VI.iv.3-4). *Techné*, however much it may resemble *praxis* in its focus on the human, rather than the divine, differs from it at first, in Aristotle's account, simply because 'making is different from doing' (*Nicomachean Ethics* VI.iv.2). Because that distinction is not intuitively clear, Aristotle goes on to explain that making and doing are different precisely because *techné*, as making, 'aims at an end distinct from the act of making' (VI.iv.3), not only (and temporarily) in a product that results from the process but, finally, in the activity of its use (Atwill 87, Johnson 11-13). The end of the *techné* of rhetoric, for example, resides only temporarily in a speech or a written text, and only in one sense—that of 'product' as form. However, even in a relatively straightforward and concrete *techné* such as cobbling, we can see that the end lies not necessarily in the concrete product—shoes or sandals—but potentially in their 'fit' with their circumstances and the purpose (walking) for which they were designed. In other words, the form that the products of a *techné* can take has been subject to outside influences—in rhetoric the counterparts of shoes, feet, and walking are speeches or texts, the expectations of the audience or readership for whom the speech or text is intended, and the coming into being of a desired state of affairs through what Aristotle called 'persuasion' (*Rhetoric* I.II.1). It is in this sense that Aristotle explains that 'the orator persuades by means of his hearers' (I.II.5); because its users' expectations constitute an end that determines the form that the matter of rhetoric—seen as words, seen as issues—can most effectively take, it is the hearer rather than the speech who constitutes the end, or final cause, of the *techné* of rhetoric (I.III.1).

The constraints offered by matter, form, and end, all brought together through the agency of the maker, make any *techné* possible by providing its tangible product with the boundaries that make them recognizable to their users. But those products, as forms, are for that reason not the end of any *techné*, and the 'boundaries' that facilitate recognition of the form are not its 'limits;' rather, recognition of the form by way of its physical boundaries facilitates the full realization of the end in the final cause, in those for whom the form has been produced. The 'limit,' called by Aristotle in the *Metaphysics* both *peras* and *telos*, is not a physical boundary but 'the furthest part of each thing...outside which no part of [it] can be found' (V.XVII.1). Thus it may contribute to 'an organization of space' but is 'never a fixed frontier or stable line' (Detienne and Vernant 288). It is, says Aristotle, the 'reality or essence' of a thing, the 'limit of our knowledge of it [that] is also a limit of the thing' itself (V.XVII.2). Because 'that which is unlimited is...unknowable,' as Aristotle claims in the *Rhetoric* (III.VIII.2), the circularity of both *epistemé* and *praxis* facilitates knowledge by encompassing it within a literal 'sphere' that also encloses its 'end,' its *telos* or *peras*. The term *peras* invokes a host of associations in ancient Greek, including the *apeiron*, or unlimited, as a circle without end or exit that accurately represents the circularity Aristotle envisions for both *epistemé* and *praxis*. It also calls to mind the *peirata*, a term that may be translated as 'tools' (Atwill 47) but that, according to Detienne and Vernant, was also literally the 'tip or end of a rope' that creates a circular bond or knot (293). Clearly, it is the end of the rope that could also be the undoing of the bond, the untying of the knot, it creates. Thus, while it is through form as the instantiation of matter 'that we recognize everything' (*Metaphysics* IV.V.21), it is only by its end or limit that we can get outside it, a position we can reach, if at all, not only figuratively but literally at the end of our ropes.

The relationship of *techné* to boundaries is therefore, as Atwill says, paradoxical. Because the end of art exists outside the 'sphere' of production, because the *peras* provides the *peirata* that can lead to its own undoing, it seems that the boundaries that make the products of art intelligible also exist in large part to be violated. In fact, according to Aristotle we can only speak of 'excellence' in art because it is also possible for art to fail. Here again *techné* differs from both *epistemé* and *praxis*, both of which can admit of error only at the expense of giving up their identities, of ceasing to be *epistemé* and *praxis*. But *techné* is 'compatible with failure' (Roochnik 52) and more: true excellence in *techné* is attributed by Aristotle to error itself. The specifically 'voluntary' error that makes for excellence in *techné* would be blamable in *phronesis*, Aristotle says; *epistemé*, as 'true' knowledge, cannot incorporate or account for error at all, cannot 'state the exception to the rule' (*Metaphysics* VI.II.13). But it is precisely the exception to the rule that is the substance of the willing error to which Aristotle refers and to which he attributes the one conclusive difference between *techné* and all other kinds of knowledge. *Epistemé* aims to be *achreistos*, whether translated literally as 'useless' or more generously as 'value-free;' *phronesis* aims to inculcate cultural values into the individual who is shaped by engagement in cultural *praxis*. But rhetoric aims to be *chreisimos*, says Aristotle, to be 'useful' or valuable precisely because of its concentration on the values of its users, the use they will make of its products, and the role of voluntary error in accommodating—or violating—both.

Detachment, Immersion, and Use: The Relative Value of Values

Though Aristotle does create hierarchies among the faculties that he recognizes in the *Ethics* (see *Metaphysics* I.I.17, where he considers 'the speculative sciences to be more learned than the productive') he also recognizes each as important for the contribution it makes to what we can know through its characteristic habit of mind. Similarly, each method of legal analysis I have introduced in this chapter makes important contributions to what we can know about law by way of the value that animates it. The scientific urge expressed from Blackstone, through Langdell, and on to Posner takes on the task of systematizing the materials of law (generally understood as statutes, constitutions, judicial opinions, and other texts) in order to infer from them an order that can, in turn, contribute to understanding the law itself. Posner, as he tells us, extends Blackstone's move to place those materials in a social context that, while necessarily and purposely diluting the presumed autonomy of law ('The Decline of Law'), allows the critical distance necessary to perceive law's characteristic structures. The detachment from law, however, stems from immersion in another culture, that of economics, that imposes its own culture, structure, and values (White *Justice as Translation* 46-51). The predictive power that Posner claims for economic analysis, in other words, stems from its commitment to the value of efficiency through wealth maximization. This value, as Posner readily admits, economic analysis is always able to find (*Problems of Jurisprudence* 365) whether the situations it examines are intuitively 'economic' in nature or decidedly not. Here economic method is like any other; seeking efficiency, it finds efficiency in large patterns of behavior or, failing to find it, recommends a corrective.

The literary urge values the very immersion (in law as well as in literature) that economic analysis vainly seeks to avoid. In the process, of course, the goals and source of critical perspective from which to understand the law changes; rather than inferring large structural patterns in the textual materials of law, literary analysis such as West's or Nussbaum's infers communal values from the perspective of literary materials, either through explicit discussions of law in literary texts or through the assumed congruence of literary and legal interpretive methods. White takes an additional step further back to a prior material, that of language itself, in order to understand law's self-construction as a community. Both of these moves lead to an awareness of outside perspectives on law that itself fosters an emphasis on the value of empathy rather than efficiency. Literary analysis thus requires a level of comfort with uncertainty that economic analysis abhors; concerned not with developing predictive powers but with uncovering the meaning embedded in and enacted through law's language, White in particular claims for the literary perspective a contribution to understanding how law 'comes to be' through its words.

Where White's work stops, rhetorical work begins. The abstract claim that a way of reading implies a way of writing begins to take concrete form through the rhetorical focus on production through the value of use. Thus *poiesis* attempts a different route out of the circle in which it, like every method, is enclosed; rather than claim detachment through a 'separate' perspective in which one is immersed, and rather than celebrate one's immersion in the hope that a close examination of one's perspective will yield critical consciousness of one's assumptions, the rhetorical perspective takes advantage of the permission Aristotle grants it to 'fail.' Seeing its end in the use of its products by those for whom they are intended, the rhetorical perspective attends closely to the manner in which they are produced and the demands of the material with which it works. Rather than attempt to exit the circle of its own assumptions through a detachment that it considers false, or even through a presumptive empathy with those outside that circle, the rhetorical perspective seeks to undo the knot creating that circle through the very material of which it is constructed. Through its acknowledgment of the contribution of its materials to its products, as well as of the unpredictable uses to which both may be put, the rhetorical approach to understanding law draws on its unique excellence— its capacity for voluntary 'failure'—to err past the bounds of its experience.

Chapter 3

The Things We Say: The Speculations of Legal Science

> This is why we say Anaxagoras, Thales, and men like them...know things that are remarkable, admirable, difficult, and divine, but useless...
>
> Aristotle
> *Nicomachean Ethics*, Book VI

A group of accomplished legal scholars at a conference on law and the humanities did their best to convince me that my focus in this chapter on Richard Posner was misleading, mistaken, misdirected, or worse. Despite his position in the forefront of the Law and Economics movement Posner's work was hardly the whole of its scholarship; in fact, they explained, his work could not even be called representative of it. Several of them had stopped responding to Posner in their own work; paying attention to his outrageous claims, they seemed to be saying, only encouraged more. But in the space of only a few minutes the tide of the conversation turned. Posner, one scholar admitted, was the most-cited figure in Law and Economics; Posner, another added, has national visibility and is widely cited even outside academic circles. Posner's book on Law and Literature, I pointed out, was at one time the most frequently used text in literature courses in law schools. (That's literature, not economics.) Posner, we all agreed, was endowed with all the power and influence that normally accrue to the Chief Judge of a Circuit Court. However 'uninformed and slipshod' his work, as Stanley Fish had said of his literary theory, and however much we might want to ignore him we seemed, with Fish, to be saying that Posner and his work must be taken into account (*Doing What Comes Naturally* 310-311).

So my focus on Posner remains, though I have learned that I cannot argue that his theoretical positions are representative of Law and Economics scholarship. Rather, it is my intention to argue that Posner's distinctive approach to the use of economic science for legal analysis exhibits a remarkable similarity to classical science, to Aristotle's *epistemé*. Further, Posner's work presupposes a 'tool use' or instrumentalist view of language that, as I will argue, is typical of much Law and Economics scholarship and leads directly to a position held by many of its scholars, that the work of legal science, understood as economic in nature, is not to deal with questions of justice—most especially, not with the justice of the current distribution of wealth.

It is for this reason that I begin this chapter with what seems a nearly offhand remark in the *Nicomachean Ethics*, Aristotle's association of philosophy—the remarkable, the admirable, the difficult, and the divine—with the 'useless' (VI.vii.5). Such a comment seems somehow callous or wrong to today's way of thinking, in which the value of knowledge is often predicated precisely on its usefulness. Yet for Aristotle, if not for Posner, it was philosophy's very inapplicability in practical matters that made it the highest form of knowledge to which human beings could aspire. As he tells us in Book VI of the *Ethics*, this lofty knowledge could be reached through a combination of human faculties, particularly through science (*epistemé*) exercised with intelligence (*nous*). When joined with wisdom, or *sophia*, science and intelligence could lead to the very threshold of undemonstrable and unquestionable first principles. The 'habit of mind' associated with *epistemé*, the *theoria* translated as both 'theory' and 'speculation,' was for that reason a primary intellectual virtue of the soul. It was, however, only one of three such virtues Aristotle recognized. Two other intellectual virtues, called practice ('doing') and production ('making'), were not speculative but calculative, and operated in the uncertain atmosphere of the human as opposed to the certainty of the divine that Aristotle reserved for theory. It was in the human realm that knowledge became of use, a realm and a purpose that Aristotle denied to science as he understood it.

Though our understandings and definitions of science have changed in the centuries since Aristotle made this statement, we continue to debate on many fronts the uses of theory and the certainty of scientific knowledge. Building on Thomas Kuhn's *Structure of Scientific Revolutions* the postmodern critique identifies the socially constructed nature of all science. Feminist critiques offer either to extend the postmodern through positions such as that of Mary E. Hawkesworth, that all epistemology hinges upon linguistic possibilities (167), or to supplement Kuhn's 'normal science' with an 'improved' version of empiricism—hence, the standpoint feminism of Sandra Harding (113). Nevertheless, values rooted in the Aristotelian tradition and in the Enlightenment respect for science free of linguistic bias—for theory over practice—have ensured that law would fight for centuries to be recognized as the former, to be known as 'legal science.' One result of that struggle, the Posnerian version of Law and Economics, is the subject of this chapter; that this particular form of legal science more closely resembles classical *epistemé* than modern science is its argument.

While it is relatively easy to understand the appeal of 'legal science,' it is hard to say precisely when (or whether) law succeeded in its claim to be known as such. Law was at first inextricably tied to classical rhetoric, itself practiced through three activities—the deliberation of the political assembly, the celebration of cultural values typical of ceremonial orations, and the dispute resolution of the law courts. Thus seen as a subset or 'branch' of rhetoric, as James Boyd White has argued it may usefully still be seen (*Heracles' Bow* 37), law was also one of Aristotle's calculative virtues and took its place in the human realm of productive knowledge—as 'making' rather than 'theory.' But rhetoric gradually lost its relevance in the calculative sphere as the establishment of empires from Rome onward began a gradual separation of rhetoric from both politics and law. Legal scholars Linda Levine and Kurt M. Saunders are no doubt correct in noting that Peter Ramus's sixteenth-century excision of logic and reasoning from the art of rhetoric made law's divorce from rhetoric desirable (110), but Ramist method merely continued a long trend that had left rhetoric confined either to ceremonial discourse or to the practice of secular and canon law through the *ars dictaminis*, letter writing (Bizzell and Herzberg 377). It was later, as poetics cultivated an identity distinct from both law and science, that Renaissance rhetoric became linked and limited to the use of figurative language largely courtesy of Ramus (473).

The successes of the physical sciences in the realm of human (rather than divine) affairs rendered rhetoric increasingly irrelevant to the very realm for which it was invented, and further eroded its status. It is not surprising under the circumstances that law should attempt to transfer its allegiance and identity to science and to profit by its link with the social values that law sought to support. In fact, those social values had by the seventeenth and eighteenth centuries themselves become 'scientific' as the New Science of Francis Bacon, Isaac Newton, and John Locke increasingly promised to accurately describe, predict, and control the phenomena of the natural world. But the proponents of legal science were faced more squarely than those of the physical sciences with a problem the latter would claim to have handled and dismissed; law, more obviously than those other sciences, was required to do its work through language. That necessity led to another, the necessity for law to develop a theory of language that would reconcile science and rhetoric in a manner both more complicated and more detailed than that required of the 'New Scientists.' In this chapter I follow that intricate move both historically and conceptually, examining claims for and beliefs about science generally, and legal science more particularly, beginning with Aristotle before moving to Sir William Blackstone and Christopher Columbus Langdell and finally to Posner, the most avid promoter of legal science today. From its use in Aristotle, where *epistemé* could refer simultaneously to both specialized and generic types of knowledge, to its translation as 'science' with all the cultural and political commitments that translation implies, our understandings of this 'approach to truth' seem to have changed dramatically. Yet certain core issues remain constant, as I hope to show, a core that is particularly evident when science becomes 'legal.' Blackstone's eighteenth-century *Commentaries on the Laws of England*, for example, followed in the classical tradition through his attempt to articulate a legal science based on quasi-Aristotelian 'first principles.' Claiming for legal science a basis in natural law that echoes the focus of Aristotelian *epistemé* on the realm of the divine, Blackstone presented a powerful and persuasive argument for the role of its language in maintaining, through its very obscurity, law's majesty.

Nearly one hundred years later, at Harvard Law School in the late nineteenth century, Langdell took on the task of modernizing the work begun by Blackstone. The first principles on which Blackstone had claimed law was based could be discovered, said Langdell, through an empirical investigation into the 'data' contained in judicial opinions. Few scholars now accept the Langdellian claim to 'legal science,' which is empirical and scientific only in a strained sense of those terms. The continuing controversies over Langdell's personal role in creating the case-method approach to law school teaching provide evidence that, as Bruce A. Kimball claims, his influence on legal education was and remains enormous (329), despite conflicting positions on the viability and presence of case method in legal education. Albert J. Harno's 1953 history of legal education claimed that few law school teachers were using 'literal' case method by that time (69); however, Brainerd Currie's survey of law school materials claimed to find that it was still the dominant instructional method in 1951, 'with minor modifications' (332). More recently, in 1981, Thomas J. Reed's history of legal education claimed that it was still the 'most popular model' for law school teaching and had been the standard for American Bar Association accreditation for sixty years (343). Even as late as 2004, the case method is highly visible in scholarship on legal education, serving as a touchstone for arguments in favor of other pedagogical models. Thus, a feminist agenda critiques the case method's 'sharp, objective rhetoric' (Proctor 577); similarly, a scholar interested in addressing questions of race in law school classrooms points out the lack of consistency in the application of the case method and thus, or so goes the claim, a lack of reliable attention to important social issues (Buckner 912). Other discussions draw on the perceived values of case method pedagogy; an argument for the use of clinical training in legal education trumpets it as 'one of the most significant and successful pedagogical developments since Langdell's case method' (Wilson 421), while another article about teaching criminal law suggests that case method has the advantage of teaching students to 'read, understand, critique, and manipulate, mostly appellate, judicial decisions.' That article goes on to claim, however, that 'the same case analysis skills are surely covered in many other first-year courses' suggesting that criminal law classes might avoid this 'rather substantial burden' (Cohen 1200).

Even strong arguments against the prevalence of case method cannot dismiss it. One argument for creative legal problem-solving points out that the tacit assumptions of the case method 'significantly constrain the options a lawyer may consider in attempting to resolve a client's problem' (Krieger 158-9), but quotes an even stronger polemic against case method that concludes, 'Should we toss out the case method entirely? Definitely not. The study of litigated disputes not only teaches the rules of law, but provides the reasoning to show how and why the cases were won. Preventive law cannot be properly practiced until the practitioner knows what must be prevented' (Kerper 371). The very same argument had begun with a complaint that case method has been 'the centerpiece of legal education' for over one hundred years despite 'extravagant claims for its effectiveness' (351). In short, 'scientific' or not, and lauded or reviled, this conceptual and pedagogical model of a 'law' firmly and explicitly located in its discourse continues to preoccupy the minds of legal scholars and, of necessity, their students.

Objections to case-method pedagogy yielded many fruits in the form of alternative pedagogies and scholarship. By the mid-to-late twentieth century case method was far less likely to be identified as 'legal science' than the approaches typical of the Law and Economics school, which argued strenuously against the autonomy that literal case-method pedagogy assumed. It is Posner's prolific scholarship that has been among the most visible in Law and Economics, both within the academy and without, for the last two decades. Strongly sympathetic to what he sees as Blackstone's real innovation, his focus on a legal system in its operational context, Posner's work places law in an economic context in order to focus, he says, on human behavior, not on what people think but on what they '*do*' (*Law and Literature: A Misunderstood Relation* 188, emphasis in original). This common tenet of legal economic science—that humans act 'rationally' and that their behavior can therefore be understood and predicted in economic or even mathematical terms—often leads to denial of the importance of rhetoric to legal language and reasoning (Wetlaufer; Panetta and Hasian). Posner is representative of Law and Economics scholarship on that score, though he is unusually cognizant of the need to argue the point. But it is not solely on the basis of his growing recognition of the role that language plays in legal thought and decision-making, if not in economics, that I base the argument of this chapter. That recognition, paired somewhat paradoxically with Posner's reliance on conclusions derived from unstated, undiscoverable 'first principles,' and an acknowledged lack of interest in their empirical verification, suggests that legal science may have come full circle, back to *episteme*. With his emphasis on the purely descriptive value of economic theory and his resistance to strong reformist movements in legal scholarship, Posner would seem to argue for the value of legal science as a value apart from 'use.'

I base my discussion of these claims on the account of the nature and realm of *episteme* provided in Chapter 2, noting the very similar continuing concerns of classical and legal science. Moving in this chapter to describe the claims for legal science, whether implicit in their discussions or expressly advanced by Blackstone, Langdell, and Posner, I then use the insights of Posner's economic theory to analyze his own judicial opinion in *Carr v. Allison Gas Turbine Division*; here I draw on the economic theory of sexuality he provides in *Sex and Reason*. Duly noting both its resemblance to classical and modern sciences and its contribution to our understanding of the reasoning in this sexual harassment case, I also note the limitations of legal science as Posner represents it. The resemblance it bears to both classical and modern sciences, I find, is primarily methodological—Posner's legal science proceeds like a science, based on scientific assumptions. But its discrepancies, though subtle, are significant. Posner's science appears to be a hybrid, an application of modern scientific method to the uncertain data provided by human behavior. Like that of classical *episteme*, this data is primarily discursive. But unlike Aristotelian *episteme*, and like modern science, Posner's legal science anticipates that its knowledge will be of use. But the economic aspiration toward use is severely undercut by the economic resistance to values. What Posner ultimately provides is precisely what he offers, a simple description, rather than explanation, of human behavior; that description is accompanied by a lucid demonstration of the assumptions of Posnerian economics about human nature and, based on those assumptions, options for human behavior. Those options are severely limited, in Posner's implicit view, by the resistance of human language to the universality and certainty that he both ascribes to it and wishes to harness for legal analysis and its production of correct (efficient) legal decisions. Posner's economic project ultimately leads to a theory regarding the relationship of legal analysis to justice that, I conclude, is in near perfect accord with the description of justice that Aristotle provides in the *Ethics*, an understanding of which ultimately grounds the 'uselessness' of Posnerian legal science.

Ethical Properties and Legal Science

One's choice of method is always made in service of an ethic. In Aristotle that ethic was of the sufficiency of knowledge apart from its interpretation by a human agent, in the presumed value of knowledge for its own sake. Absent the more recent emphasis on the value of use, *episteme* is free to engage in the luxury of speculation without practical import or consequences. This, we are led by Aristotle to believe, is one sense in which knowledge may be seen as divine. In Blackstone's equation of the human world with divine intent, the ethic shifted to one of conservatism; resonating with Aristotle's claims for the value of knowledge for its own sake, legal science became an exercise in self-preservation. Langdell's later naturalization of legal science led him to claim for it an ethic of autonomy that Posner specifically rejects. Substituting interdisciplinarity for autonomy, Posner uses economic analysis to extend the reach of law into every area of human endeavor it aspires to regulate with an eye to rendering those endeavors compatible with an economic ethic, that of efficiency.

Understood generically, a 'method' is the application of a process toward the understanding of a subject matter represented by a body of information that the method itself values and thus constructs or recognizes as 'data.' Following the development of Baconian empiricism, both Blackstone and Langdell had argued for an inductive method for legal science; whether applied to the data of legal and social systems or to those of judicial opinions, the goal of induction as each represented it was to discover legal principles that were presumed to lurk, unidentified, in the data. Aristotle acknowledged the value of an inductive method that could generate first principles, and called it *paradeigma*, or reasoning from examples (*Rhetoric* I.II.8). It was not, however, the method of *episteme*, which according to Aristotle worked deductively from those first principles in order to reach conclusions based upon them (*Nicomachean Ethics* VI.iii.3-4). And while for Blackstone and Langdell the existence and discovery of its principles were essential to their claims for a legal science, Posner rejects their necessity. The role of empiricism in legal science is not, he says, that of discovering or applying principles, first or otherwise (*Problems of Jurisprudence* 239). Because economic empiricism is, he admits, limited, Posner's own method is difficult to characterize as either inductive or deductive; he generally gathers data inductively from the vicarious experience offered by historical, sociological, or other accounts of human behavior, including statistical representations, in order to apply what we might call a deductive thought experiment designed to test a hypothesis generated from that data.

An example drawn from Posner's *Sex and Reason* may help to make these claims clear as it simultaneously illustrates his typical method. Realizing on the basis of both direct and vicarious experience that sexual mores have undergone radical transformations over the course of the eighteenth, nineteenth, and twentieth centuries, Posner hypothesizes that the role of women within and outside the home, itself radically transformed over that same period, is an intimately associated factor. Unable, of course, to test this hypothesis via a controlled process, Posner instead conducts a thought experiment, positing an undocumented three-stage account of sexual morality. In what he calls stage 1, woman's role is that of a 'simple breeder' and practices such as prostitution, adultery, and homosexuality flourish. In an intermediate stage 2, he says, woman's occupational role expands to include the rearing of children and provision of companionship to the husband, causing such practices as prostitution to become anomalous. However, in stage 3, it is not only men who 'enjoy almost complete sexual license;' women do also, a condition Posner attributes to the market employment of women and illustrates by reference to modern Sweden. Now comes the test: if his analysis is correct, Posner says, 'the sexually conservative retrenchment of the Victorian era should be associated with a reduction in the amount of female employment outside the home. It is' (*Sex and Reason* 173-4).

Having established not only that Victorian women rarely had non-domestic careers but also that one of the problems with normal economic methodology is that 'the results being predicted are known in advance' (*Problems of Jurisprudence* 365), Posner appears to be satisfied that he has also demonstrated that 'the movement toward sexual permissiveness—the sexual revolution of the twentieth century—has been due ultimately to women' (*Sex and Reason* 180). We might dispute this conclusion, of course; besides the fabrication of the presumed three-stage morality model that grounds this entire account, Posner has failed to engage the question of choice that is a critical assumption of his economic perspective, failing to consider whether women have historically been able to determine their own social roles. Indeed, Posner's assumptions about choice are one of the primary targets of West's response to *Sex and Reason*. But before we turn to West's critique, because we are primarily concerned here with the ethical implications of scientific methods, let us take note of the ways in which the methods of legal science have evolved through Blackstone and Langdell to Posner and of the role of data in their methods. In fact, as it has moved from Blackstone through Langdell to Posner and the Law and Economics movement, legal science has gradually developed a recognizably modern scientific method. Blackstone initiates the claim that there are legal first principles, an essential to the science of his day, which Langdell then says are empirically discoverable through the data of judicial opinions. Posner refines the claims further, moving away from the first principles of early modern science and toward the empiricism of its twentieth-century descendant, positing that hypotheses drawn from legal data can be tested by empirical verification and used to predict future legal phenomena. Just as Posner has argued that judge-made law conforms to the economic principle of wealth maximization in a tendency toward the increased efficiency of its decisions (*Problems of Jurisprudence* 359-60) so we might say that the very Anglo-American legal process is arguably 'scientific' strictly in terms of its method. If we conceive of judicial opinions as legal hypotheses drawn from the data provided by prior law, we can see that judges may draw on this accumulated data in order to validate, or justify, their conclusions and therefore the results in the cases at hand. They may also be seen as testing those prior opinions, validating or modifying them through the legal disputes they adjudicate and through their own hypotheses that will themselves either stand when they are cited as precedent, falter when they are remanded for further refinement, or fall when they are refuted and discarded.

There are bumps in the methodological road, however. To begin with the most obvious, none of these versions of legal science, and particularly those of Blackstone and Langdell, venture very far into the territory of concrete, physical phenomena. For Langdell the subject matter of law was the abstraction of law itself, exhibited in the data of legal opinions from which law's 'first principles' could be drawn. Blackstone's thinking was more metaphysical than Langdell's, given his belief that the forms that law took, particularly its manifestation as English common law, were divinely dictated—truly, 'Law' with a capital 'L'. As Daniel J. Boorstin's thorough analysis of the *Commentaries* points out, 'Law' functioned as both the starting point and the conclusion of Blackstone's theoretical universe, providing evidence of the nature of 'man' through legal concepts and proof of its own validity to the extent it reflected the nature it 'proved' (Boorstin 123-127). Absent from both Blackstone and Langdell, then, was any move from the abstraction of legal hypotheses to concrete testing, to their validation through pitting those hypotheses against some sort of data, however that data may be construed.

This is the contribution that Posner wishes to offer, the possibility of testing legal analysis against data that can potentially validate or refute its hypotheses. In making this offer Posner also moves away from metaphysics and closer to the realm of empirical analysis, at least to the extent that human behavior may be characterized and represented numerically as concrete 'phenomena.' But as we have seen, the testing phase of Posner's legal economic analysis resembles not so much the controlled experiment of the physical sciences as the thought experiment of analytical philosophy, presenting as 'proof' the vindication of its premises through the data with which it began. Posner is not alone in claiming the potential verifiability of conclusions drawn from the economic analysis of legal problems; he claims that he is also not alone in leaving the task of verification, if it is to be taken on at all, to others. Most legal economic analysts, he says, are much more interested in assessing the wealth-maximizing properties of legal rules and decisions than in testing the data against empirical reality (*Problems of Jurisprudence* 371).

The role and nature of data in legal science, while they may seem to have undergone significant changes, have thus actually remained relatively constant since Aristotle. Remember that while the sun, moon, and stars provided the subject matter for *episteme* they were not its data; indeed, their inaccessibility meant even for Aristotle that they could yield little, if anything, in the way of unmediated information. It may be for this very practical reason that Aristotle considered the data suitable for his ethical method to be suitable not only for metaphysics but for his science as well (Nussbaum *Fragility of Goodness* 242). Those data were, said Aristotle, *phainomena*—not to be confused with the English cognate 'phenomena,' *phainomena* were 'appearances,' says classical scholar Martha C. Nussbaum, mediated by what Aristotle frankly calls *ta legomena*, or 'the things we say' (*Fragility of Goodness* 240). In fact, *phainomena* and *ta legomena* are veritable synonyms, derived respectively from *pheimi*, the Homeric verb meaning 'to say,' and *lego*, the equivalent verb in Aristotle's time. Nussbaum argues with some urgency that 'Aristotle's appearances' are in danger of disappearing, rendered as 'observed facts,' 'data,' or 'observations' by translators falsely convinced that Aristotle's understandings of experience and of scientific phenomena were closely compatible with Baconian empiricism (244). But Aristotle's appearances have not disappeared; in fact, they are nearly perfectly preserved in the 'data' of legal science. Whether such data is drawn from legal and social systems, as they were for Blackstone; from judicial opinions, as they were for Langdell; or from the findings of the social sciences abstracted from human behavior and quantified as statistical representations, the data of legal science are certainly *phainomena* in the Aristotelian sense, 'the things we say' about ourselves as social beings governed by law.

Though he has not really managed to change the nature of legal data Posner has nevertheless extended its scope. Langdell, by restricting its 'data' to the judicial opinion, had made of law a closed system that was interested only in discovering its own first principles. In this he lagged behind his predecessor, Blackstone, who had drawn his data not just from the British common law but also from his analysis of comparative legal systems, including continental and civil law, in order to understand both 'Law' and 'Man.' Repudiating Langdell's isolated model of law while building on Blackstone's contextualized model, Posner goes a step beyond both in an interdisciplinary move that brings the perspectives of the social science of economics to bear on legal problems. The more expansive understanding of legal data is significant, for it defines the subject of legal science more expansively as well. Langdellian method, in shrinking the circle of inquiry, had restricted the subject matter of legal science to the facts presented by any given case, in the process restricting legal science to a mere sorting operation, a procedure not for distinguishing values or legal arguments, but simply for distinguishing relevant from irrelevant facts (Ames, quoted in Harno 61) in the light of the legal 'first principle' in question. But for both Blackstone and Posner law has a plausibly scientific subject matter—not nature strictly, but human nature, as Blackstone claimed or, in Posner's less grandiose claim, human behavior.

Whatever his aspirations toward certainty, Posner candidly admits the limitations of economics. It is, he says, 'weak in comparison to the natural sciences, though it is the strongest of the human sciences' (*Problems of Jurisprudence* 366). Leading not to absolute certainty but to probability, economics by necessity accepts observation mediated by human interpretation, relying on the intuition and speculation of its observers. Posner's analysis begins like Aristotle's, with a vast accumulation of appearances—'the things we say' in the form of statistical representations of human behavior. Like Aristotle, he then examines the discrepancies among them in order to determine which of these cultural beliefs are most in accord with what he sees as truth and should, therefore, be held as true. Such a method was necessary, Aristotle had said, in an undertaking where we must live with probability rather than certainty (VII.i.5, VI.v.3). What could be less certain, more contingent upon probability, we might ask, than human behavior? In the realm of *epistemé* as Aristotle understood it the existence of first principles could be unproblematically assumed, given the divinity of its subject matter. Posner clearly differs from Aristotle regarding the necessity of principles—as he must, given the very human realm in which he works. Nevertheless it is clear that he does work from first principles in the Aristotelian sense, or at least from one of them. Posner's first principle is a frequently stated and unargued assumption, a vision not of what people do but of what people are and one he shares, as he readily makes clear, with Blackstone.

This vision of humanity and human nature becomes particularly obvious in Posner's response to Blackstone's discussion of property law. Through his observation of legal and social systems in England and on the European continent, Blackstone had observed certain regularities which became for him, because of their very regularity, universal principles about law, nature, and 'man.' The law of society itself, for example, was evidence for Blackstone of the principle that man was naturally 'selfish' and competitive; much like Thomas Hobbes, Blackstone concluded that the universal fact of social order proved man's naturally violent tendencies (Boorstin 179; Posner 'Blackstone and Bentham' 573-74). In turn, the law of society became 'a kind of secondary law of nature' (Boorstin 47) and laws that enabled, or grew out of, the law of society became the same. One such law was that of private property, which Blackstone believed to be founded in a principle of natural reason and linked to that essential human trait, 'man's' selfishness. Reconceived by Blackstone as self-love, because ordained by God as part of man's nature, such selfishness became not a flaw but a principle that man not only could, but must, follow (51-2) and from which other goods derived, particularly the goods of social peace and order (53-4). Selfishness, or self-love, became a divine principle upon which man must act in order to fulfill the expectations of God and the demands of divine will (51).

By Blackstone's time the concept of property 'as a social fact,' says Boorstin, 'was undergoing striking metamorphosis' (167). In the century prior to Blackstone's, Locke had defended a concept of property that justified the ownership of increasingly intangible properties on the basis of human labor, an activity that mixed the human self with the object of its ownership (Boorstin 168). In this naturalized theory, the role of civil government was not to create property but simply to 'recognize' or 'secure' it (Boorstin 168, White *Acts of Hope* 157). Blackstone attempted to explain away the problems of intangible properties through a number of strategies, first by simply claiming that property, as a primary and absolute right, was necessarily obscure (Boorstin 167-72). Here Blackstone clearly echoes Aristotle on the undemonstrability of first principles. There was, however, a less abstract explanation available and one that Blackstone also seized upon: as a natural outgrowth of the social organization that itself was increasingly complex, the new intangible properties were deftly handled by the natural genius of English law, which managed to find 'an owner for everything that was by its nature capable of ownership' (172). The definitional problem, at least, was resolved, with property becoming anything the law protects as such (177). Blackstone's law, then, is both the measure and the reflection of the natural world, even of the world several times removed from nature.

What seems to us an obvious circularity was not, Boorstin tells us, a problem for Blackstone. Nor would it have been for Aristotle who, comfortable with the circularity of *epistemé* as knowledge for its own sake, understood first principles not only as 'the things which are most knowable' (*Metaphysics* I.II.6) but also, and precisely by virtue of their nature as the starting points of analysis, not provable 'since the starting-point of a demonstration is not a matter of demonstration' (*Metaphysics* IV.VI.2). Blackstone's necessarily obscure property laws can fit neatly into the space provided by Aristotle for first principles, requiring no explanation precisely because of their inexplicability, leading from themselves inexorably back to themselves via propositions that confirm their essential validity. With selfishness playing the role of first principle Blackstone was able to follow a line of reasoning about property to a seemingly logical and inevitable conclusion: given that the private ownership of property resulted from a natural law of society, any attempt to alter the distribution of property was an attack on nature. In fact, the very inequity evidenced by the obviously unequal distribution of property was according to Blackstone 'the surest guarantee of the property of all,' because the interests of the prosperous and powerful, those responsible for developing the law of property, in justifying and retaining their own holdings assured even the least prosperous 'that the very qualitative and quantitative differences in property relations were helping [them] to keep what [they] already had' (Boorstin 178-9). 'By this kind of reasoning,' Boorstin continues, 'the absolute right of property was shown to be perfectly realized in the existing legal arrangements of society' (178).

White, whose literary theory is in many respects a reaction against the economic perspective now so prevalent in law schools, tells us that as economies became increasingly industrial in the later nineteenth century, Locke's reasoning 'was applied to sanctify what one obtained not from nature by one's labor but from other people, and the institutions of society, by one's superior wealth, power, or skill' (*Acts of Hope* 157). This description is purposely crafted to echo a conclusion characteristic of much Law and Economics scholarship, a conclusion that is as regularly defended as it is attacked. According to Posner and other economic scholars, for example, economists cannot tell whether the existing distribution of wealth is just (quoted in Hackney 318). James J. Heckman, in his intellectual history of the Law and Economics movement, concurs with this typical conclusion, arguing that because questions of distribution lie 'outside their competence' the separation of distributional questions from those of efficiency, the special domain of economics, is 'the mark of a clear mind, not of a committed ideologue' (Heckman 328-9). Not everyone agrees that this economic blind spot is inevitable, however, or that distributional issues are 'outside the narrow confines of the law' (333); Viner argues that it is not appropriate 'from either an ethical or an economic-efficiency point of view' to assume that existing income distribution is 'the consequence of a dispensation of Providence..., as if it just "happened"' (67). Whether we believe that distributional issues are 'not analyzable' (Hackney glossing Lionel Robbins 290) or that the assumption common to legal economics that distribution and efficiency are questions separate from those of justice is itself highly analyzable, the centrality of private property rights and unabashed acceptance of their given distributions—for analytical purposes—remains typical both of Posner's scholarship in particular and much of Law and Economics generally.

Posner is thus substantially in accord with Blackstone on the nature and significance of property. Though he finds Blackstone begins his defense of private property 'inauspiciously' (by noting that it is authorized in the book of *Genesis*) he appraises the fully articulated theory as 'a competent statement of the economic theory of property rights' ('Blackstone and Bentham' 573). This appraisal is backed by Posner's selection of statements from the *Commentaries* that, purportedly concerned with the nature of property, are more obviously statements about the nature of man, in Blackstone's version, or human beings, in Posner's. This nature is characterized by a remarkably, even spectacularly, lazy self interest. Blackstone maintained, for example, that man's selfishness was of such a degree that 'no man would be at the trouble to provide either [habitations or raiment] so long as he had only an usufructuary property in them, which was to cease the instant that he quitted possession' (quoted in 'Blackstone and Bentham' 573). Not only would 'no man' work to provide shelter or clothing if he could not be assured they would be his alone—apparently no man would plant crops, either, for 'who would be at the pains of tilling [the earth] if another might watch an opportunity to seize upon and enjoy the product of his industry, art, and labour?' (573). Posner fails to consider whether these are really accurate statements about human nature— whether humans really would starve, naked, in the elements rather than share the fruits of their labor. Instead, he praises Blackstone for his 'precocious' articulation of the concept of the division of labor (573). Neither Posner nor Blackstone bothers to support these highly questionable statements because they require none within their theoretical systems. 'Man' just is selfish or self-interested, an intuitively knowable and consequently undemonstrable first principle that, immune from the necessity of proof, yields countless conclusions.

In this assessment of the essential selfishness of human beings, whether expressed as self-love or self-interest, both Blackstone and Posner depart from Aristotle who, while agreeing 'that no one voluntarily throws away his property' adds a qualifier based on circumstances. 'Any sane man' caught in a storm at sea, he continues, would willingly throw his property overboard in order to save not only his own life, but that of his shipmates as well (*Nicomachean Ethics* III.i.5). Let us not be hasty, however, in assuming that Aristotle's understanding is inherently more 'ethical' than that of Posner, who works within a framework that he considers not only rational but ethical as well, a structure provided by the concept of wealth maximization. His detailed explanation of wealth maximization and general legal economic theory in *Problems of Jurisprudence*, supplemented with illustrations drawn from the economic theory of sexuality that he provides in *Sex and Reason*, can take us a long way toward understanding and assessing Posner's rational and ethical claims.

Posner explains in *Problems of Jurisprudence* that economic analysis of law begins with a basic guiding assumption, that 'people are rational maximizers of their satisfactions...in *all* of their activities...that involve choice' (353, emphasis in original). It is critical to understanding Posner's theory to realize that satisfactions are not always monetary (for instance, that they can be sexual) and that the decisions people make are not always conscious. Nevertheless, economic theory holds that no matter how unconscious or unsuccessful such choices may be, the process of making them is rational, in the sense that people '[suit] means to ends' (354), by choosing actions or practices that they believe will get them where they believe they want to go. Wealth maximization, as the process whereby humans choose means suited to ends, therefore provides the starting premise of Posner's economic analysis. It is not a strictly individualistic assumption, as the above explanation might imply, but a statement about the behavior of individuals in markets and a characterization of the aggregate of their behaviors. Wealth cannot really be maximized by a single individual, because it is based in a process of exchange with other individuals (or in a process of exchange between groups). Accordingly, the goal of legal decision-making that maximizes wealth is not, strictly speaking, to enable individuals to do so, but to balance transactions between individuals (and groups) so that the accumulated wealth of society more generally is maximized. There can be, in other words, both winners (who maximize their individual wealth) and losers (who don't) in the process of insuring that society's overall wealth increases. The most telling example of this process of social wealth maximization that Posner provides in *Problems of Jurisprudence* is the concept of the 'cost justified' accident, where the loss suffered by an injured party is acceptable when it is less than the gain incurred by the party responsible for the injury who, for example, did not spend on measures that would have prevented the accident (357-8).

How, then, can wealth maximization be plausibly represented as an ethical process? Posner bases this claim on two properties of wealth maximization as he understands it—its requirement of co-operation and exchange among individuals and groups, and the willingness of the parties to those exchanges to pay for the benefits they seek (*Problems of Jurisprudence* 391). His reliance on co-operation seems facile—the automatic balancing of interests and exchanges in a market as Posner presents them would not seem to require the volition of some, or even any, of the parties to its transactions. Our mere presence in a market, in other words, whether we are aware of its nature as a market or not and even if we contest that nature, is sufficient to indicate our acceptance of its conditions and our 'co-operation' with them. Willingness to pay, however, is a more intriguing concept, tied up as it is both with the economic ethic of efficiency and Posner's approach to cost-benefit analysis.

Cost-benefit analysis is, in fact, the only one of the six principles Posner says can describe human behavior in mathematical terms that he discusses in either *Problems of Jurisprudence* or *Sex and Reason*. A simple description of this principle holds that we choose to 'purchase' desirable benefits if the price is right. The principle is more complex than that normally, however, because of the nature of the practices we engage in (the 'means') in order to achieve the benefits we desire (the 'ends'). For example, practices are sometimes substitutable, meaning that if one practice is made prohibitively expensive a person may well choose a less satisfactory but also less expensive practice in its place. In *Sex and Reason* Posner illustrates substitutability by pointing out the increase among homosexuals in alternative sexual practices such as fellatio or even abstinence in the face of AIDS, which has made both anal and vaginal intercourse potentially more 'expensive' than in the past (114). Other practices can be complementary, meaning that the demand for one will increase if the price of another decreases. Once again Posner's example is vaginal sex, demand for which will increase when its cost (pregnancy) decreases due to the improved efficacy of birth control methods (143). Finally, the means we adopt toward our chosen ends are influenced by at least two factors, the nature of our ends and what we perceive the cost of the means to be. A look at Posner's discussion of sexual ends can illustrate this point. Such ends, he says, are three—procreative, hedonistic, and sociable (111). Clearly, not all sexual practices, or means, will lead reliably to all possible sexual ends (oral sex is not terribly procreative, for example, though it works marvelously well as contraception). With the reminder that cost is not merely, or even very often, strictly monetary we can also see that sexual intercourse has various and multiple costs. In Posner's analysis, sexual costs can range from disease to children.

Willingness to pay, then, is the visible end of a largely invisible process whereby humans presumably, even if unconsciously, calculate the costs of the benefits they wish to enjoy and balance that cost against the strength or intensity of their desire for the benefits. Willingness to pay thus provides evidence of 'efficiency or value in the modern economic sense' (Posner 'Blackstone and Bentham' 591 fn60) with efficiency further defined (by Heckman) as the use of resources to maximize output (327). Output, of course, results in more resources, or benefits, that we desire and for which we will set asking prices and make offers, perpetuating the 'co-operation' and thus the productivity of market processes. Wealth maximization, measured as an aggregate of individual choices rather than against the results of any given individual choice, is clearly the ultimate efficient process, perpetuating itself by ensuring the continuation of exchange and co-operation in markets from the more traditionally economic to the sexual.

Wealth maximization is also the ultimate end of Posnerian economic analysis which, if it discovers a trend toward inefficiency in any of the markets it examines, will recommend a corrective. The economic theory of sexual harassment Posner proposes in *Sex and Reason* provides an illustration, not only of his emphasis on efficiency but also of its results in an intuitively non-market context. Beginning by debunking what he says is a commonplace in our culture, that sexuality belongs to the domain of the irrational (4), Posner explains that the economic model sees sexual activity as governed instead by a rational balancing of goals and the costs required to attain them in the existing market. For example, Posner contends that the high incidence of male homosexuality among otherwise heterosexual males in prisons may be fairly simply explained by the low incidence and high cost of heterosexual partners. Given the small market of females and the heavy penalties attached to acquiring them through such means as assault, smuggling, or escape, homosexual activity incurs comparatively low search and penalty costs while meeting the physical goal of sexual activity, albeit in a potentially less satisfying way (121).

This explanation is consistent with the view of sexual harassment provided in the second edition of *Law and Literature*, where Posner insists upon a rational balancing of costs with goals and on the efficient use of resources. In fact, according to Posner the problem with sexual harassment is not any moral 'wrong' that it commits, but that it is not economically efficient—it is a 'market failure,' even a 'market abuse' (192, 193) that reduces the output of both workers and their supervisors and forces employers to pay higher wages to workers to compensate them for 'the unpleasantness of the workplace' (192) in the manner of a wage premium paid to employees who choose to work in hazardous environments. Posner's analysis of the alternatives available to employers to deal with the potential for sexual harassment in the workplace is worth quoting at some length for the insight it provides into the economic analysis of both legal and sexual issues:

> Could the employer offset those additional costs by paying the supervisors less, on the theory that he [sic] has given them a valuable license to harass female workers? In other words, might the benefits to the harassers exceed the costs to the victims? It is unlikely. Sexual harassment…is generally a minor and guilty pleasure to the harasser but a source of anguish and indignation to the harassed. Because of the disparity between the pleasure and the pain and also because there are fewer supervisors than workers and most of them do not want to harass their subordinates sexually, cutting supervisors' pay is unlikely to compensate the employer fully for the higher wages he must pay his female employees to compensate them for the risk of harassment, and for the reduction in the productivity of those supervisors and workers who spend their time respectively making and fending off (or yielding to) sexual advances rather than working. Furthermore, if sexual harassment is common, women who are less sensitive or more compliant will have a competitive advantage; they will be slower to quit and quicker to be promoted. There is no reason to think they will be the better workers, so there will be an inefficient sorting of workers to jobs, just as when promotions are based on nepotism rather than merit (192-3).

This analysis works from a number of unstated assumptions, among them the happy but unlikely possibility that women receive artificially high wages as 'hazard pay' for potential sexual harassment. Other assumptions include the idea that sexual activity is straightforwardly physical, originating in sexual advances and culminating either in their refusal or in their consummation through the most efficient form of intercourse available. Assuming that prisoners engage in sexual activity solely for hedonistic purposes, or that sexual harassers similarly are pursuing only physical pleasure or release, Posner neglects alternative explanations and their implications, including the possibility that 'sociable' sexual ends can have other than positive motivations.

The abstractions, assumptions, and implications of Posner's method can be made clearer if we now turn to a more concrete context than hypothetical situations can provide, the decision Posner authored in *Carr v. Allison Gas Turbine Division*. Itself an abstraction in the manner of all judicial opinions, drawn from the data provided by testimony and arguments submitted to the court, *Carr* nevertheless sheds some light on the economic theory of sexuality while the theory sheds some light on the reasoning that led Posner to decide for the plaintiff in this case against the defendant that he calls 'mighty GM' (*Carr* 1012).

The full text of the case is provided in the Appendix, but a short summary is called for here. Posner wrote the opinion as Chief Judge of the Seventh Circuit Court of Appeals in 1994; it overturned the trial court's previous decision against Mary Carr, who had sued the Allison division of General Motors for sexual harassment she claimed she had suffered as its first and only female tinsmith. The facts of the case, most of which were not contested by the parties to the suit and which were based on Carr's own description of events, had been determined at the lower court level. Recited in some detail in Posner's opinion, they paint a picture that is familiar to frequent readers in this area of the law. Carr had begun work at the Allison plant as a drill operator but in 1984 was made a tinsmith apprentice, a capacity in which she continued to work until 1989, when she quit. Her suit contends that her male coworkers had engaged in a campaign of harassment both against her person and her property, referring to her often as a 'whore' and a 'cunt,' stealing her tools, painting her toolbox pink, cutting out the seat of her overalls, and decorating the work area with 'signs, pictures, and graffitti [sic] of an offensive sexual character' (*Carr v. Allison Gas Turbine Division* 1009). One of her coworkers exposed himself to her on at least one, and possibly two, occasions and once suggested that if he were to have an accident on the job, Carr would need to perform 'mouth to dick resuscitation' (1010). According to Posner's holding her complaints to supervisors, beginning in 1985, were largely ignored (1010, 1012).

Given this history it may be surprising that Carr lost her claim at the trial court level, but the lower court believed that she had 'invited' the behavior. Carr had a poor work attendance record, caused not only by psychological and family problems but also, she maintained, by the harassment itself. It did not help her case, however, that when she was at work she used the same foul language the male tinners used and that she occasionally participated in some of their sexual jokes—for example, by pointing (when asked) at the clitoris in a pornographic picture (1010). Based on this evidence and citing precedent in its own district, the trial court found the tinners' behavior was not 'sexual harassment' as the term is legally defined because Carr had not shown that the harassment was 'unwelcome.' Chief Judge Posner's majority opinion differed on this point, arguing that 'harassment' is by definition 'unwelcome.' A strong dissent to Posner's opinion maintained, however, that 'welcome harassment' was a legal reality created by precedent that the majority could not ignore. Concurring with the previous decision of the trial court, the dissent quoted its conclusion that '[t]he tinners' conduct, to the extent it may have constituted sexual harassment, was not unwelcome' (quoted in *Carr* 1014).

Measuring *Carr*

'Of course it was unwelcome,' Posner wrote in his opinion (1011). Despite my agreement with that conclusion I could not help, on first reading this case, being puzzled by Posner's decision. Why, given his faith in the ability of the market to regulate itself and his paired reluctance to interfere with its activity, did this generally conservative judge intervene on Carr's behalf in the operation of GM? We will not find an economic justification spelled out in the decision itself for, as Warren J. Samuels and Nicholas Mercuro have noted, Posner rarely discusses his economic theories explicitly in his judicial opinions even though they frequently ground his reasoning (110). *Carr* is no exception to that general rule. However, it is clear from a close reading of the opinion in conjunction with the principles of wealth maximization that it is Posner's economic theory that rules the day, grounding his reasoning and providing the ethical justification for his holding in the case.

Because for Posner wealth maximization is an ethical process it is not only a 'genuine social value' (*Problems of Jurisprudence* 360) but also the justification of economic analysis as the 'default rule or presumption—the right place to start' in analyzing legal problems (374). It makes sense, therefore, to begin our reading of *Carr* by considering what might have constituted 'wealth' for the parties to this dispute. Clearly, monetary considerations were not explicitly primary for Carr, the tinners, or even GM. The only statement attributed to Carr and her motivations in the opinion is what Posner calls a plausible argument, that she simply wanted to be accepted by her male coworkers (1011). To this explicitly desired benefit we might add an additional, implicit end, that in the absence of that acceptance she desired to be left alone. It appears that she shared that desire with GM, which indicated by its 'lackluster' (1012) response to her complaints a similar wish to be left alone—by both Carr and the tinners. Both Carr and GM failed, of course, Carr continually and GM ultimately when Carr filed (and it eventually lost) her lawsuit.

In fact the only winners in this scenario, for the four years of Carr's presence in the tinshop, were the male tinners. But what 'wealth' were they maximizing? Given the explicitly sexual means they employed, we are led to at least consider whether the end they sought was also sexual, specifically sexual dominance or power. This is a consideration that Posner himself would be likely to dismiss. You will recall that Posner recognizes in *Sex and Reason* three categories of sexual 'benefits,' the procreative, the hedonistic, and the sociable. Posner explicitly considers, and then quickly rejects, the possibility suggested by feminist scholarship that dominance could be a potential sexual end (113). Though he promises to discuss the question in later chapters he fails to take it up explicitly, even in his discussion of coercive sexual acts. Nevertheless, sexual dominance can be seen as a variety of Posner's 'sociable' sexual ends—a negative one, to be sure, but certainly as a 'use of sex to construct or reinforce relationships with other people' (111). Posner prefers to restrict his analysis to the use of sex to forge relationships with 'spouses or friends' (*Sex and Reason* 111) and to consider 'sexual activity' in a restricted sense that would exclude sexual remarks or even the physical 'pranks' (*Carr* 1009) of the tinners. But power seems to have been a priority for the tinners, who almost certainly exerted very little throughout GM generally but aspired to it in the limited realm of the tinshop. Posner notes that 'a frequent remark heard around the shop,' where only one woman and only one black man worked, 'was, "I'll never retire from this tinsmith position because it would make an opening for a nigger [sic] or a woman"'(1010).

Assuming that it is, as Posner might say, at least plausible that the tinners were engaged in maximizing the sexual end of (negative) sociability, we can now assess their behavior by asking about the practices they employed to determine whether their behavior was rational in the economic sense, that of suiting means to ends. It certainly appears that for the four years that Carr endured the conditions in the tinshop the tinners were acting rationally in that limited sense, enjoying a great deal of control over Carr for a minimal investment. But rationality, even in that sense, is not the only criterion by which Posner says we measure the process of wealth maximization and it is not sufficient grounding, even for him, for a decision—otherwise, Posner should have held for the tinners, the best wealth maximizers in the plant. Remember that wealth maximization is to be measured on the social level rather than on the strictly individual level, and that to be operating maximally the tinshop must demonstrate that the overall wealth of society (whether by society we mean the tinshop, GM, or some wider context) must increase. To make this analysis, we need to consider two types of maximization, an ordinary and a superior level from which the ethical evaluation of wealth maximization may be made. In the superior level, officially known as 'Pareto Superiority,' both (or all) parties to an exchange simultaneously maximize their wealth, and no one is made worse off by their transactions (*Problems of Jurisprudence* 388). This is obviously not the case in *Carr*, given that both Carr and GM ultimately failed to maximize their wealth or achieve their ends (though there is a sense, invoked by the dissent to Posner's opinion, in which the transactions can be considered as a Pareto variety, a point to which I will return shortly). But the failure of Pareto Superiority is not fatal to a finding of efficiency; the exchanges could still be wealth maximizing, though in an inferior sense, if the wealth accumulated by the tinners exceeded the loss incurred by Carr or, eventually, GM.

This last calculation is difficult, if not impossible, to carry out, but we don't need to do so in order to follow Posner's reasoning in this case. The inferior grade of wealth maximization achieved by the tinners and GM is only ethical, according to Posner's theory, if the weight of the Pareto Superiority it lacks is borne by some sort of insurance, social or otherwise (*Problems of Jurisprudence* 390). Carr's right to take legal action against GM provided the 'insurance' of last resort, with Posner's holding in her favor compensating for the failure of her employer's policies by balancing the exchanges and mitigating her losses. Of course, the decision instituted losses for the tinners and GM but those losses are justified ethically as well, given that the wealth acquired by the tinners and GM was insolvent—neither one had demonstrated the 'willingness to pay' that must back wealth-maximizing ambitions (391). Understanding willingness to pay as the practices in which people are willing to engage in order to acquire a particular kind or level of wealth allows us to evaluate the means they choose to achieve their ends. The tinners, for example, actually invested very little in the power they exercised over Carr. Not only were the anticipated penalties low, given GM's lack of interest in responding to Carr's complaints, but the tinners also incurred very low 'search costs,' an all-important measure for evaluating wealth maximization. In the tinshop the search costs were minimized by the fact that the market was so small—'the analogy,' Posner tells us in another context, 'is to transportation costs. High-value goods are shipped a greater distance than low-value ones because shipping costs have a smaller effect on the final price of the former' (*Sex and Reason* 120). In this case Posner is explaining the relative costs of call girls and streetwalkers; calling the latter 'zero-search-cost prostitutes' he concludes that 'the lowest-quality goods are consumed at home, not shipped at all' (121). Back at home in the tinshop, focused on one scarce and extremely visible female, it was ease of search that allowed the male tinners to control Carr. 'She was one woman,' says Posner, and 'they were many men' (1011). The search costs were low, the anticipated benefits high.

Carr herself appears to have been guilty of poor choice of means, given that her attempts to be 'one of the guys' were not merely unsuccessful but seriously backfired when her behavior was reviewed by the trial court. Carr, the trial court noted, was 'not merely the recipient of crude behavior and crude language—she also dished it out' (1010). The court's conclusion, essentially that she gave as good as she got, shows that the lower-court judges were just as concerned as Posner with the balance or symmetry of exchanges in the tinshop and suggests that they recognized a negative variation of the Pareto principle—a sort of Pareto Inferiority, as it were. This insight sheds new light on the requirement of 'unwelcomeness,' which now becomes a stand-in for parity, explicitly allowing admitted harassment if the plaintiff demonstrates to the satisfaction of the court that she asked for it. The majority of Posner's court, however, saw it differently. Emphasizing the asymmetry of the parties' positions, that Carr was a highly visible minority in a hostile environment, Posner seems to be saying in effect that the exchange rate was unequal, that Carr's 'money' was no good in the tinshop. Of course, the dissent pointed out one reason for that circumstance—Carr had failed to gain the good graces of the tinners because she had not exhibited willingness to pay by showing up for work (1015).

This argument sounds plausibly economic, and it would not have been surprising if Posner had held Carr accountable for her failure on that score. Why does he lay the blame at GM's door instead? Posner provides an answer to this question early in the decision, noting that the judicial review in a sexual harassment case need answer only two questions. The first is whether the plaintiff was subjected to hostile behavior that occurred because of her sex and that would have caused a reasonable person to have quit. Assuming that the answer to that question is affirmative, and for Posner in this case it is (1011), the second question is whether the employer's response to the situation was negligent (1009). Here it seems clear that Posner resorts to the standard of negligence articulated by Supreme Court Justice Learned Hand in 1947, what Posner says in *Problems of Jurisprudence* 'verges on' an explicitly economic legal doctrine (371). That formula, expressed algebraically as B < PL, means that an injurer is negligent if the burden (including the cost) of preventing an accident is less than the loss caused by the accident, multiplied by its probability (54 fn18). Once again we need not engage in complicated mathematical calculations to measure the relative costs, for Posner's decision tells us outright that the cost to GM of preventing the 'accident' that became *Carr* would have been minimal. The company's active response consisted merely of several meetings, at one of which mutual apologies were required (1012). Its numerous failures to respond are detailed in the opinion, where Posner notes that no one was ever reprimanded for the harassment, that the distribution of policies and posters dealing with sexual harassment was 'uncertain,' and that a videotape on the subject was never shown. One supervisor agreed with the trial court judge who asked if he had 'more or less, left these gals alone to develop their own methods of coping on the job.' That supervisor's superior later turned the cost around, suggesting that 'the gals' pay what for Posner should have been GM's cost by working harder than the men to prove themselves (1012). In short, GM failed to demonstrate willingness to pay for the benefits it sought, causing its attempt at wealth maximization to lack, for Posner, ethical standing and creating of the situation at the tinshop a non-cost justified accident.

The dissent disagreed on this score as well, saying that if GM could be blamed for anything, it would have been for 'not discharging an employee whose acute absenteeism syndrome was causing severe morale problems within the tinshop' (1015). Here the dissent is invoking another principle that Posner would characterize as economic, wealth maximization's claim to social value based on its emphasis on co-operation (391). Clearly, co-operation was in short supply in the tinshop. But wealth maximization is grounded in other values as well, key among them its recognition and protection of property rights and their free exchange. Compared to the intangible properties that the tinners menaced, including the right to employment guaranteed by the Civil Rights Act under which sexual harassment claims are adjudicated, 'property' in its everyday sense might seem to be a minor issue in *Carr*. Her personal integrity, protected by the Equal Employment Opportunity Commission (EEOC) regulations on sexual harassment, was also a threatened good; the potential harm to Posner's way of thinking might have been the sex theft that he sees in coerced sexual relationships (*Sex and Reason* 182). But for Posner the significance of the tinners' sabotage of Carr's tools and equipment is great; he refers specifically to the defacement of her property as 'more ominous, more aggressive affronts than mere words' (1010)—more ominous even, we must presume, than the insulting Valentine left on her toolbox and addressed to 'Cunt' (1009).

Finally, we cannot forget the ethic of efficiency and its importance to the economic analysis of legal disputes. Indeed, Posner believes that efficiency is one of the characteristics, not only of market systems, but of the common law process itself (*Problems of Jurisprudence* 360; see also Hansmann 234). If efficiency can be measured by our willingness to pay, as Posner has claimed, it was glaringly absent from the tinshop. The 'inefficient sorting of workers to jobs' (*Sex and Reason* 190) that Posner theorizes as a market abuse brought about by sexual harassment was made manifest in the person of a female welder who worked in an area close to the tinshop and testified that 'she herself had no trouble with the men in the shop—though occasionally she did have to zap them with her welding arc to fend them off' (1010). An unfair competitive advantage had thus accrued to this woman who was less sensitive to harassment than Carr but who, Posner would remind us, was not necessarily a better worker. The market had clearly failed to use its resources to maximize output; Posner therefore made the necessary adjustment, holding the highest level of authority responsible for the failure of its agents and using coercion to promote or simulate the outcome of a well-functioning market ('Wealth Maximization and Judicial Decision-Making' 132). GM had incurred, and was required by *Carr* to pay, what Posner calls 'agency costs' ('Ethical Significance of Free Choice' 1441). As for Carr, we can use simpler economic terms—she quit her job because GM just couldn't pay her enough.

Posner's economic theory thus has a great deal to tell us about the basis for his decision in this case. We have been able to mine the opinion, in other words, for a fairly deep understanding of why Posner reached the conclusion that GM must be held liable for conditions in the tinshop. But we must not forget that Posner holds out as the promise of his theory that we will learn more about the behavior of the humans in the tinshop itself, and on this count his theory is less adequate. What it has given us is simply a good look at itself—at its own principles, assumptions, values, and their use to reach a decision in this case. Whatever sympathy Posner has for Carr in this case, and it is clear that his sympathy is considerable, it is not the tinners' abuse of Carr that he punishes, but GM's abuse of the market. GM has failed to support the ethic of efficiency, an ethic that it could have promoted at minimal cost to itself if it had enabled free exchange in the market that was the tinshop by protecting Carr's right to her own property, however that term is to be construed.

The ultimate effect of this economic analysis, its interest in the promotion of efficiency for its own sake, makes Posner's legal science more than superficially akin to Aristotelian *epistemé*. Its grounding in the realm of human events and behavior, the source of its data in 'the things we say,' whether we are appellate court judges or parties to a legal dispute, and its posture of detached, 'value-free' analysis all suggest that with Posner legal science has turned toward its classical roots.

The Limits of Legal Science

Posner's scholarship presents an easy target: it is not only highly visible, but the wealth maximization it promotes is frequently taken as flat-out 'repulsive,' as Posner has acknowledged (*Problems of Jurisprudence* 373). Critiques have generally taken one of two tacks, protesting either that Posner's version of Law and Economics is insufficiently scientific or that it is excessively so. Critics friendly to the hope for legal science, whether or not to Law and Economics, simply maintain that Posner's scholarship is inadequately scientific. It is inaccurate; its characterizations of humans as rational wealth maximizers is not only counterintuitive but incomplete or reductionist; human interactions are not reliably analogous to those of monetary markets. All these objections Posner recognizes, summarizes, and, in some cases, concedes in *Problems of Jurisprudence*. In sum, these objections often boil down to the point that humans are not as rational as economic analysis assumes they are or that, even if they were, they are constrained by circumstances that prevent them from acting on their rationally motivated desires (Kelman 275-7). The strictly non-falsifiable predictions of economic analysis therefore 'cut no empirical ice,' says Frank I. Michelman in his reflections on the Law and Economics movement (198). Coming at this question from a different perspective, critiques from outside Law and Economics have suggested that social constraints on human behavior are not limitations but positive elements of human community that are productive of co-operation and empathy (West *Narrative, Authority and Law* 257-8; White *Justice as Translation* 235-7). And even where the value and possibility of economic analysis is supported, some scholars believe that the models of human behavior it develops are not necessarily useful for the analysis of every potential legal situation. Henry Hansmann has pointed out, in his survey of Law and Economics scholarship, that those models are not especially 'illuminating' for the analysis of interactions in small groups where, he says, 'prices are not mediated by markets and there are opportunities for strategic behavior' (Hansmann 230). (The tinshop, then, may not provide a sufficiently extensive site for market analysis to work, or may simply enable behavior that can circumvent the market.) Finally, economic analysis is unscientific because its findings are not demonstrable through proof, neither verifiable nor falsifiable through empirical testing (*Problems of Jurisprudence* 371). The self-interest model of human behavior, all these critiques suggest, is just too simple.

Scholars less friendly to the legal aspiration to science find Law and Economics objectionable precisely on those grounds where it most succeeds in looking like modern science. Posner summarizes these objections as well: because of its focus on objectivity and logical relationships, economic analysis fails to treat people as individuals; its moral neutrality leads it to have little interest in important value questions such as the nature of justice, the distribution of wealth, and the need for legal reform (374-82). Its focus on cost-benefit analysis, Nussbaum has said, means that economic analysis limits itself to answering only 'the obvious question,' the one that asks, in the face of a dilemma, what we should do. But it fails even to ask, let alone answer, what Nussbaum calls 'the tragic question,' which asks whether any of the options we face can be chosen without violating important moral or ethical standards ('The Costs of Tragedy' 171). Certainly that failure contributes to another, the tendency West sees in *Sex and Reason* to ignore the needs of traditionally subordinated groups such as the poor, the young, the homosexual, or the female. Economic theory, then, is simply an exercise in 'valuing that which the strong members of a community...already value' ('Sex, Reason, and a Taste for the Absurd' 2416).

As an example, West pinpoints Posner's discussion of sexual preference; though she does so in order to take issue with his reasoning about the nature and prevalence of homosexual practices, we can draw on her analysis to expose problems with his definition of 'preferences' and the related concept of choice more generally. Likening sexual preference to taste, particularly a taste for vanilla ice cream as opposed to, say, a taste for chocolate, Posner suggests that the frequency of homosexual behaviors in any given culture is not a reliable indicator of 'true' homosexuality; just as rampant consumption of chocolate ice cream may indicate not that there are large numbers of chocolate lovers in a culture but simply a shortage of vanilla, frequent homosexual practices may be due to a lack of reasonably cheap heterosexual partners (*Sex and Reason* 436-7). This analysis leads Posner to make a number of points, for example that many human preferences are 'opportunistic' rather than naturally given; that it is not the role of scientific analysis, however, to question those preferences; and that, accordingly, we should enhance the possibility for human behavior that reflects preferences through a policy of 'moral indifference' (181-3). West's point is that the conclusions of Posner's 'libertarian,' morally indifferent analysis constitute 'an astoundingly crisp endorsement of the status quo' ('Sex, Reason, and a Taste for the Absurd' 2427), from the 'don't ask-don't tell' policy of the military to the prohibition of homosexual marriage, conclusions based in the assumption that homosexuality is usually not a natural condition but a wealth-maximizing, opportunistic choice. Further, Posner's neglect of mistaken or regretted judgments misunderstands human nature through a deceptively simple account of a complex process. 'We do not know,' West concludes, 'our sexuality or our sexual preferences with anything like the clarity with which we know our tastes in ice cream' (2432).

But Posner's approach to sexual preferences is also evidence of a more widespread bias that infects his discussion of choices of all kinds. For obviously nobody, in dithering over the chocolate-vanilla dilemma, would even think to consult the ice cream. In the context of more obviously ethical choices (such as those characterizing choices about sexual activity) such questions are absolutely necessary, and they are precisely the questions Posner fails to ask. The passivity and objectification of women in Posner's economic theory of sexuality (West 'Sex, Reason, and a Taste for the Absurd' 2446) enables Posner to present a sexual project of continual search, possession, consumption, and, ultimately, elimination—the objects of search are acquired with the least possible effort and facilely discarded when they no longer serve the purpose of the active sexual agent. While it may well be that sex is not really economics, economics as Posner presents it is certainly sex, at least from the culturally assumed masculine perspective. Far from the moral neutrality Posner claims for it, the perspective of his economic theory is simply a 'studied moral apathy,' says West (2416) that fails to recognize its grounding in values precisely because they are values, those that by virtue of their adoption and promulgation by dominant social groups have come to seem 'neutral.'

West thus echoes, consciously or not, the feminist critique of science broadly understood, particularly of the modernist science to which Posnerian economics aspires. That critique has in some cases begun by questioning the basis of knowledge itself or the quest for our understanding of its sources that has come to be known, drawing on its classical roots, as 'epistemology.' While some feminist critique objects to the very concept of epistemology itself, a more common objection is to traditionalist epistemologies that, like Aristotle's, conceive of a precise separation between the knower and that which is to be known (Grant 99). The quest of the traditional epistemological enterprise in science is, says Hawkesworth, for an 'objectivity' aimed at delivering 'a grasp of actual qualities and relations of objects as they exist independently of the observer's thoughts and desires regarding them;' shifted into the realm of law, the traditional quest becomes that of 'impersonal and impartial standards and decision processes that produce disinterested and equitable judgments' (151-2). Both such quests fail, leading not to objectivity but to objectification (Mary Ann Doan, quoted in Hawkesworth 157). Eve Browning Cole points out variations in such traditional epistemologies that recognize the subjective elements most feminist critique insists upon, particularly in empirical approaches that rely on sense impressions applied to physical objects (77). Here, presumably, the radical divorce of epistemology from ontology—the separation of what a person knows from who that person is (Hirschmann 164-5)—may be tentatively overcome. But the morally indifferent, abstract empiricism of Posner's approach, relying upon non-falsifiable thought experiments, duplicates what the feminist critique faults as the primary weakness of traditional science, its neglect of the connection of knowledge to power (Cole 81) enabled by presumably value-neutral science.

Responding to such criticisms, Posner contends that 'we should not worry whether cost-benefit analysis is well grounded in any theory of value,' that we should ask simply 'how well it serves whatever goals we have' ('Cost-Benefit Analysis' 320). Posner seeks to exclude pragmatism from the catalogue of moral values to which it clearly belongs—and for good reason, because for Posner and others in Law and Economics, questions of value are not simply irrelevant but completely elude legal science. Heckman is especially clear on this point, explaining that economists refuse to take on questions of the appropriate distribution of wealth, for example, because they 'have no special competence in determining which distribution is appropriate' (328). Yet it is not simply the distribution of wealth that Posner neglects, but the whole category of equity and, correspondingly, justice. Once again, Posner is not exceptional among Law and Economics scholars on this score. James R. Hackney, Jr., glossing Guido

Calabresi's *The Costs of Accidents*, which itself draws on A. J. Ayer's linguistic analysis, maintains that justice finds its expression in 'utterances' and concludes on that basis that it is one of many 'emotive gestures adding nothing to the scientific quest for knowledge' (312). It would seem that legal science has nothing much to do with justice, in large part because of the latter's unavoidable implication with language.

Nevertheless, the decision Posner reaches in *Carr*, however firmly grounded in his economic theory, is also in nearly perfect harmony with the theory of justice that Aristotle provides in Book V of the *Ethics*. What Aristotle tells us here is that there are two types of justice, distributive and corrective. Distributive justice is the means whereby community goods, what Posner would call wealth, are distributed among its members. Justice therefore has four terms, Aristotle says, two people and two shares that are to be distributed on the basis of the merit of those who lay claim to them. Merit, he explains, is defined in terms decided upon by the community, and any person's share is in direct proportion to that person's contribution to its 'common stock.' Where shares have been wrongfully distributed for any reason, corrective justice comes into play, requiring a judge to 'equalize' transactions by imposing a penalty that takes away one party's (illicit) gain (*Nicomachean Ethics* V.iv.4-5). Like Posner, however, Aristotle refuses to engage, at least in his *Politics*, the question of how individual merit and thus shares are to be determined. 'The starting point in such matters,' he says there, 'is to train those that are respectable by nature so that they may not wish for excessive wealth, and to contrive that the base may not be able to do so' (II.IV.12).

In *Carr*, an apparently innocent party is the recipient of illicit gain—the female welder who enjoyed an unfair competitive advantage due to her imperviousness to sexual harassment (alternatively, due to her welding arc). Yet it is not she who has been unjust; an unjust act, says Aristotle, is voluntary, 'done from choice and unprovoked' (V.xi.5). And whatever culpability the trial court and the dissent to Posner's opinion wishes to pin on Carr herself, Aristotle would hold that she, too, was innocent of injustice, 'for we do not think a man acts unjustly if he gives what he got' (V.xi.5). Assuming that we may apply Aristotle's rule to a woman as well, it is clear that 'it is not possible to suffer injustice involuntarily,' a position with which Posner's finding on 'welcome harassment' concurs (and one on which Aristotle differed dramatically from Plato). The unjust act, the use of sexual power to intimidate and harass, was clearly that of the male tinners.

There are structural reasons why it is GM, and not the tinners, who must pay the price exacted by Posner's corrective justice—sexual harassment law holds that an employer is responsible for the behavior of its employees when it knows, or should have known, that another employee is the target of a hostile environment (Equal Employment Opportunity Commission 1604.11(e)). But how is justice to be measured, and how are damages to be assessed and paid? Uniformly, says Aristotle; echoing Plato, he explains that all commodities, the various forms of wealth we seek to maximize, must be measured by one standard. Where Plato had perhaps disingenuously suggested in the *Protagoras* that the measure might be pleasure, Aristotle forthrightly declares that it is 'demand...conventionally represented by *nomisma*' (V.v.11) a word that Rackham translates simply as 'money.' Derived from the singular noun *nomos*, *nomisma* are literally everyday conventions, not the 'valuable things' represented by *chreimata*, but what Aristotle explains is 'customary currency' (V.v.11). What, then, was in demand in the tinshop, and through what currency was it represented? This question is one that Posner, as an appeals court judge, is not required to answer; he must simply remand that question to the trial court with his order that it 'proceed to a determination of the remedy to which [Carr] is entitled'(1012-13). In all likelihood, those damages were monetary, and Carr may well have been satisfied that justice was done. But it seems unlikely that what Carr initially demanded, and what was denied to her by the tinners, was literally money. For what Carr said she wanted was simply to fit in, to be one of the guys, and the means she chose toward that end was her use of language. It was this 'tool' that the tinners, the trial court, and the dissent to Posner's opinion denied her. Posner, of course, disagrees about the significance of language as a tool of either community or intimidation. The verbal abuse Carr suffered at the hands of the tinners was 'mere words,' he said, while the sabotage of her more literal tools was, he believed, both more ominous and more aggressive (1010). But one of the most egregious transgressions of the tinners was that they thwarted Carr's intentions and turned her language against her, first by forcing her to speak their own and then by denying the value, in her voice, of that customary currency. It was Carr's language, no less than her toolbox, that the tinners painted pink.

It is not surprising that Posner should have failed to recognize the significance of language as a medium of exchange in the tinshop despite his belief that language, like everything else in his scholarship, operates 'like the free market. No legislature or bureaucracy,' he claims, 'prescribes the forms of speech, the structure of language, or the vocabulary that individuals use' ('Blackstone and Bentham' 603). Holding that language, '[l]ike a free market...is an immensely complicated yet private and decentralized institution' Posner fails to take into account the effect of market forces on the acceptability—the currency—of Carr's language. Though his statements about language have evolved since this rather early formulation, Posner continues to think of it in economic terms. Indeed, a careful reading of Posner's work indicates that for him unclear language resembles sexual harassment; it is not so much an abuse of those to whom it is directed as it is an abuse of the market in which it is presumed to function, what Posner might call an inefficient sorting of words to ideas. His definition of rhetoric, understood by Posner as a particular kind of language—a sort of persuasive or stylistic gloss over an otherwise transparent base—makes this assumption clear. Rhetoric, he explains in *Overcoming Law*, alternately is or simply impinges upon 'belief costs' through its ability to convince us to believe the false or disbelieve the true (529).

Such assumptions about the inherent stability and potential clarity of language (assuming the absence of 'rhetoric') are evidence of a 'windowpane' theory of language proposed by George Orwell in 'Politics and the English Language,' an essay frequently cited by advocates of 'plain language' in law and other fields. Carolyn R. Miller's analysis of this positivist view points out that the obvious function of a windowpane, literal or figurative, is transparency—with respect to language, it is the ability to provide 'a view out onto the world' through the construction of simple 'observation sentences' ('A Humanistic Rationale for Technical Writing' 612) that, the positivist view surely holds, avoid tampering with that reality. Posner's claim that 'the task of legal scholarship is to get behind the prose of the opinions' ('Killing or Wounding to Protect a Property Interest' 220); Edmund W. Kitch's claim that, thanks to rhetoric, 'law professors share with their colleagues at the bar an ability to clothe even the most absurd position in an aura of reasonableness' (186); and Hansmann's claim that 'economics provides us with a more powerful syntax and semantics for legal argumentation' than, presumably, legal language (227) all speak to an instrumentalist view of the inadequacy of language to function in the precise and reliable manner each assumes one can demand of a science. This instrumentalist view, what Langdon Winner also calls a 'tool-use ethic' (26), presumes 'an entirely obvious connection between the thing desired and the means to its fulfillment,' an assumption that, 'if one thinks about the matter for very long...is in fact the exception rather than the rule' (228).

The instrumentalist assumption of the neutrality of tools is, White reminds us, 'not right either as to language or as to tools' (*Justice as Translation* 49). It is, however, a distinctly modern position on the relationship of tools to the sciences. Just as tools employed by the physical sciences are to enhance perception, bring reality nearer, or make it more palpable, so the tool that is law's language, the instrumentalist view holds, should function. That it obviously fails to do so may be the fault of the tool (if language is inherently ambiguous), its user (who may be incompetent or malicious), or the 'weak science' that relies upon it. Where Blackstone had found a justification for the obscurity of law's language—it was a sign of law's majesty and divinity—Posner and other legal economists find in the inadequacy of law's language their own 'professional incompetence' to address questions of justice (Heckman 329). Economic analysis may well be remarkable, admirable, and difficult. But given that it is not divine, its emphasis on customary currency, or current custom, leads to a 'value-neutral' position on justice that is literally useless.

Aristotle would not have suggested that 'science' should remain free of its language. In fact, language provided classical *epistemé* with its analyzable data, the *phainomena* that took the form of cultural beliefs and sayings. Furthermore *epistemé* is reliable for that very reason, distinguishing among the *phainomena* to find and eliminate their discrepancies and, by retaining the most constant among them, to find the 'residuum of correct opinion left standing' (*Nicomachean Ethics* VII.i.5). However much Posner may have extended the notion of scientific data once that notion was imported into the realm of legal science, he has not been able to change its nature. Its method has, however, changed from that envisioned by Aristotle, especially in its insistence upon results that obtain with some certainty in the world of human affairs, a position that Aristotle found untenable. The long evolution from *epistemé* to Posner's legal science has also made evident the constant presence of certain core issues other than those of data and method. These include the reliance of science, however construed, on its language; the inability of such science to regulate the uncertainty and unpredictability of human behavior; and the effects of the beliefs of the scientist, whether in the divinity of its subject matter or the selfishness of the human agent, on what science itself can see. Legal science, like classical *epistemé*, does an excellent job of making manifest its own assumptions.

Finally, justice is as unpredictable and uncontrollable as is the medium through which it is conducted; as an 'utterance,' an 'emotive gesture' (Hackney 312) it cannot lead to the certainty Posner demands of science. Faced with the obvious disproportion of shares of the common stock found in the tinshop at GM, Posner the judge applied not distributive but corrective justice, taking away from the female welder the unfair advantage that Carr's vulnerability had given her. She, like Carr and like the tinners, was entitled only to such 'wealth' as she could fairly contribute to the common stock, a share that Posner the economic analyst (much like Aristotle) assumes will automatically be adjusted as the circumstances in the tinshop are regulated and as GM begins to exercise its proper authority over its workers. In determining what that share may be, legal science declares itself to be of no use. But in speaking with the voice of Posner, it is surely one of the most authoritative of 'the things we say.'

Chapter 4

The Things We Do:
The Activities of the Legal Imagination

> Hence it is incumbent upon us to control the character of our activities, since on the quality of these depends the quality of our dispositions.
>
> Aristotle
> *Nicomachean Ethics*, Book II

We live in a world of activity and activities, among them the language we use to talk about ourselves, others, and our relations with others. As we have seen from the analysis of *Carr v. Allison Gas Turbine Division* in Chapter 3, workplaces are no exception to this rule but are sites where activity is not restricted to the tasks anticipated by job descriptions. Like the tinshop in which Mary Carr found herself, every workplace has built-up habits of activity and language, recognizable patterns of professional and non-professional, formal and informal, behaviors. As Carr learned through sorry experience, those informal, non-professional activities and language practices are no less crucial to enculturation and success in a workplace than its formal professional structures—and newcomers are generally expected to comply with rather than to question them. This common-sense account is supported by research into the ways in which new members of workplaces learn their way into and about work communities and their value systems; noting that 'the features that make up a culture...*may be* consciously (and *will be* unconsciously) imparted to all who join a company,' Jean A. Lutz also notes that it is 'communication [that] is the primary tool through which members participate in an organization' (114, emphasis in original). Research into the relationships between gender and organizational structures also confirms the importance of communication networks to successful integration into an organization's practices, noting the ways in which women can be (and frequently are) systematically excluded from those networks (Gilbert and Ones 686). Communication scholar Patrice Buzzanell sees a clear link of organizational structure both to workplace discrimination against women and to communication systems, to the ways we talk about men, women and the workplace itself and thus 'do gender' in organizing and communication processes (328).

The presence and importance of informal activities and language practices within an organization are not only supported by research. In fact, they have sometimes carried the force of law, a condition made particularly apparent in sexual harassment decisions prior to the early 1990s. In such cases, and on a literal-minded understanding of the Civil Rights Act and guidelines for its interpretation published by the Equal Employment Opportunity Commission (EEOC), precedent in seven of the thirteen federal districts and the Supreme Court itself maintained that otherwise clearly harassing behavior did not constitute sexual harassment in its strictly legal sense unless it 'altered' the conditions of the plaintiff's employment (*Henson v. City of Dundee* 904, *Meritor Savings Bank v. Vinson* 67). Based on this interpretation such courts affirmed a legal right to a variety of mind-boggling workplace behaviors. Frequent water-gun and jelly-bean fights in a graphics department whose supervisor would sit on his female subordinates' laps and occasionally lick their glasses thus became what the courts called sexual 'horseplay' (*Spencer v. General Electric Co.* 214); intercourse that the plaintiff claimed was unwanted but that she accepted out of fear of losing her job was characterized by the Supreme Court as 'voluntary,' though 'unwelcome,' behavior (*Meritor Savings Bank v. Vinson* 18). Employees who complained about pornographic pictures or foul language at work were reminded by the courts that workers and the workplace are often 'rough hewn and vulgar' (*Rabidue v. Osceola Refining Co.* 620); furthermore, given their continuity with 'a society that condones and publicly features and commercially exploits open displays of written and pictorial erotica at the newsstands, on prime-time television, at the cinema, and in other public places,' sensitive employees were advised that they must accept the existing 'lexicon of obscenity' (*Rabidue v. Osceola Refining Co.* 620, 622) that was often justified as 'shop talk' (*Carr v. Allison Gas Turbine Division* 1010). In recent years the tide has begun to turn; in 1992 the language in *Rabidue* that required plaintiffs to show serious psychological harm was specifically vacated by the Supreme Court in *Harris v. Forklift Systems, Inc.*, and a pair of decisions issued in 1998 (*Burlington Industries v. Ellerth* and *Faragher v. City of Boca Raton*) held employers responsible for harassment that yielded no tangible job detriments in terms of promotions or salary, for example. Such decisions signal that the courts are beginning to conclude that Title VII really is intended to change 'the social mores of American workers,' contrary to the *Rabidue* court's claim (621) and despite the overwhelming presumption of precedent that, by virtue of their acceptance of employment, workers also implicitly accept the conditions already in place upon their entrance into the work site (*Ebert v. Lamar Truck Plaza* 1499).

But in 1994 Mary Carr could be seen as attempting to comply not only with custom and common sense but also with the law when she entered the tinshop at the General Motors plant in Allison, Indiana, and began to participate in the 'antics' (1016) and 'foul' language or 'shop talk' (1010) she found there. She, of course, said merely that she wanted to 'be one of the boys' (1011) and earn the acceptance, if not the respect, of her male coworkers. When her attempts to comply with the informal practices in the tinshop failed, her complaints were not taken seriously by either her supervisors or the trial court judge quite precisely because she had previously attempted to comply; while the judges at trial and at appeal, including the dissent to the majority opinion in her favor, are unanimous in condemning the behavior of the male tinners as 'vulgar,' 'crude,' and even 'abusive' (1010) the trial court and the dissent to the appeal both uphold their right to engage in those behaviors upon the presumption that Carr, through her participation in those activities, 'was just as responsible for any hostile sexual environment that consequently arose' as were the male tinners (1017). In other words, her acceptance of the pre-existing conditions in the workplace, an acceptance not only sanctioned but literally required by law, worked ironically and fallaciously to make her legally responsible for them. In simpler terms we might just say, along with the District Court and the dissent to her successful appeal, that she brought her 'problems' upon herself.

Carr's story simultaneously validates and offers a caveat to the scholarship of James Boyd White, work on which I focus in this chapter as central to the project of the Law and Literature movement more generally. What Carr seemed to intuitively understand was the role that White claims for language in forming and maintaining a culture. For White, any culture simply is the sum of its activities, the activity of language chief among them. In an environment where, Chief Judge Richard Posner's majority opinion tells us, a worker named Beckham could be 'clocked' saying 'fuck' fifty to sixty times in the space of ten minutes (1010), a rate with the potential to yield an astounding 500-plus 'fucks' per hour, Carr attempted to be a fellow traveler, though perhaps in the slow lane. The failure of her attempt to join in with the 'shop talk' suggests a number of hazardous implications for the generally positive picture White paints of culture, including the exclusionary potential of any culture's language, whether characterized as shop talk or, what is generally less controversial, professional jargon. It also illustrates Aristotle's insight, the irony that 'the actions from or through which any virtue is produced are the same as those through which it also is destroyed' (*Nicomachean Ethics* II.i.6). While for the male tinners shop talk carried the virtue of marking one's belonging in the culture, for Carr the lack of what we might call a native fluency marked her as an outsider and made her a target around which the rest of the culture could consolidate. And, finally, the trial court's holding in her case, the dissent to the appeal that reversed that holding, and the tradition established by numerous legal cases that preceded Carr's all demonstrate the tendency of culture to replicate itself through its language and to resist attempts at revision, whether that culture is the tinshop at GM or the legal culture that upholds the perpetuation of what it calls 'the conditions of employment' in the workplace community.

I focus in this chapter on an ongoing exchange among a limited group of scholars—not only on White, often acknowledged as the founder of the Law and Literature movement, but also on classical scholar Martha C. Nussbaum, constitutional law scholar Robin West, and judge and legal scholar Posner, who is both White's counterpart in the Law and Economics movement and the author of *Carr v. Allison Gas Turbine Division*, the appeals court decision in Carr's favor. My account of each scholar's work, and of that scholar's response to the work of each of the others, is intended to reveal the necessity they all face to deal with a loftier manifestation of the challenges Carr faced in the tinshop. These challenges, I will argue, are the legacy of the humanities tradition these scholars consciously adopt, whether it is to advocate or to dismiss the potential for a humanities-based approach to legal education, and are embedded in an approach to experience typified by Aristotelian *praxis*. It is not my intention to argue that this purposely limited group of scholars provides a portrait of the entire Law and Literature movement. In fact, all four are methodologically atypical, relying to varying degrees on a variety of literary criticism long out of vogue in the Departments of English that generally house literature studies—the New Criticism of the Chicago School that as Posner notes, 'arose in the 1920s, achieved great influence in American universities in the 1940s and 1950s, and then faded' (*Law and Literature* 220-1). Both White and Posner explicitly declare their allegiance to New Critical method; the work of both West (who relies on Northrop Frye) and Nussbaum (who focuses on the morality of literary form) is also clearly compatible with this critical movement. Whereas a great deal of other literary scholarship in law relies on postmodernist or deconstructive approaches, none of these four scholars is convinced of the potential for such theories to contribute to legal analysis. It seems likely that this lack of conviction stems in large part from the deconstructive tendency to problematize the construction of 'the other' through literature, a tendency that would seriously compromise the attempts by West, White, and Nussbaum to attribute empathic values to literary language and form. For Posner, its 'opacity and sheer strangeness' have combined with its appropriation by 'leftist legal scholars' to take attention away from aspects of deconstructive critical theory that could otherwise be useful; postmodernism, he concludes, 'denigrates the intelligibility and coherence of texts' (216). West appears to sum it up for this group of scholars; 'as a tool of analysis,' she says, deconstruction 'has all the usefulness of an unhinged steering wheel' (*Caring for Justice* 204).

Further, White, Nussbaum, West, and Posner not only diverge from much other Law and Literature scholarship on the basis of their methodology; their similar methodology leads them to diverging conclusions about the ethical and substantive potential for literary studies in legal scholarship and education. While White and Nussbaum remain convinced, for different reasons, of the ethical and substantive value of literature, West's later scholarship raises serious questions about her early optimism regarding both the moral and substantive claims. And Posner, whose assessment of the potential contribution of literature to law increases somewhat from the first to the second edition of his *Law and Literature*, still confines its contributions to 'style' and 'rhetoric,' both narrowly defined so as to restrict (somewhat unsuccessfully, as I will argue) their ethical and substantive use. But where these four scholars are consistent, both with each other and with the Law and Literature movement as a whole, is in the range of issues they deem literature competent or even uniquely qualified to address as well as the range of questions their literary investigations prompt them to ask. Issues regarding the validity of legal interpretation, the nature of legal authority, and the roles of texts, writers, and readers in creating legal realities pervade the movement and lead to questions not only about the validity of legal texts but of the legal system itself and of the role of its language in maintaining legal culture.

For White, who sees law as an essentially literary practice, literature is a model not only for interpretation (which his later work calls 'translation') but also for the ethical creation of law through its authoritative texts as a 'culture of argument' (*Heracles' Bow* 35). Nussbaum, too, sees ethical potential in literary, particularly novelistic, form; for her, the novel both encourages and relies upon its readers' recognition of others through an activity of 'fancy' that sets ethical standards for the 'literary judge' (*Poetic Justice* 82) and 'poetic judging' (99) by which judicial opinions may themselves be judged. But both Posner and West are less complacent regarding the potential contribution of literature to legal scholarship, theory, or practice. For Posner, the work of White, Nussbaum, and others displays a moralizing or edifying tendency (*Law and Literature* 75, 307) that he ultimately concludes is of no practical import for legal decision-makers; West's work, he says, shows us how 'a mind preoccupied with politics' (188) fails to appreciate literary aesthetics (314). West, no fan of Posner's scholarship in either economics or literature, claims the humanizing value of literary studies for law students and scholars (*Narrative, Authority and Law* 263) but seems frustrated by what she sees as the strictly theoretical or merely aesthetic nature of literature, a nature that works against her activist legal agenda (*Caring for Justice* 187). Where Posner promotes a 'clean' (*Problems of Jurisprudence* 362) economic approach to legal analysis that attempts to minimize the role of language (and thus interpretation and ambiguity) in legal decision-making, West calls for attention to silence in order to avoid the use of 'one verbal construct…to criticize yet another' (*Caring for Justice* 198).

What all four scholars seem to be aiming for is an approach to legal scholarship that has practical implications and tangible consequences, a desire that seems fulfilled to varying degrees. Yet what the work of all four demonstrates in addition is a 'practical' strain of a different type, the Aristotelian *praxis* that is marked by the value and necessity of experience, of individual immersion in the activities and language of a culture. Calling those activities 'deliberation,' and its exercise within a community *praxis*, Aristotle sees their culmination in individual *phronesis*, or 'practical wisdom.' Anticipating objections to my characterization of Law and Literature scholarship as what our culture is inclined to call 'mere' practice, in this chapter I emphasize the ways in which today's common-sense notions of 'practice' differ from Aristotle's understanding of *praxis*. One common claim of Law and Literature scholarship, for example, is that it serves students well in their preparation for legal practice; meanwhile, an equally common claim (and one that is not necessarily a complaint) is that it performs no practical function whatsoever. Such claims and complaints resonate with the assumption common to our day that practice is either antithetical (and subordinate) to 'theory' or designed merely to carry out its commands.

But for Aristotle *praxis*, while it was clearly less 'divine' than theory given its orientation to human life and affairs, was not its handmaiden; in fact, the 'practical wisdom' of *phronesis*, he tells us, itself 'issues commands, since its end is a statement of what we ought to do or not to do' (*Nicomachean Ethics* VI.x.2). It is true that *praxis* differs significantly from Aristotelian *theoria*; in contrast to the detached observation Aristotle associated with the latter (closely akin to the perspective demanded by Posner's theory of Law and Economics) *praxis* offers the total immersion in daily particulars that is essential, Aristotle says, to ethical decision-making. But *praxis* is not designed to carry out the orders of theory largely because, as Aristotle tells us, theory is a 'useless' occupation (VI.vii.5) which has no such orders to give; here Stanley Fish, a literary and legal scholar who is deeply critical of much Law and Literature work, including the work I review here, is in accord with Aristotle's conclusion if not with his premises (*Doing What Comes Naturally* 154-6). But however 'practical' it may seem, *praxis* is not intended to generate any condition or product separable from itself—such production is the responsibility of what Aristotle called *poiesis*, to which he assigned not literature, as we might be tempted to do, but rhetoric. In assigning Law and Literature to *praxis* rather than to either *theoria* or *poiesis* myself, I intend to emphasize both the sources of the ethical potential claimed for literary studies and the pitfalls of its typical approach to language, a perspective that is ultimately unwilling, or unable, to get outside itself.

In Chapter 2, I described the claims made by Law and Literature scholarship in order to note the derivation of those values from the humanities tradition as well as to question not only the equation of literature with that tradition but the purposes and effects of the claims themselves. What I found more important, however, were the striking similarities of the claims for the humanities and literature to those Aristotle makes for *praxis* and *phronesis*. In this chapter I consider the implications of Aristotle's unabashedly circular and instrumental understanding of *praxis* and the ways that the work in Law and Literature that I examine here either attempts to resolve or bypass those problems. Examining the specific properties of literature that each scholar claims enable (or disable) its potential contribution to legal studies, I then move to 'read' *Carr* as each scholar's literary approach suggests I should. Based on that reading, I conclude with a discussion of the contributions each such approach can make to our understanding of this case, offset against the limitations each approach creates through its self-definition, what I call the bounded imagination. The potential each scholar sees for literary legal study, I conclude, is directly dependent upon the language theory each brings to the study of both literature and law. And while those theories vary, each is a response to the potential it recognizes in legal texts to create realities that demonstrate, more obviously than in perhaps any other endeavor, that words literally 'matter' in law.

Literary Properties and 'Craft Values'

Today's Law and Literature scholars are by no means the first to have made the argument for literature's edifying and empowering properties. Credit for that innovation generally goes to Cicero and the ode to 'literature' that is the *Pro Archia*. In this defense of an immigrant poet named Archias, who was threatened with the loss of his Roman citizenship, Cicero argues not so much for Archias but for the value to Rome of his art. The list of literary virtues Cicero recites may seem almost trite today but apparently, given his apologies to the jury for his unusual argument, had both the benefits and the drawbacks of novelty at the time. Literature, Cicero said, provided him with refreshment, repose, and inspiration; even considered purely as entertainment, literature was valuable, for 'in the home it delights, in the world it hampers not' (vii.16). But Cicero needed to promise more because the Romans, as Bernard Knox reminds us, were 'an immensely practical people' (79). So, as he told his audience of jurors, literature was useful, 'abound[ing] with incentives to noble actions,' encouraging emulation, and molding character (vi.14-15). And if such rather abstract usefulness to the individual were to be deemed by the jury insufficient, Cicero added that literature served the Republic itself as the means by which the reputation of the Roman people was made manifest abroad. 'Whithersoever our arms have penetrated,' Cicero declared, 'there also our fame and glory should extend' (x.23) and poetry, it seemed, was just the means to accomplish the feat.

Cicero's claim for the direct link of poetry to culture, not only to its preservation but also to its extension, remains 'the standard apology for the manifold social import of the humanities' today (Pantazakos 31), an argument taken up and carried forward for centuries. The strengthening of this argument and of the bond between literature and culture itself coincided with a weakening of the bond between classical rhetoric and Aristotelian-style deliberation, a deterioration helped along by the end of classical democracies and the rise of empires and regional monarchies. As rhetoric's substantive implications diminished, taken over by literature's new importance to cultural imperatives, the balance of power in their own relationship shifted. For the Sophists, arguably the inventors of rhetoric, literature had provided cultural fodder for substantive rhetorical arguments; for Cicero, it had provided the 'inspiration' and 'cultivation' that served primarily to strengthen his 'oratorical powers' (vi.13). As literature began to be seen as the 'better half' in their relationship, rhetoric, confined primarily to the promulgation of church law through the *ars dictaminis*, or letter writing, eventually began to be seen as mere ornamentation. This relationship would be formalized by Peter Ramus, who excised the reasoning component that Aristotle had offered as a corrective and extension of sophistic rhetoric and grafted it onto dialectic in the sixteenth century (Bizzell and Herzberg 473). With the unabashedly inventive rhetoric of the Sophists forgotten along with their writings; with the characteristic mode of reasoning that Aristotle attributed to rhetoric denied; with Cicero studied primarily as the elegant writer that he was, rhetoric became nothing but 'style,' a literary property.

The supremacy of literature in the university curriculum was, however, short-lived. By the 1870s in the United States, social and educational structures were changing and broadening; law schools were not immune, and found themselves somewhat involuntarily democratized by an 'influx of lawyers without classical education' (Page quoted in Gemmette 289) that eventually affected the professional Bar as well. The calls that issued late in the nineteenth and early in the twentieth century for a revival of literary skills among lawyers thus echo Cicero as they plead for the retention of culture through classical and otherwise canonized literatures that the broader democracy in legal education and the Bar was threatening. Eugene Wambaugh's list of law-related literature published in 1889 (Papke 421 fn2), and the better known 'List of Legal Novels' published in 1908 by John Wigmore, Dean of the Law School at Northwestern University (Gemmette 285; Pantazakos 38), appear to be part of a last ditch effort to guard against the democracy represented by the 'hordes of immigrants' (Reed 347) that were invading the profession. Described in Gary Minda's *Postmodern Legal Movements* as 'the first to combine literature with legal studies' (307 fn3), Wigmore saw himself as defending the profession against particularly virulent lay criticism; while he claimed that lawyers should read the works he recommended to better understand the human condition through 'the gallery of life's portraits' literature could provide (quoted in Pantazakos 38) Wigmore also noted the contribution an awareness of the profession's 'uncommissioned portrait' in such works could make to understanding, in David Papke's take on Wigmore's purpose, 'what quirky laymen were thinking about law and lawyers' (Papke 422). Papke's conclusion, that Wigmore and Wambaugh were promoting a 'fundamentally humanistic' agenda (422) emphasizes a subtle distinction between their agenda and that of today's Law and Literature movement—that is, if Michael Pantazakos is correct in his assessment of the 'general unity of the [current] movement in [a] rebellious form of humanism' (38). Certainly, Wigmore's and Wambaugh's agendas promoted and maintained the privilege of a currently empowered elite rather than calling to subvert it, as is often claimed for more recent literary legal scholarship.

These early pleas for the revival of literature studies were transformed significantly by the work of Benjamin Cardozo who in 1925, as a judge on the Court of Appeals in New York, wrote an essay titled simply 'Law and Literature.' While he shared with Wigmore and Wambaugh an individualistic approach to literary advocacy, calling not for the addition of literature to the law school curriculum but for individuals' private reading of great literature, what Cardozo provided differed substantially from their lists in purpose; according to Richard H. Weisberg, Cardozo's essay provided 'a poetics of the judicial function' that recognized the role of style (still, at this time, frequently equated with rhetoric) as the 'drive to express through the opinion's form the essential *rightness*' of the decision in the case (Weisberg 311, emphasis in original). Understanding form not as something 'added to substance' ('Law and Literature' 5) but as a judicial opinion's 'very bone and tissue' (26) Cardozo maintained that its logical organization was the key to the opinion's ability to provide a conclusion that 'follow[s] so naturally and inevitably as almost to prove itself' (33).

Cardozo's 'fundamentally literary slant' (Pantazakos 38) prefigures the approach taken by White since the publication of his *The Legal Imagination* in 1973, both the book and its author widely cited as the impetus and inspiration for the modern Law and Literature movement (Minda 149; Pantazakos 39; Posner *Law and Literature* 4; West *Caring for Justice* 181). White's attempt to build on Cardozo to develop a literary concept of judging was explicitly intended to consider the consequences of assuming that 'the literature of the law,' as White explained in later work, 'really were literature' (*Justice as Translation* 17). White's work in what is often called the 'law *as* literature' branch of the movement earns the skepticism of West, whose own work grows out of the 'law *in* literature' orientation visible in the Wigmore and Wambaugh lists, and who eyes White's re-creation of the 'man of letters' with considerable suspicion for its traditional and elitist implications, as we have seen. But most approaches to literature in legal studies, whether of the 'in' or 'as' variety, share a project to explore the potential for a literary understanding of the nature of interpretation to expand the interpretive capabilities of those who read legal texts, a project that itself builds on each scholar's understanding of the very nature of literature and literary properties. The conclusions reached by White, West, Nussbaum, and Posner regarding the potential for literary legal studies are thus grounded in what are related but significantly different assumptions about literary properties themselves. The first assumption, appropriately enough the position of the economist Posner, assumes that its 'properties' are something literature owns, capacities it 'has' and can, accordingly, exercise. The second, implied in West's discussion, assumes that its properties are less external to literature, that they make literature what it 'is.' Finally, White's thought shows that for him literature's properties are neither its possessions nor its characteristics, strictly speaking, but its activities, what literature 'does.' Nussbaum, whose discussion of novelistic 'features' in *Poetic Justice* most resembles the position of White, nevertheless maintains, as White does not, the value of economic contributions to legal understanding and, as we will see, of Posner's judicial writing in *Carr* as an example of ethical judging by literary standards.

It is important to remember, in reviewing Posner's discussion of literary properties, that he sees little of value for legal interpretation or analysis in the Law and Literature movement as a whole. In its theoretical manifestations he says Law and Literature has not shown that literary interpretation is analogous in any meaningful way to legal interpretation (*Problems of Jurisprudence* 203); in fact, says Posner, 'we do not need, and can I think make little use of, the concept of interpretation to understand and evaluate the common law' (261). Furthermore, according to Posner, law is irremediably distinct from literature because legal texts such as statutes and constitutions are 'commands,' while literary texts 'are the opposite' (394). But Posner does allow one exception to his position that legal texts generally are not literary, and that exception is the judicial opinion (remember, Posner is a judge). As a legal decision-maker who must be persuasive in order to be successful, the judge is free to be both 'rhetorical' (394) and 'literary' (*Law and Literature* 276) in the unique meanings and significance both terms take on in Posner's work.

The relationship Posner sees between literature and rhetoric has both evolved and continually contradicted itself since his first publication of *Law and Literature: A Misunderstood Relation* in 1988. In the revised edition, titled simply *Law and Literature* and published ten years later, Posner has obviously modified his position on the value of literary to legal studies, though not much. In sorting out the relationships among literature and its content, meaning, and style, Posner develops a system; calling the literary properties of the judicial opinion its 'style,'

Posner defines rhetoric as the subset of those stylistic devices intended specifically to persuade (*Law and Literature* 255). Literary properties, deprived of both content and persuasive intent, then become simply 'the smooth capsule or the flavor additive that makes the medicine easier to swallow and hold down—or,' he adds, 'that makes some readers want to throw up. But it is also the earmark of "good" writing (that is, not "just rhetoric"), whether or not the writing has any persuasive purpose other than to keep the reader reading to the end' (256). Finally literary properties, what Posner also calls the 'craft values' of impartiality, scrupulousness, and concreteness, together create the 'aesthetic integrity' of the judicial opinion (282-95).

Posner at least consistently limits the claims he makes for literary properties and the value of literature itself, for his claims for the craft values eventually add up to very little. Impartiality, which he defines as 'detachment, balance, an awareness of the possibility of other perspectives' boils down to an admonition against hyperbolic writing or loading the dice against what an opinion figures as its villains (282-3). Posner's discussion of the second craft value, 'scrupulousness,' is even briefer than that of impartiality, defining it as 'the search for the exact word and phrase,' illustrated by quotations from T.S. Eliot and Shakespeare (284-5). Concreteness, however, receives more extended treatment and is linked by Posner to a clearly ethical end. Defined as the 'use of visual or tactile imagery to drive home a point' (285), concreteness is illustrated, he says, by the prose of Oliver Wendell Holmes—and very few others. Its general avoidance in legal prose holds for Posner an ethical implication, allowing judges to 'lose sight of the consequences of their decisions' through euphemizing and insensitivity (286-7). Posner finds judicial examples of aesthetic integrity, or lack of the same, in what he calls 'high' and 'low' or—drawing on Robert Penn Warren's poetic distinction—'pure' and 'impure' judicial styles. The distinction, which he characterizes as that between 'inward'- and 'outward'-directed styles, seems to be primarily that between more and less traditionally professionalized judicial language. The implications Posner claims for this otherwise intriguing observation are, however, minor. The 'imperfect correlation' he finds of the 'pure' and 'impure' styles with formalist and pragmatic judicial stances leads Posner only to note that, while a judge may construct a character through language as White has claimed, that character is a façade, nothing more than an indication of 'what the judge thinks is an admirable character for a judge to have' (294). It is clear that the bottom line on Law and Literature for Posner has changed little between the published editions of his literary theory: From his 1988 conclusion that, in understanding the importance of form, 'judges and law clerks might pay more attention to the style of their opinions' and thus improve their writing (*Law and Literature: A Misunderstood Relation* 297) Posner moves only to the grudging acknowledgement in 1998 that it 'might not be the worst method of teaching legal writing to assemble an anthology of descriptions of legal doctrine found in works of imaginative literature' (*Law and Literature* 266).

West draws more substantive implications from formalist theory than does Posner from his craft values, perhaps because for her formal properties—the 'narrative methods' and 'world visions' she takes from Frye—constitute not something literature 'has' but what it 'is.' And because legal theory, she says, 'contains a substantial narrative component that can be analyzed as literature' (*Narrative, Authority and Law* 345) she is confident that the anatomy of criticism Frye develops in his 1957 book of that name 'can be easily fitted to Anglo-American jurisprudence' (351). As it is recounted in West's extensive discussion, Frye's anatomy is based on a division of literature into two narrative methods, the romantic and the ironic, that are analogous to two world visions, the comic and the tragic. The romantic method, based in an assumption of 'innocence,' creates narrative through a metaphoric method that exhibits an 'apocalyptic' (optimistic) world vision. The ironic method, based in an assumption of 'experience,' creates narrative through realism and leads to the pessimistic world vision that Frye calls the 'demonic' (348-51). West's own analysis links natural law jurisprudence to romanticism, comedy, and the apocalyptic belief in the convergence of law and morality; legal positivism, she concludes, is linked to irony, tragedy, and a demonic belief in the divergence of legal and moral considerations. One of West's conclusions based on this analysis is that Law and Economics jurisprudence is rooted in the most tragic extreme of positivism, that combined with 'a thoroughly demonic assessment of the world' (356). But Law and Economics has a 'peculiarly schizoid aesthetic posture,' she believes, its normative vision of the world both romantic and comic in its belief in the possibility of individual autonomy but its descriptive vision, asserting the fundamental selfishness of that autonomy, both ironic and tragic (385).

Based on this summary we may or may not agree with West that Frye's theory 'can shed new light on the substantive debates that presently dominate jurisprudential literature' (409). While I find her account of Frye plagued with difficulties, I do find her account of the schism between the normative and descriptive visions of Law and Economics at least plausible within the context of *Carr*, as we will see. In any case it is clear that for West literature's formal properties count as more than devices that literature and writers can deploy as they see fit, as in Posner's account. Literature and law simply are narrative in West's view, and that narrativity ultimately accounts for the contribution that literature can make to both legal theory and the development of individual morality. The narrative element in jurisprudence, she says, 'uniquely allows the theorist to transcend history through imagination and speculation,' allowing 'choices not open to the empiricist' and, ultimately, bringing us 'face to face with our moral selves, our moral options, and our capacity for moral action.' Frye's anatomy of criticism leads to an anatomy of legal ethics that requires us to take responsibility for 'the worlds we, as theorists, create with words' (416).

This claim is both bold and a bit of a leap from the evidence West has provided. For some support, however, we can turn to Nussbaum who, as Posner argues, improves on the moral claims of most edifying literary criticism through the 'concreteness' of her own approach to literature, a concreteness that clearly differs from his earlier definition of it as simply the apt use of imagery. The key to Nussbaum's 'concreteness' rests in her insight that literature itself is concrete, in the sense that it focuses on the plight of clearly drawn and fully developed individuals in everyday circumstances. It is, however, what Nussbaum calls the 'play back and forth between the general and the concrete' (*Poetic Justice* 8), between the human condition and the condition of one human in particular, that allows the novel to construct, in her words, 'a paradigm of a style of ethical reasoning that is context-specific without being relativistic' (8), and that in her earlier *Fragility of Goodness* she says characterizes 'most good examples of Aristotelian deliberation' (316). The argument that it is 'the very structure of the genre' (*Poetic Justice* 8) that enables its contribution to morality forms the foundation of the argument that Nussbaum develops throughout *Poetic Justice*. Literature, she says, 'is a morally controversial form, expressing in its very shape and style, in its interaction with its readers, a normative sense of life' (2). Literature thus 'focuses on the possible' (5) and 'promote[s] identification' (6) in ways that develop 'insights' and 'moral capacities without which citizens will not succeed in making reality out of the normative conclusions of any moral or political theory, however excellent' (12). And literature does all this through its various 'features,' arguably its literary properties—its nature as story, and that story's inclusion of distinct characters who display an inner life leading to unique responses to problems that we share. All this, says Nussbaum, constitutes an ethic that is committed to the separateness of persons and the importance of what happens to them (27-32).

Another key to the ethical claims Nussbaum makes for novelistic form is a faculty she calls 'fancy' that bears more than a passing resemblance to what White calls 'the legal imagination.' Fancy, as a 'fiction-making imagination' (36), can endow perceived forms with 'a rich and complex significance,' and generously construct the scene in which events take place (43). In describing fancy as an 'activity of mind' (36) she echoes word for word White's description of the 'object'—in the sense of the goal—of authority: it is, he says, 'an activity of mind and imagination and art' that is created performatively through language (*Acts of Hope* 306). Defining 'imagination' as the sum of the ways we 'conceive of and talk about experience' (*The Legal Imagination* xix), White seems to be saying that it simply is 'literary,' a word that for White indicates an attitude that is 'tentative, always incomplete,...in part a function of the context in which we live, always imperfectly perceived and always changing' (*Justice as Translation* 41). As examples of 'literary' texts White offers not only poetry but also law; while law and literature are not identical, the differences between them are in his final analysis 'largely in emphasis and in the degree of explicitness with which these things are done' (*Heracles' Bow* 96). Both literary and legal texts (Gibbons' *Rise and Fall of the Roman Empire* and Frankfurter's opinion in *Rochin v. California*) are performances that realize 'capacities for being and acting' in their readers (94) and even act upon their own language in order to give their words 'a significance...that they would otherwise lack' in ordinary discourse (83).

This capacity of the text to act, and to realize such capacities in its readers, evinces an understanding of literary properties not as something a text owns and deploys, not as features that can be isolated and identified, but as activities

(*Heracles' Bow* 49)—as 'practices' (*Justice as Translation* 245) or 'performances' (*Acts of Hope* 270) and therefore as something a text does. The literary or legal text is therefore a speech act, 'a way of being and acting in the world that makes a claim for its own rightness' (*Acts of Hope* xi). The implications of this position for White are, first of all, that 'we should direct our attention towards the practices we engage in, with the object of making them more self-conscious' (*Justice as Translation* 20). This claim is far stronger than is Posner's similar statement, that judges and law clerks should 'pay more attention' to their style. Because for White (much like Aristotle) we create our characters through our textual performances, the admonition carries ethical weight, not only for 'us' as producers of texts but for those who read them through the invitation our texts extend for the practice of the reader and, especially for legal texts, for their 'comprehension' of the multiple voices for which they speak (*Heracles' Bow* 114). Key to the text's ability to thus recognize the perspective of the other is its metaphorical ability, understood as a way of recognizing 'the other...as a center of meaning apart from oneself' (*Justice as Translation* 257). In this sense, White says, not only law but even life itself is the activity of 'seeking to make texts that will establish meanings and relations with others' (20).

For West and Nussbaum as well, the metaphoric capacity of literary texts is key to the ethical, empathic promise of Law and Literature. As the ability to 'see one thing in another [or] to see one thing as another,' the metaphorical imagination points 'to something beyond itself,' says Nussbaum (*Poetic Justice* 36); for West's earlier work metaphor (and narrative) provide the means whereby 'we come to understand what was initially foreign,' 'understand the inexplicable,' 'see what is hidden,' in short, how we come to 'grow' (*Narrative, Authority and Law* 259). West claims that literature thus offers what economics denies is possible, the 'intersubjective comparisons of utility' (253) that, by allowing one individual to understand the preferences of another, could also make room for meaningful empathy between them. And while his legal economic theory seems to deny such empathy, even Posner recognizes not only its existence but the contribution literature may make to its creation as well. It is, however, empathy of an extremely impoverished variety. Relying on Carol Gilligan's description of male and female moral development, Posner seems to suggest that empathy is a weakness, a stance that prevents girls (who, he says, are described in Gilligan's work as generally more empathic than boys) from pursuing the settlement of disputes because they want to avoid the 'hurt feelings' that 'an attempt to decide the merits of the case' might cause (124). Here Posner misreads Gilligan to his own purposes, for the description provided by *In a Different Voice* of boys' and girls' responses to infractions of rules during games concludes not that girls are more 'empathic' than boys, but that girls are more committed to maintaining relationships than they are to the games themselves, which they are likely to abandon should disputes over rules threaten their continuing relationships with their playmates (9-11). In line with Jean Piaget and Sigmund Freud, who are both described by Gilligan as having questioned the female 'legal sense' or sense of 'justice' based on girls' willingness to bend or abandon rules that threaten relationships (18), Posner construes empathy as a weakness of principle that nevertheless yields a strictly strategic advantage. It is empathy, he says, that can help the legal advocate consider not only what clients might say on their own behalf, given the opportunity, but how both opposing advocates and a judge might respond (283). Thus for Posner, unlike West, White, or Nussbaum, empathy is not valuable in its own right. It is not, as Gilligan's work suggests, an alternative female ethic that is as morally valuable as the male sense of 'justice' but, he says, 'amoral,' a way of working oneself into another person's mind (327) that 'great demagogues'—including Hitler—could master 'all too well' (316). If literary study can indeed deliver 'the goods,' those goods are not empathy, community, or relationships, but preferences, tastes, or properties that neither law nor literature are competent to assess.

Though we lack a consensus regarding the precise nature of literature's properties or the values those properties support, we have found that the discussion of both seems to be an essential feature of attempts to sort out the relationships between law and literature. With that limited and provisional consensus in mind, I now move to use the various claims for literature advanced by all four of our scholars to judge the value—and values—of Posner's judicial craft in *Carr*.

Reading *Carr*

Reading Posner is rarely a refreshing exercise. In his writings on Law and Economics (as in *Problems of Jurisprudence*) he is, at least to humanist ears, ponderous and dull. In his writings on literature (*Law and Literature*) he is occasionally ludicrous, producing what Fish is comfortable to characterize as the occasional 'howler' (*Doing What Comes Naturally* 310). And in his writings on sex (*Sex and Reason*) he is all of these and more—ponderous, dull, ludicrous, and infuriating. But when we come to the judicial opinion in *Carr v. Allison Gas Turbine Division* we find Posner at his best, by turns witty, clear, and even understated, clumsy in one paragraph and artful in the next, with a distinctive style that mixes archaisms with slang and laces strings of citations with the occasional memorable phrase. It may not be great literature, but in it I have found some favorite phrases, and I can read it again and again. Were I to judge its 'craft value' here, I would turn Posner's own criteria against him and suggest that he read a bit more literature in order to avoid mixing the 'pure' and 'impure' styles; nevertheless, Posner presents an absorbing story with distinctive characters, a gripping plot, and even (for me at least) a surprise ending.

Were I to judge the substantive value of the holding itself I would certainly approve. When I first stumbled upon this case I held out little hope for Mary Carr as I read through the narrative, and Posner's holding in her favor surprised me. Why, I wondered, had this conservative, non-interventionist judge interfered in the operations of General Motors on behalf of an obviously flawed 'low-level' (1009) employee? Were Posner's narrative explanation to be presented in generic terms (a fault, it should be noted, that he does not commit) it would be the tale of a damsel in distress, tormented by a group of vulgar villains, left to those wolves by the callousness and ineptness (Posner will call it legal negligence) of those in a position to save her, rejected even by her one potential ally, the 'other' woman who spurns her as a tramp. She loses hope and gives up her cause, but then seeks revenge; thwarted at first, she is finally vindicated by the *deus ex machina* of the Seventh Circuit—Richard A. Posner, Chief Judge, presiding. The particulars do vary somewhat from this schematized plot: Carr apparently made a rather poor 'damsel,' described by her former employer as 'vulgar, confrontational, profane, lazy and vindictive' (1010). She fares a little better with the district court judge, who finds her 'vulnerable [and] emotionally fragile...with...many personal, non-job problems' (1011) but only achieves full damsel status through Posner's description of the details of her 'troubled life' (1011). The male tinners with whom she worked and about whom Posner has not one favorable comment, appear to have 'loaded the dice' against themselves through their own words and actions and are described by Posner as 'tormentors' (1012). Chief antagonist Beckham (a fittingly Dickensian surname and villain) exposed himself to her—twice. Having learned that he once suggested Carr might need to perform 'mouth-to-dick resuscitation' (1010) we suspect that he also participated freely in such pranks as the sabotage of Carr's tools and the 'gift' of an obscene Valentine card. After a series of complaints to which her supervisors failed to respond adequately—indeed, one response was to require Carr and Beckham to apologize to each other—Carr quit her job and filed suit. The happy ending, in which Posner reversed the lower court's decision against her and ordered it to determine 'the remedy to which she is entitled' (1013) was a long time—five years—in coming.

The opinion is resplendent with craft values, as Posner defines them. Concreteness is chief among them, as Posner details the conditions under which Carr worked in solidly empiricist terms. The sexual pranks are recited in detail, down to the illustration and sentiments of the Valentine card and the uncertainty regarding Beckham's position (in front of Carr? behind her?) when he exposed himself the second time. No such uncertainty prevails regarding the consequences of the latter episode, however—the worker who had bet Beckham he wouldn't do it lost five dollars (1010). The opinion is so relentlessly concrete that its style even draws a protest from the dissenting judge who, disturbed by Posner's recitation of exposures, public urinations, obscene posters and direct quotations ranging from 'cunt' to 'dickhead' writes, 'I choose not to recite the language [Carr] used because I do not believe that quoting vulgar language contributes to the development of the body of law' (1015). Clearly, Judge Coffey does not see Posner's concreteness as driving home a point; further, it is not even 'concreteness' in the full sense in which Posner himself would define it, given that its visual and tactile images are excruciatingly literal rather than figurative, as they are in the examples he provides from Holmes. Yet in part through such recitation Carr herself has become vivid and real, at least as others saw her. That vividness is also due in part to Posner's careful avoidance of the common judicial fault that he and so many others criticize—he never refers to Carr and General Motors in generic legal terms as 'plaintiff' and 'defendant.' That sin against concreteness, he has told us, is worse than euphemizing; it is an insensitivity that fails to see the object it is naming (*Law and Literature* 286). We meet the leading characters, at least, and get to know them in some detail; we see (regrettably) Carr's chief tormentor Beckham, one of whose 'charming comments,' Posner says, was that he would gladly have paid the electric bill for the execution of Carr's foster son (1011). We see Routh the supervisor who, when he heard statements that might have offended women, was so perplexed that 'he would just chuckle and bite down harder on his pipe' (1010). And we see Carr, in all her faults and trials, psychiatric problems and family tragedies, through Posner's eyes.

Posner's understanding of the ethical value of concreteness—its contribution to making a legal argument and its sensitive recognition of the individuality of the parties to legal disputes—is developed more fully by Nussbaum, who has told us that the contribution of novelistic form to ethical reasoning lies in the 'play back and forth' between what she calls the general and the concrete (*Poetic Justice* 8). Such 'play' becomes visible in literary texts in the invited realization that the protagonists whose daily circumstances and inner lives we observe are caught up in larger dramas that speak to shared problems of the human condition. But a legal text, even a 'literary' judicial opinion, is not a novel, and Posner must work with formal constraints against much inner revelation or conscious philosophizing. The only inner life to which we have any access at all is Carr's, and that through one reference to her explanation for her own actions, her wish to fit in with the other tinners (1011). Posner makes no attempt to reveal or even consider the 'inner life' of the male tinners, and appropriately so—intent is legally inadmissible as a defense to a sexual harassment claim, which must show only that the contested behavior had either the 'purpose' or the 'effect' of harassment in order to succeed (EEOC 1604.11(a)). Beyond three references to the perspective of a 'reasonable person' that are customary (and highly questionable) in sexual harassment cases (1008, 1011, 1012), Posner also makes no explicit attempt to describe the human condition. He does, however, engage in some of the general-to-particular play that Nussbaum discusses as he argues that Carr's situation went beyond 'the merely vulgar' to the 'deeply offensive' (1010). 'Defacing a person's property (even if it is hers just to use while at work),' he says, 'and mutilating her clothing (even if it is hers just to wear while at work) are more ominous, more aggressive affronts than mere words' (1010). We are invited here to join in his normative assumption as he places Carr's individual reactions within the context of an assumed generalized description of human response.

In fact, Nussbaum cites this very passage as partial support of her claim that Posner, in his opinion in *Carr*, exhibits the characteristics of the 'judicious spectator,' the model for judgment she has derived from Adam Smith. This 'artificial construct' provides what Nussbaum calls a 'filtering device' by which we may decide which of our emotions we may trust as reliable (*Poetic Justice* 72); it exercises what we might call an unbiased empathy based in a vivid imagination, but goes beyond it in order to assess the situation at hand based on what Nussbaum calls 'appropriate' emotions (74). It is this last condition Nussbaum sees met in Posner's assessment of the comparative threats of property damage and 'mere words,' because in making that assessment he has cited Patricia Williams's

Alchemy of Race and Rights (*Carr v. Allison Gas Turbine Division* 1010). This book, an example of the narrative jurisprudence whose truth value Posner generally questions, undergoes a great deal of criticism in his *Law and Literature* (355-7). But for Nussbaum, this citation demonstrates that 'it was perhaps not easy for a judge in Posner's position to decide, on the basis of his own judgment and experience, whether the intimidation reported by Carr was reasonably based in the objective facts of her situation,' that 'his complete assessment of Carr's contention requires comparison with other narratives from people in relevantly similar positions of social inequality' (108). I would argue, however, that what Nussbaum sees here is not a principled refusal to bend to personal bias, but Posner's compensation for his own assumed inability—Nussbaum says it herself—to empathize, a compensation that is wholly consistent with the assumptions of Posner's economic jurisprudence. Further, Posner's personal bias is rather obviously showing here, and not only in the 'empathic impotence' that West has noted is characteristic of economic thought (*Narrative, Authority and Law* 253). What personal bias other than that of Economic Man (or a child reciting 'sticks and stones') would insist that, universally, property damage committed in one's absence is 'more ominous, more aggressive' than 'mere words'—'Cunt,' especially—flung in one's face?

This, I contend, is a failure of both empathy and the imagination, but again Nussbaum sees the opinion differently. For her there is a 'good deal of "fancy"' in the opinion, appropriately tied to both Title VII of the Civil Rights Act and the facts of the situation (*Poetic Justice* 105). Unfortunately Nussbaum has misunderstood Posner's holding on the lower court's determination of those facts, assuming that he has found clear error in the facts themselves (105) rather than, as he explains, the application of the legal standard to the facts (*Carr v. Allison Gas Turbine Division* 1009). Based on this faulty assumption Nussbaum credits Posner with the reconstruction of the facts themselves, rather than of their relationship to the legal standard, and thus with a 'willingness to go beyond the evidence' that she says is characteristic of fancy (38). It seems highly unlikely that Posner would ever boast of such fancy, and his statement that 'we must treat [the facts] as largely undisputed' (1009) makes it clear that he is exercising no such fancy here. And even if we overlook Nussbaum's technical misreading, her insistence on the imaginative faculty in Posner's statement that he has 'trouble imagining a situation in which male factory workers sexually harass a lone woman in self-defense as it were,' finding it 'incredible on the admitted facts' (1011) seems a bit of intentionalist fancy itself, reading into the statement an imagined prior and earnest attempt to imagine the situation of the male tinners rather than what it purports to be, a simple statement of disbelief.

Other implicit and generalized assumptions creep into the opinion as well, and they lend some credence to West's argument that the normative vision of Law and Economics is 'comic,' optimistically assuming individual competence and autonomy, while its descriptive vision is 'ironic,' pessimistically assuming total self-interest and empathic incompetence (*Narrative, Authority and Law* 385). In his normative (ironic/realistic) mode Posner explains that it is 'unrealistic to expect management to be aware of every impropriety committed by every low-level employee' (1009) but that, in his descriptive (comic/optimistic) mode 'General Motors was astonishingly unprepared to deal with problems of sexual harassment' (in normative, ironic/realistic mode) 'foreseeable as they are when a woman is introduced into a formerly all-male workplace' (1012). With a comic faith in the efficacy of size and top-down power, Posner invites our incredulity at a 'situation in which for years one of the nation's largest enterprises found itself helpless to respond effectively to an egregious campaign of sexual harassment directed at one woman. No reasonable person,' he concludes, 'could imagine that General Motors was genuinely helpless' (1012). With a stroke of his ironic pen Posner prescribes the comic happy ending that 'mighty GM' (1012), in its incompetence and negligence, failed to produce.

Posner's legal imagination is here actively at work despite such admitted failures. But to see that imagination at work we must think of it neither as belief nor credulity, as Posner uses the term in *Carr*, nor as a 'going beyond the evidence' as Nussbaum describes 'fancy,' but in the sense in which White sees imagination, as an 'ability to make sense of what [one] does by looking beyond it' (*The Legal Imagination* xix-xx). This sense of imagination points to the world Posner both assumes and constructs through the words of *Carr* as he looks beyond conditions in the tinshop to an assumed larger order. What might the world be like if, as Nussbaum suggests, we '[s]ee the world in this way, and not in that,' if we were to '[l]ook at things as if they were like this story' (*Poetic Justice* 43)? What we find, as White might tell us we will, is that Posner's text creates a world in an enactment of its own assumptions. *Carr* tells an implicit story about an imagined top-down world in which institutionally sanctioned authority has the right, the ability, and the responsibility to set and maintain standards by which 'low-level' employees are to live. Failing that responsibility, such authority can lose the right and cause a four-fold tragic ending in its own failure, the failure of the lower court holding, the failure of the normative vision of economics, the failure, finally, of the stance of non-intervention that Posner's jurisprudence advocates. Yet the top-down world is maintained by the Seventh Circuit itself, through whose holding all failures but the last can be reversed. Posner tells us that the position of 'us appellate judges' in scrutinizing the lower court decision is to be 'deferential, but...not abject' (1008). Enacting a second craft value through a scrupulously chosen vocabulary, Posner's deference is almost entirely to the precedent he cites rather than to the lower court, and he is clearly not abject. Where White describes the coherence claimed by the literary imagination as 'tentative' (*Heracles' Bow* 125), where Nussbaum claims that answers presented by fancy are 'guesses' (*Poetic Justice* 42), Posner expresses no doubt as to his conclusion in *Carr* or anything leading up to it. The legal imagination at work here differs considerably from the portrait painted of it by either White or Nussbaum. If the literary imagination realizes its own incompleteness and fancy delights in going beyond the evidence, Posner accepts—as he must—the version of the facts given him by the lower court, questioning only the application of the legal standard to those assumed facts (1009). And where the literary imagination realizes it constructs its version of the world through language, a medium that is 'contingent and imperfect' (White *Heracles' Bow* xii) Posner (even if his position is nothing but what he would call a 'façade') expresses no doubt that Carr violently resented the conduct of her male coworkers, that factors other than that harassment impinged on her own conduct, that 'negligence was proved,' indeed that all the above and the evidence itself were perfectly 'plain' (1011-12).

What, then, has our reading of *Carr* as literature been able to tell us? Relying on Posner's own rather limited theory, we have been able to see the contribution his concrete (in the sense of literally descriptive) language has made to our ability to picture the situation in the tinshop vividly. Nussbaum has made it possible for us to appreciate greater ethical implications than Posner has claimed for that concreteness, and to question the implications the opinion tries to draw from it, by pointing out the ways that the play back and forth between concrete particulars and general statements about the human condition, however masked they are in the opinion, contributes to our empathy. West's anatomy of jurisprudence suggests that the foundations of the opinion in an economic ethic, already uncovered by an overtly economic analysis in Chapter 3, are also apparent in the ways that the opinion constructs its narrative. And through an examination of the 'fancy' or 'imagination' visible in the opinion, despite disagreements about where and how those faculties are exercised, we have been able to discern that the facts presented in the case, and the manner of their presentation, create not only their own relationship but a world in which 'facts' function as facts only in conjunction with an imagined ethic that expresses values consistent with the value-neutrality or moral agnosticism Posner claims for economic analysis.

But the framework provided by the literary or legal imagination, like any framework, necessarily encloses some perspectives and insights while leaving other possible conclusions outside the frame. Understanding that framework as what White calls 'culture' and what Aristotle called its results—*phronesis*—our task in the next section is to consider the limits of that bounded imagination.

The Bounded Imagination

What Law and Literature has provided us is, as White has promised, 'a conception of reading' (*Heracles' Bow* 77) that is intimately linked to the creation of a community and a culture. Whether that way of reading may be called interpretation, and whether literary interpretation provides a legitimate model for legal interpretation, are questions on which the scholars whose work I have examined here, like scholars in the Law and Literature movement in general, are divided. For West, the focus of a great deal of scholarship on questions of literary interpretation fails to take into consideration genuine and significant differences between law and literature, primary among them the social fact of law's imperative authority. Here, at least, Posner and West agree; in large part because of the power legal texts exercise, Posner concludes that 'legal and literary interpretation have nothing *useful* in common' (*Law and Literature* 250, emphasis in original). The most powerful statement of law's imperative nature is provided by Robert Cover, who explicitly links his claim that legal interpretation 'takes place in a field of pain and death' ('Violence and the Word' 1601) to the nature of such interpretation as practical wisdom in the sense in which Aristotle speaks of it in the *Nicomachean Ethics* (1610 fn23). Judicial interpretations are mandates 'for the deeds of others,' he says, and as such are not 'only practical, [but] themselves, practices' (1611). This essential agreement with White, combined with the recognition that legal speech acts 'generate credible threats and actual deeds of violence,' including the death penalty, leads Cover to conclude that White 'systematically ignore[s] or underplay[s]' the connection of legal interpretation to violence (1601-2 fn2). And, adds Cover, '[I]f it seems a nasty thought that death and pain are at the center of legal interpretation, so be it. It would not be better were there only a community of argument, of readers and writers of texts, of interpreters' (1628). Such criticisms suggest that White's avowed project, not to 'subvert authority' but to distinguish more and less valid forms of it, may inadequately account for law's real coercive power.

Whatever our position on such questions, it is clear that a literary approach to legal texts has allowed them to be asked in a manner that, differing from the traditionally legal manner, provokes valuable discussion. We may say the same for the value claims for literature advanced by White, Nussbaum, and West's early work though, to the extent such claims make ethical—what Posner calls 'moralizing' or 'edifying'—arguments, they are difficult to evaluate. The values that support the premises of literary studies render impossible any real verification of the 'humanizing' effect West claims for literary studies upon law students or their professors, for example; the claims of the humanities tradition since Cicero for the refreshment, repose, and cultural value of literary study, visible not only in West but also in the work of Nussbaum and White, are of a kind that value argument and discourse above the demonstration claimed for economics and other social sciences. But Nussbaum, explicitly, and White, implicitly, make another kind of ethical claim, the claim that Aristotle makes for *praxis* and the role of the individual agent who may acquire *phronesis*, or practical wisdom, thereby. The essence of the 'ethical' claim in Aristotle is its focus on *ethos*, what in Nussbaum's description is the particularity of an individual immersed in everyday circumstances (*Fragility of Goodness* 310-11) and what is often translated, prefiguring White, as 'character.' Whether the effect of the literary emphasis on metaphor is to bring into being the faculty of empathy on the part of its reader as the 'edifying' strand of ethical arguments holds, we cannot tell. But its emphasis on individual circumstances and their interplay with the milieu of a community brings into focus the reciprocal nature of individual and cultural *ethos* and suggests both the ethical promises and compromises that literary analysis may bring to its legal counterpart.

The inextricability of individual from cultural character that Aristotle and White both recognize can lead, however, to their differing conclusions—that 'practical wisdom' in a culture is essentially good, as Aristotle believed, or that it is a 'radically problematic fact of our moral life,' as White admits (*Heracles' Bow*

86). It is the latter conclusion that West's later work recognizes, a recognition shared by much other feminist work in legal studies. A great deal of such feminist scholarship notes the goals it shares with the Law and Literature movement, including those of relevant social and political critique (Goodwin), the provision of a wider 'emotive scope' that can be both radical and demanding (Cohen 351-2) and an imperative to 'shake up the order of things' (Minton 47). Other feminist scholarship hopes to build on or expand the focus of Law and Literature scholarship in order to reflect the 'lived experience' of women (Baron 177) through the incorporation of women's voices and narratives (Resnik 340). But all of these feminist goals are blocked by the widely recognized problem of 'canonicity' (Cohen 353), boundaries set around the group of texts considered worthy of legal attention. Characterizing the Law and Literature movement as the attempt of 'white men...to speak for us all,' Carolyn Heilbrun and Judith Resnik conclude that 'the new canon is the old' (27); and while some scholarship calls upon feminist legal theorists to provide leadership in redefining the canon (Goodwin 614), other scholarship notes that feminists tend to 'sit out' debates such as those involving Fish and Posner on the large question of the very nature of literature (Cohen 354). The results pinned to such limited feminist participation, or of its limited effectiveness, cover a broad range. Resnik notes the invisibility of female theorists in law school classes in law and literature—particularly the absence of West from such syllabi, based on 1995 survey results showing that, among feminist literary theorists, only Williams (cited by Posner in *Carr* 1010) made the law school reading lists (349). Even West, as Heilbrun and Resnik have earlier noted, uses literature primarily to write about law rather than to 'cast light on the conditions of women' (20). With women thus unrecognized as potential authorities, Resnik concludes, feminist narrative exists only 'at the periphery' of the Law and Literature movement (352).

It is, in fact, the distinctly non-feminist nature of the humanities tradition that leads West to formulate her objections to White's work in particular as a rejection not just of culture, but of 'high culture' (*Caring for Justice* 182), as what she sees as an almost purely aesthetic project on his part. Almost—for her objection to what she sees as White's invitation to an aesthetic project is not simply that it is 'the sort of invitation of which feminists—or anyone interested in more radical reforms of the law—should be extremely cautious,' nor simply that it may not be a 'workable ideal for the goals or practices of the legal *reformer*' (187, emphasis in original). The larger problem is that the particular aesthetic of White's work, '[s]upplementing the legal sensibility with a literary one...depends entirely on the content of the canon, and on the liberality of the liberal sensibility, and on both scores, history does not provide reasons for optimism' (184-5). The literary and legal canons, then, are loaded with social and political implications beyond the aesthetic. Duly recognizing the 'liberal, progressive, and egalitarian' (182) intentions behind White's project, West believes his work cannot be divorced from its historical legacy. Indeed, White's choice of canonical literary and legal texts has been widely criticized; Susan Mann argues that his choice of 'a small, selective sample of "classic" texts' (963) 'systematically emphasizes the importance of linguistic and personal aspects of life over social and cultural ones' (981). And while we may point out that for White the linguistic and personal create the social and cultural, by his choice of texts White does, indeed, demonstrate his commitment to 'a way of life' (*Heracles' Bow* 107) that has not traditionally been turned to the work for which he intends it.

That work, and the work of West and Nussbaum as well, depends in great part on the claim each makes for the contribution of literary texts to the development of empathy. It is an assumption of empathy that allows White to defend his use of canonical texts by arguing that they can, indeed, be used for purposes for which they may not have been originally intended. Responding, for example, to criticism of his assumption that the phrase 'We, the people...' in the U.S. Declaration of Independence may be interpreted inclusively despite the obvious restriction of its original focus to propertied white males, White declares that the promise inherent in the phrase goes beyond the limitations of those who drafted it, that the phrase functions as 'a promise, or a pledge' against which both the past and the future may be tested ('The Rhythms of Hope and Disappointment in the Language of Judging' 47-8). I have already noted that schools of literary criticism more recent than the New Criticism on which White, West, Nussbaum, and Posner all rely would be skeptical of such empathic claims, but an even stronger argument questions the value of empathy itself. Cautioning that the emphasis in the feminist movement on empathy is steering us toward simply a 'new and improved version of liberalism,' Cynthia V. Ward calls the invocation to empathy 'misguided,' confusing two conceptions of empathy with contradictory aims (930-1). 'Projective' empathy, she argues, aims toward an understanding of others through the projection of an 'abstract, universal' self into the situation of the other and leads to an interest in equality based in an assumption of sameness (940-1). 'Imaginative' empathy, which she links to a methodology of storytelling, encourages a contextualized placement of oneself in the shoes of others, a 'spectator' role she draws from interpretive anthropologist Clifford Geertz and that leads to 'the conscious *setting aside of the self*' (946-8, emphasis in original). In this model of empathy that seems especially compatible with the view advanced by Nussbaum, the other is seen as a completely separate being and differences are appreciated—with the result that the connection of empathy to equality 'disappears' (949). Whatever our position on the possibilities and limits of empathy of any definition, it seems clear that we should question this connection of empathy to detachment, whether it occurs in the model of the judicious spectator Nussbaum advocates or in the detachment of the 'animalistic' self, in which West places her faith, from its political and social contexts.

Questions about the ability of language (or at least of literary language) to develop a capacity for empathy aside, of critical importance for my purposes is the connection of each scholar's beliefs about language, however it may be understood, to corresponding beliefs about law and its potential link to justice or legal and social reform. In contrast to the positivist view of language that is typical of Posner and much other Law and Economics scholarship, the view that the function of language is to provide a 'windowpane' onto reality that avoids distorting what are reasonably clear data (Miller, 'A Humanistic Rationale for Technical Writing' 612), most Law and Literature scholarship holds a view of language that recognizes, and in some cases celebrates, the inherent and unavoidable ambiguity of language. White's evolving scholarly project eventually leads him to set aside questions of the nature and proper processes of interpretation in favor of a process he calls 'translation' that bypasses the necessity of 'proper' readings and permits instead readings for 'confidently shared understandings of what [texts] mean' (*Heracles' Bow* 82), including readings of historical legal texts for what they may be made to mean in later times and contexts (*Justice as Translation* 229-269 *passim*). White's claim for a method of making a space between texts, between languages, and between times leads West, highly suspicious of law's 'wordy' nature (*Caring for Justice* 192) to accuse him of a transcendent, hence unrealistic, view of language (185); we might also note that the process of enabling historic texts to speak to the present has the potential for both conservative and moderate approaches to legal reform. And while there may be some question as to the potential of such a system to contribute to significant social, political, or legal reform, there is no question of the centrality of language to any such project for a scholar like White, whose belief in the ethical potential of the legal culture rests entirely in the ethical and cultural potential of its central texts. Going beyond Nussbaum's ethical project calling for the immersed perspective of an 'involved reader' ('Skepticism about Practical Reason in Literature and the Law' 743) White calls for a legal education that makes of law school 'a kind of language school, working by total immersion' (*Heracles' Bow* 110) in order to create not just competent legal readers but ethical legal speakers as well.

Despite his general optimism White has acknowledged that language, by providing a set of both resources and limits (*Heracles' Bow* xii), is itself a system of authority that can be coercive (*Acts of Hope* 303). We must speak legal language 'as it is,' White says, and because of the restrictive nature not only of legal language but of all language, some things become 'unsayable' (*Heracles' Bow* 121); 'not everything can be said,' then, in the language that is law (*Acts of Hope* 224, *Heracles' Bow* 241). Nussbaum, too, recognizes the limits imposed by what Aristotle called *phainomena*, 'the appearances' that were based in 'cultural beliefs and sayings' (*Fragility of Goodness* 245). And like Aristotle who, Nussbaum tells us, made no attempt to describe human behavior in 'language free of interpretation' but left us 'with the order that is *in* our language' (*Fragility of Goodness* 243, 262, emphasis in original) both Nussbaum and White are comfortable with the order and the limits that language—and through language, law—provides. Legal speakers may, indeed, be created by the language and culture of law, as White affirms, but they may also, he argues, remake both (*Justice as Translation* 23). The language of law, he claims, is 'open to challenge on every point' (*Heracles' Bow* 241); in large part because law is a language, he says, we always have the 'freedom to turn and walk away' (99).

It is precisely on this point that literary (first) and legal (second) theorist Stanley Fish enters the fray—or perhaps more accurately, it is at the point where

Fish enters that it becomes a fray. In speaking against the optimism of White and others who seem to offer hope for a position outside of our language, if only through a perspective such as that White suggests, self-consciousness (*Justice as Translation* 20), Fish argues that 'critical self-consciousness,' understood as produced within 'a mind capable of standing to the side of its own ways of thinking in order to critique them' is impossible (*Doing What Comes Naturally* 437). Interpretation, then, 'can never be free,' as Cover has said, but is bound to professional and cultural practices ('The Bonds of Constitutional Interpretation' 820). Not only does such 'bonding' make self-consciousness impossible, however, but according to Fish distinctly undesirable, for thought and speech are only made possible by the restrictions and limitations that make our ideas intelligible (*There's No Such Thing as Free Speech* 108-111). Sounding a great deal like White, Fish argues that speech only occurs in communities and is inseparable from conduct (108, 106). But he defines communities more narrowly than does White, arguing that the contemplation regarding legal values White says is the work of the legal culture is not the project of one engaged in the 'practice' of law. 'Those who are immersed' in a process, says Fish, 'do not characteristically act with the intention of furthering [the kind of] remaking' White calls for (173). Arguing against those in both literary and legal studies who, he says, have made a profession of arguing against professionalism, Fish defends the value of a profession in giving speakers something intelligible and coherent to say.

Nussbaum takes Fish seriously to task for this attitude, what she calls (despite her concession that he would reject the label) his 'skepticism' ('Skepticism about Practical Reason in Literature and the Law' 716). Fish's ultimate position, that professional and political interests provide the grounding for our judgments, is taken by Nussbaum as an excuse, not only for inaction, but for a lack of normative principles; according to Nussbaum, Fish believes we cannot act according to principles in the absence of 'universal agreement' based on 'transcendent normative standards' (726-7). West, too, is dissatisfied with Fish's contention that expressions of value (he calls them 'abstract concepts') have 'no "natural" content but are filled with whatever content and direction one can manage to put into them' (*There's No Such Thing as Free Speech* 102), an alternative that again, according to Fish, boils down to politics (110). Describing Fish's position as a simple celebration of power (*Narrative, Authority and Law* 149), West concludes that what she calls law's 'wordy' or 'verbose' nature is evidence that 'the entire patriarchal apparatus of male control [lies in the] attempt of men to use the power of the "word" to attain what they cannot naturally lay claim to' (*Caring for Justice* 193).

Both Nussbaum and West misunderstand Fish, whose famous declaration that his anti-foundationalist position 'will lead to nothing'—in fact, that it 'is *supposed to* lead to nothing' (*There's No Such Thing as Free Speech* 307, emphasis in original) is intended not to suggest that we can neither reach conclusions nor make recommendations but that such recommendations grow out of our pre-existing communal commitments as we exercise judgment, that it is only within 'institutionally articulated spaces [that] actions become possible' (*Doing What*

Comes Naturally 239). The fact that there may be no 'nonideologically constrained speech' (*There's No Such Thing as Free Speech* 116) does not mean, for Fish, that there is no speech, but precisely the opposite, that speech only becomes intelligible within the framework of a community of speakers. Defining politics as the '*source of principle*' rather than its absence, as the exercise of an unavoidably '*partisan vision*' (117, 116, emphasis in original), and recognizing that our needs and values cannot and do not exist apart from 'socially organized activities' (*Doing What Comes Naturally* 234) Fish understands, as does Aristotle, the inescapable connection of politics to the *polis*. Rather than the skepticism Nussbaum sees in this argument, what I see is a value-charged and inherently ethical understanding of all professions, including the legal, as an exercise of practical wisdom that Aristotle would call *phronesis* and the recognition that Fish shares with Aristotle, that practical wisdom does not exist to serve theory but that our 'practices,' of which the discourse of theory is one (14), create and contain their own imperatives.

It is, finally, an attentiveness to such values as make the substance of legal disputes significant in human lives that marks the literary perspectives of White, Nussbaum, and West as 'ethical.' None of them have claimed, for example, that literature or literary analysis can guarantee a good, in the sense of 'correct,' outcome in a legal case. For White, in fact, the outcome of a case is 'merely substantive' (*Heracles' Bow* 118), while the ethical significance of a judicial opinion rests in the manner in which that holding is reached and communicated. Even the reformist position of West, who emphasizes the moral responsibility of the creators of texts and, thereby, worlds (*Narrative, Authority and Law* 416) uses literary theory to argue not for particular outcomes in cases but for awareness of the nature of the legal theory that forms the background from which legal outcomes emerge. Nussbaum also bases her praise for Posner's judicial craft in *Carr* not on its outcome, which she mentions but does not evaluate as such, but on the manner in which that outcome is expressed and the inferences she makes regarding the process by which it was reached. What they each seem to promise instead of 'good' legal texts or 'good' legal outcomes is that immersion in the literary allows us to produce better versions of ourselves, modeled after the values grounded in the culture that both produces and is produced by its texts. This last understanding is a recognition of the power the verbal exercises; language, then, has its 'dangers,' as White has said (*Justice as Translation* 48-49). If our language, shaping us as it shapes our experience in our communities, is itself, as Fish has claimed, 'the origin of the world' (*Doing What Comes Naturally* 348, glossing Jacques Derrida) what has this world become? For Posner, clearly, it has become (he would maintain it has always been) a market characterized by an overall balance of exchanges on both individual and organizational levels. For both West and Fish the world has become one of 'politics,' though their assessments of that outcome differ. And though Nussbaum sees the world as inherently ethical, characterized by the decisions individuals make regarding the relationships they maintain with each other, it is primarily in the work of White that we see the world presented as created by 'acts of hope' that take place primarily through our languages.

But if our language is to be consciously used to 'imagin[e] an ideal into partial reality' (*Acts of Hope* 307) that feat is only possible if we are able to engage in the struggle that White says allows us to 'modify the expectations that shape our minds' (226). This is precisely the feat that Fish denies is possible, an assessment with which Aristotle would seem to agree. If we become professionals, especially legal professionals, by virtue of our immersion in and acquisition of the language that is law we may well find ourselves, by virtue of that immersion, enclosed in the boundaries we create with our tools, as the derivation of 'experience' from the Greek *empeiras*, literally bounded by one's tools, or one's limits, suggests. Certainly, as Fish has argued, it is only because we speak within a profession that we can speak to it at all. Literary legal scholarship, then, is as bound by its conventions and the limits of its tools—by the boundaries of disciplinary 'shop talk'—as surely as was Carr by the prevailing modes of discourse (to engage in a bit of shameless euphemism) in the tinshop. But while that perspective may be limited, it is not thereby illegitimate; even Fish finally insists, 'our practice *can* make perfect...and we already know more than we think' (*Doing What Comes Naturally* 355, emphasis in original). As Aristotle struggled to make sense of the circle of *phronesis*, he concluded that it was among those things that we value for themselves; we would choose to engage in culturally good practice, he said, even if it produced no effect at all. But, he immediately continued, it does. *Phronesis*—the disposition, the habit of mind, the character of those who engage in good practice—leads to 'the complete performance of [our] proper function' (*Nicomachean Ethics* VI.xii.6), the struggle not to determine finally the nature of the good generally or even the good legal outcome but, through good deliberation, to become good ourselves. And in this sense the moral claims of the Law and Literature movement become plausible for, through the experience it offers and the deliberation it invites, literature engages us in the practice that for Aristotle is proper to us, that makes us, finally, human. The promise of literature may well be to show us how inevitably and continually we are compromised by the things we say as they lead us, one way or another, to the things we do.

Chapter 5

The Things We Make: The Productions of Legal Rhetoric

To pursue an art means to study how to bring into existence a thing which may either exist or not.

Aristotle
Nicomachean Ethics, Book VI

Though Mary Carr is the tormented heroine of the narrative in *Carr v. Allison Gas Turbine Division*, it is another woman, who did not work with Carr but in an area close by, who provides us with a glimpse of an effective rhetorical performance in the classical sense. Unnamed in the majority opinion, where she is described simply as 'a female welder,' this woman testified on behalf of General Motors and against Carr's sexual harassment claim because, she said, Carr was 'a tramp' who used 'the F-word' and told dirty jokes. Chief Judge Richard Posner suggests in the Seventh Circuit Court of Appeals opinion that the lower court decision had relied not only upon this woman's testimony but also upon her example, finding that had Carr been more 'ladylike' (*Carr v. Allison Gas Turbine Division* 1011), had she refused to participate in the sexual pranks instigated by her all-male coworkers in the tinshop, she may have suffered less abuse at their hands. Yet this female welder, who testified that 'she herself had no trouble with the men in the shop,' had the advantage over both Carr and the tinners because she was armed with a rhetorical agility that demonstrates what the ancient Greeks would have called *metis*. This 'cunning intelligence,' a resourcefulness that allows a weaker force to overcome a stronger, shows us that the male tinners did not simply leave her alone—for, as Posner wryly notes, 'occasionally she did have to zap them with her welding arc to fend them off' (1010).

When we move from science and practice into the realm of production—in Aristotelian terms, when we move from *episteme* and *praxis* into *poiesis*—we also move from knowledge deemed certain and secure into ever more open and potentially unstable territory. When we move from *episteme* to *praxis* we move from knowledge deemed divine, universal and certain into the human, particular, and thus uncertain realm of practice, but we remain in a closed conceptual circle; like *episteme*, the pursuit of knowledge for its own sake, *praxis* concerns itself primarily with its own perfection as *eupraxis*, the 'good practice' that is determined by the values of the community in which it occurs. With *poiesis* we not only move into the realm of the human and particular but we also open up the conceptual circle, for production is never aimed solely at its own performance. The point of production is to bring about some result outside itself, whether that result is a product as concrete as those made in the tinshop, or a performance such as the female welder's, or a state of affairs such as the sense of security and rectitude she brought about for herself in her work space. And though such production is often aided by systematic procedures, those procedures themselves exist in a changeable realm and must be open to modification that often occurs spontaneously and under contested circumstances. Rhetorical performances thus often draw upon the cunning intelligence named for the goddess Metis, the pregnant first wife of Zeus, whose craftiness so threatened his own that he swallowed her. Through this attempt to eliminate elements of 'unpredictability and disorder' (Detienne and Vernant 305) Zeus also internalized and appropriated for himself her cunning—and, in a demonstration of the 'forethought' that characterizes the realm of *techné*, gave birth to their daughter Athena, by necessity, through his forehead.

The female welder also demonstrates that effective procedures often violate their own rules, using the welding arc to commit an 'error' that, Aristotle tells us, would be unthinkable in *episteme* and unforgivable in *praxis*, but that in art is either 'not so bad,' as Rackham translates this section, or even 'preferable,' as does Ross (*Nicomachean Ethics* VI.v.7). The boundaries established by a *techné*, whether it is the art of welding or the rules of decorum in a workplace, are often inventively and effectively circumvented by the *techné* itself in its very capacity as *techné*. The certainty established by so-called 'technical' rules is thus of a distinct and temporary type, using boundaries as tools—or, as we see in *Carr*, tools as boundaries—in a way that explains why our word 'limits' can be rendered in the classical Greek as both *peirata* and *peras*, as paradoxically both the tools we use to accomplish our goals and the limits we use them to push against (Atwill *Rhetoric Reclaimed* 47).

In this chapter I argue that 'art' understood in Aristotelian terms, as *techné*, differs from the 'art' associated with the Law and Literature movement in that it focuses not on the interpretation of text but on its production—in the female welder's case not on her assessment of her circumstances but on the swift, improvised, and effective intervention that altered them. With *techné* we find not only rules and limits but also the means to violate them in order to achieve a previously thought-out, but not pre-determined, goal. As I argued in Chapter 2, Aristotle's consistent use of *techné* as a location from which to argue for the system of the four causes he provides in the *Metaphysics* helps us to see in *techné*'s relationship to those causes an explanation for rhetoric's agility with its tools, an agility based on the differences between Aristotelian 'forms' and the 'ends' he also called 'limits.' In this chapter I provide a fuller history of *techné* both pre- and post-Aristotle, and pair it with a brief joint history of rhetoric and law; here I focus on rhetoric's evolution from *techné* to 'technology,' and on law's related 'divorce' from rhetoric, through trends in perceptions of the nature of style that become visible in the development of a rhetorical heuristic known since shortly after Aristotle as *stasis*. This rhetorical form, often translated as 'issue,' allows me to contrast literary analysis with rhetorical synthesis by first analyzing and then 're-producing' Posner's argument in *Carr* to focus on a question Posner purports to dismiss early in the opinion—that of 'welcome harassment.' In doing so I willingly 'err' outside the bounds of the established legal discourse that, pre-Posner and *Carr*, never noticed its own construction of this problematic term and that, post-Posner and *Carr*, refuses to take its own construction seriously. My focus, then, is on how some 'thing,' the existence of which is clearly optional rather than necessary, is brought about—on the female welder's production of boundaries of personal integrity, physical and ethical; on the legal production of 'welcome harassment' as a demonstrable phenomenon with concrete rhetorical effects; and on a re-production of *Carr* that uses the 'tools' of legal language to stretch the boundaries of legal concepts. Finally, I return to the question of limits in order to develop an understanding of the ways in which they differ from limitations, the role they play in *techné*, and the roles that *techné* can play in using limits to begin to undo some of our limiting beliefs about legal language.

Rhetorical (Im)proprieties

To this point I have been speaking as though *techné* were a static, frozen, easily delimited term 'invented' by Aristotle—a strategy on my part that is no more than a convenient and temporary fiction. *Techné* had had a long history before Aristotle attempted to re-conceptualize it in the *Ethics*, *Metaphysics*, and *Rhetoric*, and his own definition of the term was itself a compromise between two active and competing senses held by his contemporaries, most visibly represented by Plato and the Sophists. Further, Aristotle did not achieve a resolution of the conflict between those competing terms so much as a dynamic and contradictory blend, a compromise position that contributes to the confusion generated by this term and its descendants across succeeding centuries. David Roochnik provides a history that elaborately documents the pre-Platonic evolution of the term and can contribute to an appreciation of the Aristotelian compromise (*Of Art and Wisdom*). But that understanding is only half of our problem, of course, for in the centuries succeeding Aristotle the meanings of *techné* continued to change, to the point that *techné* itself seems to have vanished. Translated away through Latin *ars* into English 'art' and barely visible as the truncated root of modern 'technology,' *techné* is nevertheless not so much gone as it is forgotten by its two descendants. Each bears what Trish Glazebrook, summarizing Heidegger's position on technology, has called 'a trace' of ancient *techné* (98), however considerably reduced. In prevailing common-sense beliefs about technology we see *techné*'s flexible rules of thumb made rigid; in equally common-sense notions about art we see its spontaneous inventiveness reduced to an impotent 'aesthetic' (West *Caring for Justice* 188). As I will argue in more detail later in this section, in rhetoric's eventual consignment and restriction to the element of style we see both such tendencies—rigid, mechanistic approaches to the study of rhetorical figures facilitated by poorly supported arguments for the irrelevancy and impotence of 'mere' aesthetics. Finally, in the rhetorical form known as *stasis* that I will use to re-produce *Carr* we see both a mechanistic approach to 'identifying' presumably pre-existent rhetorical issues and an alternative that, recognizing the end outside the form, attempts to extend legal argument by inventing new issues and thus undoing its limits.

Relying on both Roochnik and Joseph Dunne's study of *phronesis* and *techné* in Aristotle, I will begin by pointing to two contrary senses of *techné* that both pre-date Aristotle and remain visible in his thought. It is tempting to connect what have been called by Roochnik (in a move that for me irresistibly echoes Dr Seuss) '*techné* 1' and '*techné* 2,' and by Dunne Aristotle's 'official' and 'kairotic' versions of *techné*, to the two descendants just mentioned, 'technology' and 'art.' However similar they may seem, though, there is no straight chronological or conceptual connection between *techné* 1 and technology, or between *techné* 2 and art, as I will explain. Given that my goal in tracing the history of *techné* is primarily to illuminate the nature of rhetoric and its relationship to law, I focus my history, pre-Aristotle, on the developing meanings of *techné* up to his intervention via the *Ethics*, *Metaphysics*, and *Rhetoric* and, post-Aristotle, on the political and social implications of rhetoric through continuing controversies over style. This focus, in turn, leads me to conclude that the oscillation of perceptions of rhetoric between *techné* 1 and *techné* 2 is partially determinate of the relationship rhetoric maintains at any given period of time with law. This oscillation is especially visible in changing perceptions of the nature and significance of style, for long periods of its post-classical history claimed as the whole of rhetoric.

But style has always had political implications, and for that reason has never been innocent; indeed, as law began to distance itself from rhetoric 'style' was seized upon almost as an excuse for that separation. The fact that stylistic elements could be used in precisely that way, however, demonstrates not only their political potency but also their substantive relationship to another major issue in the history of rhetoric, that of its sheer and problematic inventiveness. It is precisely that inventiveness that led, then as now, to perceptions of rhetoric as primarily deception; its reputation as both aesthetic and imagination worked jointly to mitigate the certainty law associated with rhetoric's developing rival, science—and law, as we have seen, wished to appropriate a quasi-scientific reliability to itself. The increasingly frequent argument that law was deceptive primarily because of its language, coupled with the assumption that law could divorce itself from that language given sufficient will (or skill) of its practitioners, worked strategically to divert attention from the literal inventiveness of legal method. To illustrate both the potential inventiveness of law's language and attempts to domesticate it, I turn at the end of this section to a heuristic through which such legal inventiveness may be alternately either evidenced or disguised. Depending upon the proclivities of the age, *stasis* either identified a presumably already existent issue at the heart of a legal dispute, or it invented one—the latter in terms most conducive to a desired legal outcome. In reviving *stasis* preparatory to my re-production of *Carr* in the next section, I hope to return it to rhetoric proper, from which it has long been lost. But given its revisionary potential, I must own to the desire to use *stasis* to discover the limitations of the boundaries of the legal discourse in *Carr*—in other words, to return it to rhetoric 'improper' as well.

Centuries before it became formally associated with rhetoric in the time of Aristotle, Plato, and the Sophists, *techné* had developed two apparently contrary senses. The root term is the Indo-European *tek*, or *tekton*, which referred strictly to woodworking (Roochnik 19, Mitcham 117). The direct descendant of *tekton* and forbear of *techné* in ancient Greek was *tikto*, which meant either literally to give birth, or more figuratively to bring something into the world. Clearly, then, *techné* had both concrete and metaphoric roots, a fact that was evident by the time of Homer where *techné* could refer to what Roochnik calls 'productive skill or craft,' such as Odysseus's ability to build and navigate a ship, or to a 'more ambiguous, and less tangible' ability to develop plans or stratagems (Roochnik 23). Odysseus thus possesses both *techné* 1 and *techné* 2, both a fairly predictable and concrete skill that follows procedures specifiable in advance of the activity itself (20); and another skill that proceeds according to less rigidly predictable rules (52)—the heuristics that may be translated as 'rules of thumb.' As one possessed of a *techné* 2 Odysseus is continually described by Homer as *polumetis*, possessed of the many wiles typical of the cunning intelligence of *metis* (Detienne and Vernant 22). Just as Aristotle would later say that *techné* was the 'habit of mind' characteristic of *poiesis*, so we might now say in retrospect that *metis* was the habit of mind characteristic of *techné* 2, the less concrete and codified 'stochastic' (Roochnik 50) or kairotic (Dunne 253-61) *technai* such as medicine and rhetoric. Working on the basis of a probable reasoning that proceeds according to informed guesswork, an ability expressed by the Greek verb '*stochazomai*' that means to aim at or to conjecture, such *technai* are also dependent upon proper timing, an ability to perceive and seize the opportune moment that the Greeks called *kairos*. As the ability to exercise such well-timed and well-informed guesswork, *metis* operated 'more or less below the surface' (Detienne and Vernant 3) and became manifest as skills or expertise, often exercised opportunistically or by means of deception. It applied in situations that were transient, ambiguous, or outside the parameters of exact measurement (3-4). In such unstable circumstances *metis* worked by creating such limits as could be drawn by the weaker of competing forces in order to dominate stronger forces by way of cunning (27-29). *Metis* was therefore an ability both to construct plans and to guide people through them (248); deriving its advantages directly from the unpredictability of circumstances (228), *metis* made possible a flexible, adaptable *techné* 2.

In Aristotle's time the most visible traces of *metis* are those that appear in the phenomenon of the Sophists. The link between *metis* and language that appears in Odysseus is writ large in the Sophist Gorgias, who was renowned for his ability to produce long, poetically hypnotic improvisations and whose *Encomium of Helen* claims for language the persuasive effects that he says are 'comparable to the power of drugs' (41). It is also in the Sophists that the link between *metis* and *techné* becomes particularly visible, for the Sophists called themselves rhetoricians, and rhetoric itself a *techné*, both in their oral performances and in the handbooks—themselves called *technai*—they produced for their students. To the extent that *techné* had by that time come to denote a professional expertise that was both certifiable and advertised by way of a metaphorical 'shingle' (Roochnik 25), the Sophists did, indeed, possess one. And to the extent that the codification provided by those handbooks or sets of instructions was also a *techné*, the Sophists did, indeed, supply a few (though we know them today only through a few remaining fragments). In the phenomenon of the Sophists, then, we witness *techné* 2 united with *techné* 1, an improvisational ability perceived as magical by some and deceptive by others, and an attempt to codify that ability in professional practices through a body of instructions—a move Roochnik identifies as partly motivated by a desire for the 'epistemic legitimation' a *techné* 1 could provide (64).

But the Sophists provide yet another important link, that of rhetoric and, therefore, *techné* to law. To the extent the Sophists can be called 'professionals' it is on the basis of their role as professional rhetoricians, not as lawyers, that we could make that claim. Recognizably 'legal' functions did exist at the time, primarily in the forms both of legislation (or politics) and of litigation, identified by Aristotle as two of the three rhetorical fora, or types (with ceremonial rhetoric as the third). But 'law' had not yet become a profession; what legal services the Sophists could be said to provide took the form of logography, the writing of speeches for citizens who would then deliver those speeches themselves in their advocacy of social policy and their prosecution or defense of lawsuits. As Athenian laws provided a subject for rhetorical speeches, so Athenian law courts provided a site for rhetorical performances. 'Law' was inseparable from rhetoric itself.

Neither legal function of rhetoric would endear it to either Plato or Aristotle, though both took rhetoric quite seriously. For Aristotle, the use of 'legal' rhetoric in the law courts was clearly less noble than the deliberation it could foster in the Athenian legislative assembly which, he says, 'lends itself to trickery less' than purely forensic rhetoric (*Rhetoric* I.I.10). But Plato's legendary and historically determinative objections to the Sophists grew out of his mistrust of the very same function that Aristotle held in high esteem, that of the Athenian democracy. Socrates, as Plato represents him, was 'appalled,' says Roochnik, at the thought of serious questions 'being settled by a vote' (2), a poor substitute in times of social crisis for the informed expertise of a true *techné*, understood always by Plato as a *techné* 1 (Roochnik 198). To Plato, as evidenced in several of the Socratic dialogues but most clearly in the *Gorgias*, the Sophists' use of rhetoric (by many later accounts a *techné* 2 and by Plato's own account not a *techné* at all) literally made a mockery of justice. When the quasi-historical Gorgias of this dialogue, goaded by Socrates (who puts the words in his mouth), claimed not only a specific subject matter for rhetoric but that this subject matter was 'the just and the unjust' ('Gorgias' 459d-460b) Plato, as Roochnik tells us, had him (190): only to the extent Gorgias was willing, duped or not, to claim that rhetoric had some distinctive content was Plato able to refute the argument, demonstrating through Gorgias's example (if not his assent) that the rhetorician is no expert in matters of justice. The rhetorician, in Plato's terms, is not an expert because he does not possess a *techné*, again understood as *techné* 1. Unwilling to grant the possibility of a less rigid, more stochastic or kairotic version of *techné*, Plato claims that rhetoric is to justice as cookery is to medicine—mere flattery (463b) masquerading as expertise.

But for Aristotle, less offended by the Sophists than disappointed by what he saw as their exclusive focus on stylistics, rhetoric is indeed a *techné*. His statement in the first sentence of the *Rhetoric*, that it is an 'offshoot' or 'counterpart' of dialectic, is an aggressive polemical move, says Harold C. Gotoff, intended to refute Plato's position by affiliating rhetoric with the latter's 'treasured art of dialectic' (41). But it was also intended to supplement the sophistic emphasis on style with Aristotle's own systematic approach to logic, claiming for rhetoric a distinct variety of reasoning in a highly developed system of proofs that included logical deduction and induction (through the enthymeme and example, respectively), ethical credibility (through the speaker) and emotional sustainability (through the assumed values of the audience). Developed in excruciating detail in Books I and II, the Aristotelian system seems, at last superficially, nearly pure *techné* 1, and reflects the influence of Plato that Dunne sees in what he calls Aristotle's 'official' version of *techné* (249).

But in the definition of rhetoric Aristotle provides in Book I, in the relationship he claims there for rhetoric to justice, and in the analysis of style he provides in Book III, we see strong evidence of a more sophistic, less rationalized, more kairotic understanding that provides a strong basis for claims that Aristotelian rhetoric is at least partially a *techné* 2. Rhetoric, he says, is not the 'art of persuasion,' a definition that persists and is erroneously attributed to him even today, but an art of finding out or discovering 'in each case the existing means of persuasion' (I.I.14). Rhetoric is not the study of justice, as Plato had led Gorgias to claim, but may facilitate it 'because the true and the just are naturally superior to their opposites' (I.I.12). Though there has been extensive scholarly debate on the correct translation and thus meaning of this particular passage (Grimaldi *passim*; Warnick 300) it is clear that Aristotle is determined not to make the mistake of the fictional Gorgias; rhetoric, he says, has no distinctive subject matter because it is applicable 'to any subject whatsoever' (I.II.1).

Furthermore, Aristotle maintains that style has clear substantive implications. 'Appropriate style,' he explains in Book III, 'makes the facts appear credible' (III.VII.4), a proposition whose implications are perhaps best illustrated by Aristotle's treatment of the metaphor. As a source, along with enthymemes, of 'smart and popular sayings' (III.X.1) a metaphor provides the means to 'set things before the eyes,' to 'signify actuality' (III.XI.2) not only by its derivation from objects proper to it but, says Aristotle, 'from misleading the hearer beforehand. For it becomes more evident to him that he has learnt something, when the conclusion turns out contrary to his expectation and the mind seems to say, "How true it is! but I missed it"' (III.XI.6). Deception, including the 'deception' of rhetorical style, is both a persuasive and a pedagogical method that leads, paradoxically, to understanding. For Aristotle, then, rhetoric is not an either-or, neither *techné* 1 nor *techné* 2 exclusively, but both simultaneously. Like a *techné* 1 it is systematically productive, but like a *techné* 2 it cannot properly be called a 'science' in Plato's sense of that term; neither justice nor any other content area provides rhetoric with a subject matter of its own. And its style, while it can be systematically studied and applied in the manner of a *techné* 1, functions both substantively and deceptively to enhance the persuasive and educative functions of rhetorical performances in the manner of a *techné* 2.

This complex blend of the formal and informal, of the structured and the spontaneous, gave way in succeeding centuries to a much simpler strategy, to perceptions of rhetoric as either one or the other brand of *techné* according to the political and social exigencies of any given era. The controversy, however, would center not on Aristotle or his theory of style, but on that quintessential Roman lawyer and politician Cicero, whose tri-partite stylistic theory (a *techné*-1 structure incorporating grand, middle, and plain styles) failed to accomplish its immediate objective but became influential and remained so for centuries thereafter, including our own. This legacy is not without its ironies for, as Gotoff tells us in his analysis of the grand style in the *Pro Archia*, the theory is 'a highly unreliable guide' (32) to Cicero's own practice and actual beliefs. Instead, says Gotoff, Cicero invented the three-tiered structure in his *Orator* in order to 'put forward ideas and attitudes with contemporary social and political ramifications' that were far more important to Cicero than the presumptive theory itself (19). Cicero's ascent to power and influence in Roman society, and his death as well, were 'all occasioned by his greatness as an orator' (17), the direct result of his prominent position in what had become a well-developed legal profession in which success depended directly on the advocate's oratorical powers. But by 46 B.C.E. Cicero found himself in a precarious position as the result of his alliances with various political factions. However politically motivated they were, the attacks on Cicero were nevertheless conducted through his rivals' attention to the nature (and presumed deficiencies) of his oratorical style. These enemies of Cicero, self-proclaimed 'Atticists,' characterized their own oratorical style as 'spare, plain, and to the point,' at the same time that they accused the style of 'Asianists,' (primarily Cicero himself) of being orotund, mincing, artificial, and effeminate (22-3).

In the face of this stylistic controversy, far more ominous than we might realize today, Cicero's invention of three distinct styles was intended to allow him to identify his own oratory with all three rather than solely with the grand style of which he stood accused, and thus to deny the charge that his 'mastery of a comfortable, harmonious, all too neat and perfected style' was a sign of his 'acquiescence to the status quo' (25). Cicero thus confronted an irony—that his very success as a member of the political opposition meant both his style and his politics had 'become Establishment' (25)—with a fantasy, a mechanistic stylistic construction that bore little resemblance to his own rhetorical fluency. The failure of this attempt was made obvious by his later assassination and mutilation. Nevertheless, the theory of the grand, middle, and plain styles survived for centuries and became linked to corresponding purposes and types of rhetoric. The 'patently oversimplified formula,' an attempt to turn style into a *techné* 1 and that thus belied Cicero's own nuanced practice, was used not only by Cicero but by numerous later scholars to make a number of 'facile correspondences,' says

Gotoff, ranging from the use of the grand style for political oratory, the middle for ceremonial, and the plain for judicial (42). Cicero, we should note, was not the first to associate legal language with a plain style—the Sophist and logographer Lysias had been renowned for his simplicity. Nor would he be the last, as the existence of our own 'plain English' movement attests. He was simply the most influential for centuries.

The controversy over Ciceronian style did not end with Cicero's death. It erupted again in the sixteenth and seventeenth centuries with neo-Ciceronian and anti-Ciceronian (or 'Senecan') stylists who were generally associated with particular religious and political positions—the neo-Ciceronians with the monarchy and the Catholic Church and the anti-Ciceronians with republicanism and Protestantism (Bizzell and Herzberg 480). This overtly political and religious debate followed a long period during which both rhetoric and style had been perceived as relatively uncontroversial, perhaps due to the conscious efforts of rhetoricians who had learned their Ciceronian lessons well. The 'arts,' including rhetoric and style, had been closely linked to social orders from the time at least of Plato and Aristotle (Atwill *Rhetoric Reclaimed* 126, 166); their institutionalization as school subjects for the young from the medieval period through the Renaissance and beyond led to a mechanistic, *techné* 1-style approach to both pedagogical method and the content to which it was applied. The age of Quintilian, some one hundred years after Cicero, responded to the political irrelevancy of rhetoric initiated by the fall of democracy in Rome with 'school rhetoric,' a stylistic excess that restricted oratorical performances to 'a form of private entertainment' (Bizzell and Herzberg 34). That Quintilian, a lawyer and consummate educator, aspired for more than the politics of his age could easily provide is evident in the person of his *vir bonus*, the rhetorician as the 'good man skilled in speaking' (*Institutes of Oratory* 347). Here style is once again linked, though covertly, to social imperatives, for a good man speaking well may very well be a man speaking to, through, or subtly against the proprieties of his age. Style, in other words, while always political, may or may not be revisionary. The 'commonplace' tradition of rhetoric that eventually rose out of the ashes of Rome played its part in the conservation of the political and social status quo; through its use of handbooks (the successors of the *technai*) listing rhetorical figures systematized and classified in minute detail, this tradition encouraged medieval and Renaissance schoolboys in their acquisition of *copia*, or copiousness, the remarkable ability to make the same culturally authorized statement in literally dozens of ways, customizing the form of the statement while absorbing its content.

The predominant tendency across centuries, then, even among those who would seem to relegate rhetoric to the realm of the decorative, has been to conceive of rhetorical method in mechanistic, nearly algorithmic terms that make of it a *techné* 1; the consequence of this tendency is to divert attention from the potential inventiveness of style seen as *techné* 2 through a focus on the reproduction of rhetorical (and cultural) figures and forms. Style had become, rather than art, a technology in Heidegger's terms, a way not of 'bringing forth' in co-operation with one's materials but of 'challenging,' of putting demands upon the available matter (in the case of style, its language) to stand as a ready reserve, a supply of energy that can be stored and called upon at the will of the maker (14-15). Thus, when in the sixteenth century Peter Ramus performed radical surgery upon Aristotle's once-again influential *Rhetoric* and allocated all but its discussion of style to logic and dialectic, he simply brought to a culmination a trend begun with the collapse of democracies and the growth of empire and monarchy. Trends in succeeding centuries, including the development of 'new science' in the seventeenth and of Enlightenment reason in the eighteenth, then encouraged the culmination of a parallel trend, law's development of an identity separate from that of rhetoric and the transfer of its allegiance and aspirations to science.

The professionalization of law, already evident in the Roman advocacy of which Cicero is the prime example, did not inevitably require its separation from rhetoric—again, Cicero is the prime example. But just as political realities meant that rhetoric became irrelevant for deliberation, so the lack of legislative and forensic opportunities for rhetorical performances meant that law needed to make a move. A substantive study of rhetoric initially made the move with law, leaving stylistics behind and providing the early Catholic Church with arts of both preaching, the successor to ceremonial or epideictic rhetoric, and letter-writing, the primary means by which canon law was promulgated. But as civil codes developed and Roman civil law became the subject of study in early medieval universities, law attempted to forge an allegiance with dialectic and thus a professional identity separate from that of rhetoric. With little success—for in the early Renaissance, Sir Thomas More would banish not law but lawyers from his 1516 *Utopia*, believing that absent the artifice of lawyers, 'whose profession it is to disguise matters,' law could be expressed 'in the plainest meaning of which words are capable' (61-2). Perhaps the retention of law in Utopia could be attributed to More's confidence in language itself, or at least of a language like the Utopians', a language remarkably similar to the ancient Greek, through which 'a man [could] fully express his mind' (46). Once rhetoric lost its substantive relationship with language and became formally the study only of style, and once 'rhetorical style' became the stuff of 'mists and uncertainties' wrought upon knowledge, as Thomas Sprat's 1667 *History of the Royal Society* would indignantly declare (112), law was ready to abandon 'rhetorical' language for the allegedly non-rhetorical 'plain' style the Royal Society claimed for itself and for science. In the following century John Locke, inspired by Francis Bacon, the Royal Society, and perhaps by More's *Utopia*, drafted a constitution for the colony of Connecticut that would do its part to build on their momentum, to make a utopia of North America by banning the legal profession from the colony (Mellinkoff 208). The propensity of lawyers to abuse words, Locke maintained, rendered language even less useful than its own defects made inevitable, 'a gift,' he wryly noted, 'which the illiterate had not attained to' (129).

Whether we agree with the analysis of S. Michael Halloran and Merrill D. Whitburn in their analysis of the plain style, that Cicero's three-part stylistic theory is both 'symphonic' and 'subtle' (61-2), or with Gotoff that Cicero's *Orator* was a 'polemical work parading as a critique of oratory' (30) and the theory it advanced insincere, to say the least—and my sympathies are with the latter—these contrary positions and their successors point to a number of significant conclusions. First, style is clearly not innocent but always evidences or responds to an innately political or cultural exigency. Further, it seems specious to argue that a truly plain style actually exists, whether by 'plain' we mean either entirely unornamented or entirely clear. The plain style eventually claimed for both science and law, as Cicero had argued, is notoriously difficult to achieve; 'nothing,' he said, 'is more difficult' (*Brutus, Orator* xxiii.76), a conclusion in which we may assume he was actually sincere. And, finally, claims for a *techné*-1 approach to style and thus for a controlled and predictable process periodically fail, with more or less disastrous results, in such attempts. Style, rather than the whole of rhetoric, is simply one of the forms that find their real end—or limit—in their reception not only by those for whom they are intended but by their antagonists as well. To illustrate this claim I now turn to a classical concept and a very current situation, to the use of the rhetorical form and classical legal method known as *stasis* and vestiges of that method in a series of late twentieth-century sexual harassment cases. Here, I argue, the recognition of the *peras* or 'limit' of rhetoric, its end in a product separable from its own processes, leads to the discovery of the *peirata*—the end of the rope that also serves as the tool of invention and the means to loosen the bonds of legal language.

As a heuristic system, *stasis* can be described and summarized fairly easily. It was first provided in full form by Hermagoras in the centuries following Aristotle (Bizzell and Herzberg 30); his treatise has been lost but it was summarized in such detail by others in succeeding centuries—including the Romans Cicero and Quintilian and the Greek Hermogenes—that it can be almost completely reconstructed. As their lengthy treatments attest, Hermagoras and *stasis* had 'enormous' influence on Roman rhetoric (Dearin 3); in fact, Patricia Bizzell and Bruce Herzberg's history of the rhetorical tradition contends that the development of *stasis* theory was the most significant development in rhetorical history in the two centuries following Aristotle (30). Most scholarship also notes, however, that *stasis* theory was older than Hermagoras. In fact, a number of scholars have pointed to elements of the theory in Aristotle himself, in his much earlier *Topics* and *Categories* (Thompson 134) and in his biology and physics, a derivation that makes *stasis*, like *techné*, a mix of the concrete and abstract, a 'metaphoric use of a clear and precise term of physical science,' as Otto Dieter would have it (352). The word itself, Dieter tells us, is derived from the root *sta*, meaning 'stand' (347), invoking the sense of the stand or standpoint taken by adversaries, the standing required to file or judge a legal complaint, or the standstill resulting from the opposition of either physical or rhetorical forces. But classical *stasis* is far from the dead space we may associate with English 'stasis.' In Aristotle's physics it is a dynamic space, a very temporary standstill infused with the potential for the reversal of energies—a useful illustration is the high point in the swing of a pendulum. In rhetorical theory *stasis* is a metaphoric space, the 'issue' in which is contained the possibility of the resolution of contrary argumentative positions—or the success of the position presented most persuasively by its advocate.

Stasis was used in classical times primarily for forensic, or legal, rhetoric, where it provided a method for either identifying or, depending upon one's perspective, inventing the central issue on which a case turned. It did so by leading the legal advocate, generally conceived of as defense counsel by the classical accounts, through a series of four questions, each one subordinate, or subsidiary, to the question before it (Nadeau 67, Hohman 176). The first question, generally translated as the issue of 'fact,' asks simply whether something (for which a defendant is presumably being held legally responsible) actually happened. If the defendant must concede that the event did, in fact, occur and by his or her agency, the advocate will proceed to the *stasis* of 'definition' in order to determine how that event may be legally classified. The classic example is that of a death charged as a homicide, but clear examples exist in sexual harassment law as well. A 'he said-she said' situation such as the confrontations between Clarence Thomas and Anita Hill during the 1991 U.S. congressional hearings on his Supreme Court nomination is one stalled in the *stasis* of fact, with no agreement that the given event (the infamous discussion of the porn movie 'Long Dong Silver,' for example) ever occurred; had that event been conceded, discussion is likely to have proceeded to the question of whether a conversation about an offensive movie could be defined as 'harassment on the basis of sex' as Equal Employment Opportunity Commission (EEOC) regulations require (1604.11(a)).

Even if both fact and definition are conceded, the third *stasis*, known as 'quality,' provides plaintiffs, defendants, and decision-makers with the opportunity to assess the event in terms of its extent or seriousness and to similarly assess a number of justifications or legal defenses for the defendant's actions. In sexual harassment law the *stasis* of quality appears in the EEOC regulations that require a plaintiff to show that workplace harassment has 'unreasonably' interfered with work performance (1604.11(a)). Judicial decisions have elaborated on this provision, requiring plaintiffs to show that the harassment has been 'severe' or 'pervasive,' for example (see *Meritor Savings Bank v. Vinson* 67; *Ellison v. Brady* 873; *Harris v. Forklift Systems* 21) or that they have suffered serious psychological damages as a result. This latter requirement, set for some time by *Rabidue v. Osceola Refining Co.*, was invalidated by the Supreme Court's 1992 decision in *Harris v. Forklift Systems*, which articulated the standard that Posner applies in *Carr*, requiring only that the plaintiff show 'that her conditions of employment were adversely affected,' even if those conditions were 'too mild to be described as "suffering"' (1011). Quality, however, is not only an element of the accusation; as the *stasis* concerned with the severity of a legal problem it is also the most complex of the four (Nadeau 55) and provides a location from which defendants may either excuse or justify admitted behaviors, including harassment. In the frequent argument that harassers are acting in accordance with normal male behavior, for example to 'woo' the plaintiff, we see what the qualitative *stasis* called blame-shifting (recognized and rejected in *Ellison v. Brady* 880); in the defense claim that they intend no harm or are 'only joking' we find classical counterplea (*Harris v. Forklift Systems* 18); in the defense that any injury the plaintiff received was justified, the primary defense in *Carr*, we see classical counatercharge. Harassment, it appears, ranges across a full spectrum of varieties: it can be 'well-intentioned' (*Ellison v. Brady* 880 fn19; *Johnson & Hiss v. ITT Industries* 75 fn19; *Torres v. Pisano* 633 fn6), it can be 'equal opportunity' (*Pavone v. Brown* 16, *Hardin v. S. C. Johnson, Inc.* 346) and it can even be, despite Posner's hyper-rational protest, 'welcomed,' as the dissent to *Carr* argued (1013).

Finally, if even the ever flexible *stasis* of quality fails to provide an adequate defense, a rather troublesome fourth *stasis* provides the opportunity for what I call a jurisdictional defense. Sometimes rendered in English as 'translation,' the fourth *stasis* allows the argument that the venue in which the complaint has been brought is inconsistent with the nature of the actions charged, allowing a defense through the implication that the charges themselves are therefore trumped up or that the complainant lacks the standing necessary to bring them. A modern example of classical 'translation' appears in the case of *Staton v. Maries County*, a suit through which Charlotte Staton, an ambulance dispatcher, claimed the county sheriff had made frequent sexual advances and eventually raped her. For the usual reasons (she had been 'close to and confided with' the sheriff; she may have 'invited' the behavior) the trial court had been unable to decide whether Staton had actually been raped. The Court of Appeals, with recourse first to the *stasis* of quality, decided it didn't matter: because Staton had worked ten shifts after the 'act of intercourse,' it had not interfered with her work sufficiently to qualify as sexual harassment (*Staton v. Maries County* 998). Staton's work environment, it would appear, had not been 'sufficiently hostile' (Adler and Peirce 794). But also, the court pointed out in an appeal to the *stasis* of jurisdiction, a special prosecutor had earlier found insufficient evidence to pursue a criminal charge on the rape allegations (998). Had the event really occurred, or had it been sufficiently hostile, Staton should have been able to make a successful claim in another jurisdiction.

The fully articulated development of *stasis* as a rhetorical concept post-dates Aristotle, but all four of what would later be called the rhetorical 'issues' are visible in Aristotle's *Rhetoric* itself, though they are neither presented systematically nor labeled as such. Wayne N. Thompson, quoting Cope's introduction to the *Rhetoric*, claims that Aristotle's discussion of *stasis* there remains 'in an "embryo stage"' (141) because it is focused not on developing a system of analysis but on providing students with 'broad principles and specific applications' for preparing speeches (136). This claim is backed up by Antoine Braet's later examination; it is also taken further as Braet claims for Aristotle the insight that the *stasis* of 'quality' was linked to the *telos*, or end, of any given speech ('Aristotle's Almost Unnoticed Contribution to the Doctrine of Stasis' 411, 417). Based on this assumption, Braet credits to Aristotle the insight that *stasis* was valuable for all three of the types of rhetoric that his rhetorical theory recognized rather than limited to forensic or 'courtroom' practice, as most of the later classical texts tend to claim. Current research shows the application of *stasis* theory to argumentation in political and scientific areas as well (Hohman; Hultzén; Fahnestock and Secor, 'The Stases in Scientific and Literary Argument'). Because the historical record is, as is often the case, incomplete Thompson claims that there is no way to prove his own position, that Aristotle's *Rhetoric* served as a source for much of what Hermagoras and later writers on *stasis* produced (140). But Braet is convinced by his own detailed examination of the representations of *stasis* in Aristotle and Hermagoras (the latter as evidenced by citations to Hermagoras in Cicero and Quintilian) that there is 'little or no specific Aristotelian influence' in Hermagoras (427). Indeed, the influence claimed for Aristotle by Braet remains so invisible in the Roman scholarship on *stasis* that he can justifiably call it 'Aristotle's Almost Unnoticed Contribution' in the title of his 1999 essay (430).

It is possible, however, that Aristotle made another and equally subtle contribution to *stasis* theory, and one that (like its rhetorical counterpart, as Braet's reference to the *telos* of a speech suggests and as I will shortly explain) is also tied to his characteristic focus on causality. Kostas Kalimtzis directs his book-length attention to *stasis* not as a rhetorical heuristic but as 'political enmity and disease' the causes and prevention of which, he says, were explored by both Plato in the *Republic* and Aristotle in the *Politics*. In fact, Kalimtzis takes to task the scholarship I have just reviewed for its acceptance of the meaning of *stasis* as a 'stand,' arguing that it is better understood as an 'arrest' (18); he thus argues against Dieter's much earlier claim that *stasis* is easily translated (Dieter 347), claiming that there is no accepted definition of the term (though he offers 'civil war' and 'sedition,' among other alternatives); English translations, he ultimately concludes, are misleading (Kalimtzis xiii, 3). While Kalimtzis may be unnecessarily literal, given that the meanings of 'arrest' and 'standstill' seem sufficiently similar in the metaphorical terms employed in rhetoric, it is clear that Aristotle's *Politics* is focused on a type of *stasis* that differs from the rhetorical version that would later become dominant in Hermagoras. As a political phenomenon, *stasis* is a sometimes violent eruption of discontent with the prevailing order, most particularly with the balance of power (what Kalimtzis calls 'equality') it sustains (112). Coming at the question from the angle of Aristotle's four causes, Kalimtzis argues that the final cause of *stasis*, the goal of those who engage in civil strife, is gain and power (131). While dissatisfaction with the balance of power provides such *stasis* with its material cause, its efficient cause is located not necessarily in the individuals who engage in it but in a complex of 'movers' that range from honor, gain, fear, hubris, and disdain (170-7). The formal cause, he says, is for the Greek *polis* an unusual structure, the 'private character form of *stasis*' (150) that manifests through an aberrant focus on individual rather than collective interests. The four causes of political *stasis* as recounted by Kalimtzis thus bear a visible relationship to the four questions of rhetorical *stasis*. The factual issue creates efficiency, the source of (legal) motion in an event admitted to have occurred. The definitional and jurisdictional issues supply the formal cause, a determination of the event's 'type' in the legal structures and venues provided, while the qualitative issue supplies the material cause, an evaluation of the nature and extent of the act. The final cause, or 'end' of the process, is the legal outcome that then may provide an efficient cause when it is used as precedent in succeeding cases. The four questions, then, bear a resemblance to the four causes that evidences at least a general Aristotelian influence on the shape of *stasis* as rhetorical heuristic.

Also interesting, however, is the pathology of *stasis* as a political disease, the effects of which include the dissolution of social bonds such that the political organism may cease to function (8). This dissolution appears to have been accompanied by a shift in cultural values that Kalimtzis sees clearly evidenced in Thuycidides' historical accounts of political unrest and *stasis*, accounts that link both to changes in the 'customary valences of words' and to a loss of meaning accomplished by the 'corruption of *logos*,' of language itself (10). What *stasis* as a rhetorical heuristic may offer, then, is a remedy in response to this political disease, an imposition of form and method intended to produce (or re-produce) the political coherence threatened by the dissolution of social bonds. It does so through the very medium that political *stasis* has ruptured, through language and *logos* and the re-imposition of the meanings of words through the valences that the heuristic form creates and insists upon. The social and political coherence that is ruptured by private interests acting in political *stasis* is either maintained or re-drawn through the collective negotiation provided by rhetorical *stasis*.

As codified by Hermagoras and as reported by the Latin tradition in Cicero and Quintilian, *stasis* purportedly was a method of simple identification, of the refinement of legal arguments to the point where 'the' issue at the heart of a legal dispute could be uncovered and resolved. As such, *stasis* acted in systematic and predictable ways within the boundaries of a highly articulated legal system. But as Braet points out, and as today's legal practitioners undoubtedly understand, a legal issue is as often created as identified, invented by legal advocates whose cases stand a higher chance of success if a judge can be convinced that their articulation of an issue is indeed 'the' issue at the heart of a case. *Stasis* thus provides a set of 'potential' issues that are made 'actual' by advocacy ('The Classical Doctrine of *Status* and the Rhetorical Theory of Argumentation' 89). Applicable to legal argumentation from legislation to adjudication, *stasis* works both systematically and flexibly, providing a process within the bounds of legal norms that, locating its 'end' in the use of its formal result outside those bounds, simultaneously uses that end to undo them.

Re-producing *Carr*

Stasis theory can be used both analytically, to re-construct the reasoning of an opinion regarding what it considers to be the most valid legal issues evident in the dispute, and heuristically, to construct an argument. In this section I use *stasis* to do both, with particular interest in the latter, less commonly demonstrated, function. I begin, however, with the more common analytical function. Analytically speaking, all four issues generally have a role to play in any legal dispute, and they do, indeed, appear in all the elements of *Carr*, from the accusation to the defense, the majority opinion, and the dissent. In what follows I summarize the arguments of the defense, the lower court, the majority decision and the dissent with respect to appeals to the classical *stases* as they appear in the discussion of the two legal questions that the majority recognizes, the question of whether Carr was subjected to sexual harassment as it is legally defined and, if so, whether General Motors was negligent in its response.

I must emphasize here that what I provide in this analysis, as well as in my own revision of the opinion, is not necessarily a legal argument as a legal professional would characterize it, but a rhetorical argument that differs from the strictly and professionally legal in its aims and, therefore, in what it finds significant. One good example of this difference is provided by the concept of 'unwelcome harassment' itself. Judge Posner recognizes what a rhetorician or even any fairly logical and conscious user of language would also recognize, that the two elements of this construction are redundant given their dictionary definitions. He also recognizes that one implication of this term is the presumed existence of its opposite, 'welcome harassment,' the two elements of which are contradictory and thus constitute an oxymoron. Having reached that conclusion Posner purports, on the basis of its logical flaws, to disbelieve its existence. It is precisely for this reason that the term becomes of rhetorical interest, however, for any number of sexual harassment cases have used this term since its appearance as early as 1982 (*Henson v. City of Dundee* 903) in the list of conditions a plaintiff must establish to provide a legally successful argument. A rhetorically aware legal analysis might go so far as to note that Posner's assertion regarding the oxymoronic quality of 'welcome harassment' is a convenience that allows him to avoid opening up a can of precedential worms, and then perhaps go on to consider the implications for succeeding cases. To my knowledge, however, no other cases have investigated Posner's assertion, preferring to rely on the discussion of 'welcomeness' in the Supreme Court's opinion in *Meritor Savings Bank v. Vinson* without questioning its curious link to 'harassment.' But the question is of the utmost importance rhetorically, perhaps first because it demonstrates that oxymorons are, as I have said elsewhere, somewhat more than merely amusing, and somewhat less than logically false (Ranney 'What's a Reasonable Woman to Do?' 2). Furthermore, this particular oxymoron reflects a cultural assumption about female nature that too many judges have been happy to quote precisely because they fail to notice their acceptance of its assumptions, let alone the implications of that acceptance.

To proceed with the application of *stasis* to *Carr* analytically we begin at the factual level, where it is clear that GM had disputed Carr's account of events in the tinshop. However, it is equally clear that the trial court judge had resolved any conflicts among the account in Carr's favor (1009). This resolution is a structural characteristic of the U.S. legal system and one that only a strong argument to the fourth *stasis*, jurisdiction, can overcome. While GM apparently petitioned the Appeals Court to question the lower court's resolution of factual issues, both the majority and the dissent to *Carr* state that they are bound by the lower court's authoritative version of the facts in the absence of 'clear error' in its findings (1009, 1013). Nevertheless, factual issues continue to play a role in the case, for while the majority does accept the facts as given in the lower court ruling, it questions the court's application of the legal standard to those facts—and the dissent objects not only to that position but to what it calls the majority's 'sugar coating' of the facts themselves (1015).

Just as fact and jurisdiction are closely linked in this case, so the *staseis* of definition and quality are difficult to separate. The EEOC definition builds in elements of quality, defining sexual harassment not only as sexual advances but as advances that are qualitatively and demonstrably unwelcome, and that unreasonably interfere with the plaintiff's work performance (1604.11.(a)(3)). The defense strategy that we can infer from Posner's opinion seems to have been to attempt first a defense on the basis of definition, claiming that events in the tinshop were simply 'shop talk,' or 'vulgar pleasantries' (1010). As classical theory would anticipate, however, the defense seems also to have provided a fallback position in the *stasis* of quality, claiming that Carr had willingly participated in some such events and thus had invited others (1014-5).

The oscillation throughout the opinion between quality and definition is obvious, as each party to the argument attempts to refute its antagonist's characterization of 'the' issue of the case as lying in one or the other of those two *staseis*. Posner's strategy is to counter the definitional defense of shop talk with a qualitative assessment of events as 'deeply offensive' and 'targeted' on Carr (1010). When it comes to the qualitative defense, that Carr had invited the behavior of her coworkers, Posner counters with an additional qualitative consideration, the asymmetrical power positions in the tinshop, before re-defining Carr's behavior—from the 'invitation' expressed in the trial court's decision to 'provocation,' the latter of which he then concludes cannot justify harassment (1011). To the qualitative defense regarding the second question—that GM had responded adequately to Carr's complaints—Posner counters with what we might call factual negation, a list of potential actions nevertheless not taken by GM and a qualitative assessment that the company was 'astonishingly unprepared' to deal with what he calls foreseeable problems (1012). This qualitative assessment—of the facts and of their proper definition—leads, in turn, to his conclusion that both definitional burdens have been met. Carr, he concludes, was indeed sexually harassed and the response of GM to that harassment was indeed negligent. The dissent objects to both of those conclusions, relying on Carr's own factual evidence to make the qualitative claim that she had participated willingly in what it calls 'sexual hijinx [sic]' (1014) and that GM's response was adequate. But the dissent's objection to the holding in *Carr* is primarily jurisdictional. Not only should the Appeals Court be bound by the lower court's determination of facts and its application of the legal standard to those facts, Judge Coffey protests, but the court is also bound by its own prior ruling that, he says, upholds the reality—legally, if not grammatically, plausible—that harassment can be welcomed (1013).

I have argued, however, that rhetoric's unique contribution is not the analysis of text but the means it provides for its production. Rhetorical analysis taken too far verges on the commission of a fallacy, the assumption that authorial intent can be inferred from a text. In this case that intentionalist fallacy would be due to a use of Aristotle's rhetoric for the interpretation of a text rather than for its production, the task for which Aristotle saw rhetoric most suited. However difficult it may be to conduct a visible process of rhetorical synthesis, of the production of a text within a text, such is my purpose in this section. *Stasis* is not, of course, the only rhetorical heuristic available for this purpose; it is, however, a particularly visible system whose use for legal argumentation over several centuries augurs well for its use here.

Braet has argued that *stasis* provides a model of legal reasoning not only for the prosecution and defense in a criminal trial, the most frequent assumption in the classical scholarship, but for the judge as well ('The Classical Doctrine of *Status* and the Rhetorical Theory of Argumentation' 82). In each case, whether that of the plaintiff, the defendant, their advocates, or the judge, *stasis* is linked to 'the doctrine of the burden of proof' in modern terms, providing 'a series of points which have to be established' by any of the parties in accordance with the demands of the applicable legal system and to the satisfaction of the judge (87). In the process that follows I will be taking the part of the judge, re-writing the opinion in order to re-focus the issue on the question of 'welcome harassment' that Posner's opinion discounts. My sympathies are with the plaintiff but, as Judge Coffey's dissent to the opinion demonstrates, the issue of welcomeness has been argued by the lower court in order to find against Carr and in favor of the defendant, General Motors. As I work my way through this process, then, I will be working against both the majority and the dissent—not to mention a body of precedent that seems to have accepted, however unreflectively, the notion that harassment can, indeed, be welcomed and, therefore, deserved. In the paragraphs that follow I provide a first-person, present-tense account of my progress through the steps of *stasis*, engaging each issue heuristically in order to decide what potential each may provide to persuasively advance the argument I want to make, that the most rhetorically, if not legally, significant issue in the case is that revolving around the question of unwelcome—and thus also of welcome—harassment.

The Facts

At the outset, I know that the classical paradigm holds that the four questions of *stasis* are coordinated both progressively and in successive subordination, meaning that questioning begins with the first *stasis*, fact, and proceeds to definition, quality, and jurisdiction in that order—if, and only if, agreement is reached on each preceding step. But I also know that the *staseis* are not that distinct and that in sexual harassment cases the facts, like the applicable definitions, are always shaded by references to and assumptions of quality. Furthermore I, like the Court of Appeals, am constrained by the official version of the facts contained in the District Court's ruling. What is worse, I am further constrained by the representation of those facts in the majority opinion, which recites the actions taken by Carr and those not taken by General Motors, as well as by their representation in the dissent, which correspondingly recites the actions taken by General Motors and those not taken by Carr. Because my knowledge of the facts is several times removed from the actual events and filtered by multiple perspectives, and because I am more interested in the legal definition to be applied to those facts,

I clearly cannot contest any of them nor benefit from doing so. While Judges Posner and Coffey clearly differ concerning which facts are significant, and why, neither formally contests the account provided by the District Court.

Definitions

The two most important terms to be defined are, of course, 'sexual harassment' and 'negligence.' Here I am concerned with the definition of sexual harassment as it has evolved from its first articulation in the EEOC regulations through case law, and potentially with providing a definition of 'welcome sexual harassment' that can contest Posner's dismissal of the mere idea early in the opinion (there are hazards, I assume somewhat intuitively at this point, to trying to define the latter term). In graphing out the definitions from the EEOC and from *Rabidue v. Osceola Refining Co.*, an influential 1986 case, I can see that the language of the regulations has been 'refined' in ways that continually up the ante for plaintiffs. To me, the most striking change is the shift from 'unwelcome sexual advances' (EEOC Sec. 1604.11(a)) to 'unwelcome harassment.' The earliest occurrence of this redundancy that I have been able to find in the case citations is in *Henson v. City of Dundee*, a 1982 Eleventh Circuit Appeals Court case that claims merely to be summarizing the EEOC Guidelines issued in 1980 (903-4) and that is routinely cited in courts in seven of the thirteen federal districts up to and including the Supreme Court (*Meritor Savings Bank v. Vinson* 66).

I know that one of the functions of case law is to interpret, explain, even elaborate or extend regulatory and statutory requirements—but, I wonder, shouldn't such functions be explicit? Shouldn't they be argued and supported? It seems to me that I may need to make an argument to jurisdiction, to contend that judge-made case law must be held accountable to the authoritative texts it interprets (I know this issue has been contested since our court system began and, so to speak, the jury is still out on the question). For now, though I decide to hold off on trying to define 'welcome harassment,' I keep in mind Posner's re-definition of the District Court's finding that Carr had 'invited' the tinners' behavior. She did not invite it, presumably an action that could justify the reaction, but she 'provoked' it (1011). It is a short step logically, I realize, from 'provoked' to 'deserved.' That connotation seems significant to me. Can the tinners legally call Carr a 'cunt' if she deserves it, if she behaves like one, if the descriptor is accurate? (How does a 'cunt' behave? I wonder.) Such, from a rhetorical perspective, seems to be the essence of the District Court's holding.

Quality

Carr contains surprisingly little discussion of quality in the exact terms set by the EEOC language, through its references to unreasonable interference with the plaintiff's work or the intimidation or hostility of questionable behaviors (under what circumstances, it occurs to me to ask, would interference with someone's work be 'reasonable'?). Perhaps this absence comes about because all of the decision-makers, from the District Court to the majority and dissent at the Court of Appeals, agree that the conduct of the tinners was highly questionable—'appalling' and 'disgusting' are the words the dissent uses (1013), while the district court and the majority add 'abusive,' a term the dissent echoes even as it characterizes the abuse as mutual (1016). Posner, it seems, allows his excruciatingly detailed recitation of events to answer the questions of interference, intimidation, and hostility for him. The lower court, holding against Carr, had said that the tinners' conduct 'may have constituted sexual harassment' (1011), and though GM had argued that the tinners' behavior constituted normal, vulgar 'shop talk' (1010, 1016) neither Posner nor Coffey entertain this possibility as an excuse. Both the factual existence of the events and their nature, then, seem nearly conceded. Instead, the question of quality eventually centers almost exclusively on Carr's response to the tinners' behavior because, as the District Court had concluded, to the extent the tinners' behavior 'may have' been sexually harassing 'it was not unwelcome' (1011).

Posner brings up and then immediately drops the question of why the tinners treated Carr as they did, 'why "unladylike" behavior should provoke not a vulgar response but a hostile, harassing response' (1011). Remembering Braet's characterization of the *staseis* as 'four points in the burden of proof,' I realize that the burden is on Carr to excuse her own behavior, not on the tinners or GM to excuse theirs. In a reversal of what the EEOC seems to anticipate, the element being held responsible for altering the terms or conditions of employment in the tinshop is not the harassment, because—should we take 'shop talk' and 'sexual hijinx' seriously—harassment is the status quo. With the attention focused on the question of whether Carr followed a complaint protocol that was all but invisible at her work site, the case seems rather to consider whether she may be held responsible for altering the conditions of employment of the tinners. And why, I now ask myself, does no one question whether the tinners followed some sort of protocol for registering complaints about Carr? I cannot raise this question, because the factual record contained in *Carr* does not. But why not?

Jurisdiction

As I considered the definition of sexual harassment I also considered the possibility of raising a jurisdictional issue, that of the right of judges to revise regulatory language and the conditions under which they may do so. It seemed to me then, and seems to me now, to be a rather weak argument, and given the possibilities for an argument of quality I decide that I will simply report the definitional history without questioning the jurisdictional issue—if, indeed, it could even be maintained as such.

In the space of a few pages generated by several hours of thought I have gone from worrying that my argument was pointless (Carr, after all, eventually won her case when the majority concluded she had not welcomed the tinners' behavior) to believing the argument is worth making (the law, after all, should not require women to routinely disprove an assumption that they welcome harassment; nor should it hold them culpable for 'changing' the circumstances of employment of their harassers). There are no doubt strong considerations against advancing this argument on behalf of a vulnerable plaintiff and Carr was certainly vulnerable, as the references throughout both the majority and the dissenting opinions to her own vulgarity and absenteeism (1010, 1015-16) attest. Posner himself, no doubt, had strong reasons to refrain from patently arguing the point he makes early in the opinion, his statement that 'welcome sexual harassment is an oxymoron' (1008) with the paired assumption that it consequently cannot exist. But because I believe someone needs to make the argument, I decide to amend Posner's opinion in a few respects. I begin, however, with Posner's initial summary of the issues, verbatim:

> The district judge [Posner begins] believed that in a case such as this in which the harassment is by coworkers rather than by supervisors, the principal questions to be answered are whether the plaintiff was in fact sexually harassed to a degree that could be said to affect adversely the conditions under which she worked, whether it was unwelcome harassment, and whether management knew or should have known about the harassment yet failed to take appropriate remedial action. The only exceptionable entry in this catalog is the question about unwelcomeness. 'Welcome sexual harassment' is an oxymoron; if as we concluded in Reed v. Shepard, 939 F.2d 484, 486-87 (7th Cir. 1991), the employee demonstrates by word or deed that the 'harassment' is welcome…it is not harassment. So there really are only two questions in a case such as this (1008-9).

In arguments to both definition and jurisdiction, I begin to differ from Posner with the final two sentences of the preceding excerpt (my revisions appear within brackets):

> 'Welcome sexual harassment,' [while it is an oxymoron, undoubtedly exists; it has been created by precedent in seven of the thirteen District Courts through the incorporation of its opposite, 'unwelcome sexual harassment,' in the factors a plaintiff is required to show for a finding of sexual harassment. Wanchik v. Great Lakes Health Plan, Inc., 6 Fed. Appx. 252 (2001); White v. The Money Store, 1998 U. S. App, Lexis 5495; Robinson v. Jacksonville Shipyards, Inc., 760 F. Supp. 1486 (1991); Rabidue v. Osceola Refining Co., Inc., 805 F. 2d. 611 (1986).] So there [are three] questions in a case such as this. The first is whether the plaintiff was, because of her sex, subjected to such hostile, intimidating, or degrading behavior, verbal or nonverbal, as to affect adversely the conditions under which she worked…. The second question is whether, if so, the defendant's response or lack thereof to its employees' behavior was negligent. [However, both of these questions may become irrelevant upon a determination regarding the third question that the plaintiff welcomed the behavior, which is the finding of the District Court judge in this case.]

Leaving intact Posner's discussion of the first two questions and his narrative of the facts in the case, I take up my argument to quality where Posner begins to address whether Carr had 'invited' the behavior, including his first paragraph on this topic, verbatim:

So the behavior of Carr's coworkers was harassing, yet the district judge concluded that it was not actionable, because it had been 'invited.' 'She was not merely the recipient of crude behavior and crude language—she also dished it out.'...The district judge said that 'she contributed just as much abusive language and crude behavior as did the male tinners, and therefore was just as responsible for any hostile sexual environment that consequently arose.' 'The tinners' conduct, to the extent it may have constituted sexual harassment, was not unwelcome' (1010).

[But we need not determine whether it was unwelcome in order to conclude that the behavior of the tinners constituted harassment. The statutory and regulatory language applies the 'unwelcome' standard only to 'sexual advances;' we do not see anyone, Carr or GM or the District Court, making the implausible argument that the behavior of the tinners can be characterized as such. All the regulations require Carr to show is that the tinners engaged in verbal or physical conduct of a sexual nature that had the purpose or effect of creating an intimidating, hostile, or offensive work environment. 29 CFR 1604.11. We do not need to assess Carr's response to that behavior in order to make our determination, but simply to exercise our own judgment regarding its purpose or effect.]

[GM's 'shop talk' defense, which seems intended to justify the tinners' behavior and divert attention from its effects, relies on an additional requirement created by judicial precedent, that conduct, to be regarded as harassment, must 'alter' the terms or conditions of the plaintiff's employment. *Meritor Savings Bank v. Vinson* 477 US 57 at 67. What we have here, however, is a situation where the plaintiff, contesting the viability of 'shop talk,' is attempting, however unsuccessfully, to alter the terms and conditions of the defendants' employment. So be it; were she to succeed, it would not be an actionable offense under sexual harassment law.]

Finally, what the judge found rather [than an invitation on Carr's part], was that Carr had provoked the misconduct of her coworkers (1011), [with the implication that the harassment was, therefore, deserved. By the logic of all of these arguments, the role of the law and judges would appear to be not to prohibit harassment in the workplace, but to determine what level of harassment may be permitted based upon the level of such harassment that is traditional in any given location and the extent to which a plaintiff wants, deserves, or—in the euphemism provided by the lower court—'invites' it. Surely this is not the intent of the law and regulations. H]er words and conduct cannot be compared to those of the men and used to justify their conduct and exonerate their employer (1011).

The potential hubris of re-writing an esteemed Federal judge's opinion requires that I repeat the point, if I have not yet made it strongly enough, that I do not fancy myself as an Appeals Court judge on the level of Judges Posner or Coffey; nor do I consider myself an advocate making a legal argument that would have been in the best interests of Carr, had she been my client. Legal advocates must choose their battles wisely. While Posner characterized the arguments advanced by Carr's advocates for a holding of clear legal error at the trial court level as 'strained' at best (1008) those arguments prevailed—possibly because Posner found the arguments advanced by GM's counsel not even 'remotely plausible,' even 'incredible on the admitted facts' (1012, 1011). As a rhetorician rather than as a legal advocate or judge, my intention has been to attend closely to the ways in which the language in *Carr* and other such cases has brought into existence a category of behavior titled 'welcome harassment' that is not, legally, an oxymoron. If I have committed some kind of error in using rhetoric productively in this case, so be it—in fact, according to Aristotle, so much the better. But that is the topic for our final section, a discussion of the contradictory and productive relationship the makers of any *techné* establish—through its forms, materials, and 'limits'—with its limitations.

The Use of Limits

In recent years there has been evidence of a turn to rhetoric in legal studies. It would be an exaggeration, however, to claim a Law and Rhetoric 'movement' on the order of either Law and Economics or Law and Literature. Furthermore, the 'rhetoric' that is of interest in most examples of legal scholarship is not 'rhetoric' in the sense developed in this chapter, but grows out of the Law and Literature movement and thus bears its mark in its interest in the interpretation of text rather than in its production. Highly visible legal scholars such as James Boyd White and Stanley Fish, who have taken a substantial interest in rhetoric from primarily classical and contemporary perspectives, respectively, come at the question of law's relationship to rhetoric through a prior and, in White's case, overriding interest in literature. And while Austin Sarat and Thomas R. Kearns have gone farther than most in providing a collection of essays devoted to *The Rhetoric of Law*, as it is titled, their approaches and those of their contributors also tend to focus almost exclusively on reading and thus the interpretation of text. Given the celebration of verbal play and display that Sarat and Kearns note in a great deal of 'rhetorical' work in law (2), it is not surprising that they also note the anxiety-arousing effects of the approach to language they see as characteristic of rhetorical analysis. Though they find such anxiety primarily among traditional, conventional, or mainstream legal scholars, they could have pointed to anxiety among scholars arguably less mainstream, particularly feminist legal scholars, as we have seen in the case of feminist constitutional scholar Robin West's suspicion of 'the wordy forms of law' (*Caring for Justice* 192). Clearly, claims that law is rhetoric, or even that law merely uses rhetoric, whether by 'rhetoric' one means deception or simply textual analysis, can be unsettling (Sarat and Kearns 1).

I should point out that the literary route to rhetoric is not unique to legal scholarship; indeed, it is typical of the traditional approach to rhetoric developed in U.S. university English departments since the early twentieth century, leading to a lingering perception of rhetoric as a 'property' (both literary and economic) of literature. It is not, however, inevitable. The Aristotelian understanding of rhetoric, as we have seen, conceives of it as an undertaking both distinguished from that of literature and prior to it, a priority that comes about because of the productive nature of Aristotelian *poiesis* and *techné*. In other words rhetoric, while it drew upon the existing 'literature' of traditional poetry and drama, was not interested in interpreting it but in appropriating literature as a property that yielded material for rhetorical arguments. The 'traditional' paradigm that dominates literary studies thus reverses the classical; transported into legal studies, it does little to counteract treatments of rhetoric less perceptive than those of Sarat and Kearns, those myriad law review articles referring to the 'rhetoric and reality' of topics ranging from welfare reform to the tax code and beyond. Used unreflectively either as the opposite of 'reality' or as a simple synonym for language, rhetoric becomes (or remains) divorced from both intention and reality as it is simultaneously linked with misinterpretation or outright manipulation; the result is an impoverished understanding of both language and rhetoric—rhetoric in its 'mere' sense. Such beliefs feed positions such as Posner's, that rhetoric functions as a sort of 'belief cost' in our search for reliable information (*Overcoming Law* 529), and West's, that rhetoric is not much more (or less) than 'obfuscation, masks, legitimation, or other forms of disingenuity' (*Caring for Justice* 187).

    White's position on the nature and potential of rhetoric grows from the classical and comes close to my own, particularly as he construes 'the task of the lawyer' and the practices through which it is accomplished as 'arts, or what the Greeks would call *technai*' ('What Can a Lawyer Learn from Literature?' 2022). To my knowledge, however, White has not undertaken to develop this isolated reference to *techné*; preferring to use its English equivalent, he endures critiques such as West's that assume the impotence or exclusionary nature of 'art.' In his early *Heracles' Bow*, White speaks often of the art of rhetoric as integral to legal practices, as an 'organized form of knowledge' that acknowledges both its limits and the conditions of uncertainty with which it works (44). In the later *Acts of Hope*, however, White prefers to conflate the literary and the rhetorical. The necessity to deal with 'contraries and contradictories,' along with the recognition of limits, uncertainty, and the root of all of these conditions in particularity, are 'rhetorical or literary,' he says (133, 147) or again, 'literary or rhetorical in character' (151). By the time of the even later *Justice as Translation* White has largely merged the rhetorical into the literary, maintaining that the necessity to deal with a tentative and incomplete coherence that is the function of context and that is therefore always changing is a characteristic of 'the literary conditions on which we live' (*Justice as Translation* 41). And though he never abandons the rhetorical understanding that speakers and writers must make, re-make, and be made by their languages, White has little to say about the productive process that generates the literal texts on which he focuses so much of his attention. Concentrating his energies on working out a 'conception of "reading" [that] is a way of writing as well' (*Heracles' Bow* 77) White prefers to locate the act of writing within the minds of readers who find or create meaning in interactions with texts that pre-exist their own. Whether construed as interpretation, as it is by much of Law and Literature, or translation, as it is by White, this process supports the mystification of a productive process that remains invisible until such time as it manifests in a literal text from which the process may presumably be inferred. For if 'reading is always writing, always done by an individual mind' (*Heracles' Bow* 97) writing itself can be no more than a way of reading.

I do not mean my criticism of White to suggest that he has little to offer our understanding of the role of language in law. Instead, I intend simply to point out that his conflation of the rhetorical with the literary, and with a literary that offers 'an experience, not a message' (*Justice as Translation* 42) conceives of that experience as its Greek equivalent, *empeiras*, suggests he should, as an enclosure within boundaries that language itself tends to create. Nor do I mean to suggest, however, that readers are able to produce 'first' texts, that we may make statements that are free from interaction with other texts. Both Fish and White have not only noted the constraints enacted by the contexts within which we endeavor to speak, but the positive role those constraints play. Claiming that 'restriction...is constitutive of expression,' Fish explains that without it, 'without an inbuilt sense of what it would be meaningless to say or wrong to say, there could be no assertion and no reason for asserting it' (*There's No Such Thing as Free Speech* 103). White would seem to agree, holding that law's provision of 'a set of terms and texts and understandings [gives] to certain speakers a range of things to say to each other' (*Heracles' Bow* xi) and thereby makes our disagreements not only 'intelligible' but also 'amenable to resolution' (*Justice as Translation* 179). Where White differs from Fish is on the relationship of or balance of power between texts and communities, for where Fish (according to White) argues that all meaning is a function of community, White believes that it is the text that creates the community rather than vice versa (*Justice as Translation* 99). But where Fish differs most substantially from White is in the position each holds on what Fish has called 'critical self-consciousness,' a position he maintains is impossible. Where White insists on the possibility that we may remake our languages and thereby maintain a 'greater sense of control over what we do' (*Heracles' Bow* 40) Fish calls White's hope for our awareness of our limits 'not rhetorical, but transcendental'(*There's No Such Thing as Free Speech* 174), a 'fully developed romance' that mistakenly conflates 'the perspective from which one might ask questions about the nature of law...with the perspective from which one might ask questions in the hope that the answers will be of use in getting on with a legal job of work' (172-3). Those immersed in any process, contends Fish, are characteristically not concerned with the kind of remaking of which White speaks.

Whatever their differing positions on these issues, such insights suggest the importance of attending to facets that both White and Fish leave out of the analysis. First, we need to attend to the very real and not entirely invisible means by which writers and speakers create the texts that come in for most legal 'rhetorical' analysis. Second, we must also keep in mind the nature of those texts as forms rather than as the ends, in the Aristotelian senses of those terms, of the creative process. Finally, we need to understand the end of that process as *peras*, as a limit that is not a limitation but the 'end of the rope' that, concealed by the circular processes of *episteme* and *praxis*, is made visible by the separability of the products of any *techné* from its processes. *Techné* is thus neither *apeiron*, a circular process from which there is no visible exit, nor *empeiras*, embedded in the constructions of its own 'tools.' Its 'complex relationship' to experience, to tools, and to the boundaries those tools can both create and transgress are all 'at the heart of its inventive power,' as Janet M. Atwill has told us (*Rhetoric Reclaimed* 70).

Techné's inventive power, however, is neither transcendent, as Fish would remind us, nor automatically benign. Dunne notes that the separability of *techné*'s products from its processes and makers leads to the potentially dangerous belief that we are distinct from our products (Dunne 342); in modern terms, this belief leads to the technological determinism that concludes 'the things we make' are autonomous, outside our control and even in control of us (Winner; Miller 'Technology as a Form of Consciousness'). Feminist contributions to rhetorical scholarship in the disciplines of Communication and English point out that the classical tradition does, indeed, have serious limitations that derive from its birth and growth in male argumentative traditions. As early as 1973 Karlyn Kohrs Campbell noted that 'the rhetoric of women's liberation' was an 'oxymoron,' Aristotelian in form ('The Rhetoric of Women's Liberation: An Oxymoron?' 78) but wavering between the rhetorical and the anti-rhetorical in its ambivalence toward the value (and values) of 'persuasion' (84). In the thirty-some years following this groundbreaking article, feminist research in rhetoric has taken on a number of tasks, including the restoration of silenced women's voices from antiquity through the twentieth century. Though this 'additive' (Jarratt 'Speaking to the Past' 193) strategy has been criticized for its creation of an alternative canon that looks suspiciously like 'tokenism' or even 'affirmative action' to some (Biesecker 141-2) it has led to articulations of feminist or woman-based rhetorics such as those of Sonja K. Foss and Cindy L. Griffin from the discipline of Communication; characterizing the traditional Aristotelian approach to persuasion in Kenneth Burke's work as 'a rhetoric of domination' ('A Feminist Perspective on Rhetorical Theory' 343), they offer a feminist 'invitational rhetoric' that is co-operative and non-adversarial, focused not on changing an audience through persuasion, used not to 'make a case [but] to discover more cases' ('Beyond Persuasion' 16) and alternative ways of understanding rhetorical situations.

In English scholarship, Susan C. Jarratt also cautions against the creation of 'a women's canon' in favor of historical work not only about women but also about 'the category of gender' ('Speaking to the Past' 191). Her considerable contribution to both projects focuses on parallels between the situation of the Sophists in fifth-century BCE Athens and the situation of women both then and now. Noting the historical exclusion of the Sophists from the rhetorical canon that derived much of its energy from Plato, she also points out the sophistic interest in irreconcilable or contradictory positions (known as the *dissoi logoi*) and their emphasis on contingency and the disruption of usual categories such as Aristotelian genres ('The First Sophists and Feminism' 34). While she stops short of claiming that the Sophists were feminists, she points out that 'current feminists are becoming sophists' through their focus on 'describing rhetorical solutions' to theoretical problems that can change women's lives (39). However, it is in the link she establishes between feminist rhetorics and error 'in the non-moral sense' (38) that she ties the feminist work of Campbell, Foss, and Griffin to hers while simultaneously bringing us back to Aristotle. Campbell had argued in 1973 that the purpose of the rhetoric of women's liberation was 'violating the reality structure,' what we could call an 'error in the non-moral sense' as it argued against prevailing 'norms of decorum, morality, and "femininity"' (81). Foss and Griffin similarly argue for what S. Gearhart had called in 1982 're-sourcement,' characterized as 'a swerve, a leap to the other side' that leads to 'a vocabulary which is (at the moment) incommensurable with the old' (quoted in 'Beyond Persuasion' 9). Rhetoric, concludes Jarratt, is as it was understood by Friedrich Nietzsche, 'always on the side of "error,"' always understanding 'the "real"...in terms of future possibilities, specifying "real" for whom, under what conditions, and toward what ends' (38).

Feminist rhetoric itself has limitations, of course. Foss and Griffin are especially aware that the invitational rhetoric they formulate functions best in circumstances marked by 'safety' (10), by a view of one's audience as composed of 'unrepeatable individuals' (11) and where the task itself is co-operative rather than adversarial (15). Legal rhetoric, in its emphasis on adversarial relationships between parties understood in generic and functional roles, may not be able to avail itself of invitational rhetoric except in limited or unusual circumstances. But the feminist interest in 'error' recalls not only Nietzsche but also Aristotle, whose understanding of the relationships among form, material, and limits meant that 'deliberation' took place through 'forethought' specifically intended to generate a systematic plan for working with more or less dependable and malleable materials. Because the materials themselves exert an influence on the form they may take, our prior experience with them leads us to recognize and appreciate characteristic forms they may take, their limits. But the limits of *techné* are not limitations. Instead, they are composed of both the ends to which characteristic forms may be put and the 'tools' that may be used to shape them, creating those forms while simultaneously providing a way out of the boundaries they normally take on. This circumstance explains why Atwill can say that *techné* 'is never reducible to an instrument or a means to an end,' but 'intervenes when a boundary or limitation is recognized, and...creates a path that both transgresses and redefines that boundary' (*Rhetoric Reclaimed* 48). It is the sheer inventiveness of *techné*, reinforced by the craftiness of *metis* with which it is so often associated (Detienne and Vernant 28), that allowed the female welder who worked near Carr—close by, but not in, the tinshop—to use a tool to simultaneously establish a boundary and cross it, 'zapping' the tinners whenever she need to, as Posner quaintly puts it, 'fend them off' (*Carr v. Allison Gas Turbine Division* 1010).

Again, it is the sheer inventiveness of *techné* that not only encourages but requires, if one wishes to demonstrate excellence in art, the exercise of such willing error. Where error was unthinkable in *episteme* because, said Aristotle, 'there is no such thing as error of knowledge;' and blamable in *praxis* because, again according to Aristotle, 'correctness of opinion is truth' (VI.ix.3), art is not only 'compatible with failure' (Roochnik 52) but draws on it. For if in art 'he who errs willingly is preferable,' as Ross translates the passage (*Nicomachean Ethics* VI.v.7) it is not truly because its failures may be attributed to the 'limits determined by the nature of its subject matter' (Roochnik 50) or even because failure demonstrates the artist's mastery over those materials and thus 'reveals the control one has over [the] exercise' of the *techné* (Dunne 266). Far more significant is the room Aristotle's understanding makes for innovation and change through an artist's response to the materials with which she must work. In other words, in re-inventing the central issue of *Carr* I hope not only to have shown how rhetorical heuristics can contribute to the production of a text, but to have illustrated Aristotle's position that 'voluntary error' in art is a virtue, if not necessarily sound legal strategy, because its concern for what may be otherwise opens up the possibility for the production of some 'thing.' In rhetoric that 'thing' is a discursive reality created out of what was previously 'unsayable;' protests that sexual harassment is 'the crime invented by [Catharine] MacKinnon,' or more generally that 'feminists invented sexual harassment' (Letwin 36; O'Beirne 20) thus underscore, even if negatively, the reality of rhetorical inventions. The recognition of excellence through error, then, may provide some relief from the anxiety produced by literary approaches to rhetoric, for it implies that we are both made by and remake our languages, as White has said (*Justice as Translation* 23); while we cannot stand completely outside our own assumptions, as Fish has told us, we can find in the limits of our rhetorical productions the 'end of the rope' that can begin to unravel them. Unfortunately, this method contributes to the creation of a different anxiety, one produced by the open-ended rather than circular nature of *techné*. The knowledge that our legal texts, once created, take on lives of their own encourages the belief that we are helplessly and ethically compromised by law's necessity to work with and through rhetoric. This last is the usual criticism leveled at rhetoric, that the separability of its products from their producers makes of it an inherently amoral, if not immoral, enterprise. But we might just as easily argue, as I do, that the end of rhetoric in the uses to which its products are to be put make rhetoric an inescapably ethical enterprise because, in Roochnik's description of Aristotle's position, 'it is in the using of things...that ethical value becomes visible' (31). In the requirement that makers co-operate with the materials given, and in the compatibility of art with error, we find room for a purposeful wandering along the boundaries of the acceptable that can change the meaning of both acceptability and boundaries.

Rather than accepting the pre-existence of text, as literary hermeneutics does, rhetoric contemplates 'human actions' as among the things that could be 'other than they are' (*Rhetoric* I.II.13-15). The promise of this synthetic rather than analytic approach to text lies in what Robert R. Johnson calls its 'central investment,' its dedication to 'revealing the unconscious and uncovering the mysterious for the end of transferring knowledge in a democratic and an ethical manner' (xv). The Aristotelian conception of rhetoric cannot bypass current insights recognizing the ambiguity of language; nor does it counter Fish's position, that we are unable to overcome our situatedness or that there is no space outside our own discourse from which we may self-consciously regard it (*There's No Such Thing as Free Speech* 347-8). It may, however, offset both those insights with its own, that the 'typified rhetorical action' represented by professional discourse and its genres (Miller 'Genre as Social Action' 151) may not only be consciously learned but also that its enabling constraints are subject to the transgressions of *techné* (Atwill *Rhetoric Reclaimed* 48), to the willing error that Aristotle saw as the mark of true art. In its co-operation with and respect for the materials it is given; in its anticipation of results through planning and forethought—and the willingness to abandon all three in favor of a ripe opportunity; in its acceptance of the contradictions and ambiguities of language and its recognition of the potential they provide for violating the real but shifting limits language provides; in all these ways rhetorical art recognizes that the things we say and the things we do are both the causes and the effects of the things we make.

Chapter 6

Erring for Justice

[I]n art he who errs willingly is preferable...

Aristotle
Nicomachean Ethics, Book VI
(Ross translation)

It is time to return to the 'Reasonable Woman' if we can find her—if, indeed, she exists. In this chapter I will eventually look for her in *Carr* but like any good anthropologist—or zoologist—I will first need to turn to reports of early sightings, to descriptions of her appearance and characteristics based on hints and quick glimpses. This method requires that I follow her tracks from an early suggestion of her existence in an anonymous 'Comment' in the *Harvard Law Review* in 1984, to her fleeting shadow in the dissent in *Rabidue v. Osceola Refining Company* in 1986, and finally to her first full public sighting, in the majority opinion in *Ellison v. Brady* in 1991. She created quite a stir through her appearance in *Ellison*, suggesting for the first time that the idea of 'reason' in 'woman'—conceived as different from 'reason' in 'man'—could and would be taken seriously. This event, hailed in some law review articles as a way to allow justices to 'borrow' (Brenneman 1301) the perspective of the 'usual victim' (*Rabidue v. Osceola Refining Co.* 626) of sexual harassment, was lamented by others in the public press as signaling a feminist 'attack on all rational discourse' (Letwin 34). Despite this early and somewhat grand entrance, however, and despite occasional sightings in judicial opinions over the succeeding ten-plus years, it remains to be seen whether the Reasonable Woman can live up to the revolutionary potential, for better or for worse, claimed for her.

For all my interest in the Reasonable Woman and her colleagues—the Hyper-Sensitive Female, the Reasonable Person and the Reasonable Man, the Well-Intentioned and Equal Opportunity Harasser, all of whom people the world of sexual harassment opinions—she is not the main object of my interest in this chapter, but simply the vehicle by which I wish to pursue another. By searching for the Reasonable Woman in *Carr* I hope to show that she, like any other discursive construct, can demonstrate precisely how and why the pursuit of justice is itself pursued by beliefs about language, in many or most cases even by a flight from language that makes justice itself seem difficult-to-impossible to achieve. Law, to the regret of many and the hope of a few, must do its work through language—for some, like James Boyd White, law *is* a language. For those to whom law really is a distinct language characterized by its own grammar, vocabulary, syntax, and aesthetic there is no doubt that justice, if it is to be done, must be done by and through language. Some, like White, respond to that knowledge with optimism. Others, less optimistic, nevertheless respond with celebration and 'play,' while others, the least optimistic, respond with calls for attention to silence. But even for those to whom language is simply something law uses rather than something it is, this 'tool' leaves a mark that may as easily disable as enable justice; law's language, something law should own but which appears rather to own law, may simply obscure but may also distort and deface justice. Given that the 'tool' cannot be discarded—or at least not quite—can it really be used to 'do' justice?

I therefore begin this chapter with a backward glance at the jurisprudence of the three figures who have occupied most of our attention to this point, to the legal theories of Richard Posner, James Boyd White, and Robin West. I do so to see how each answers the foundational questions of jurisprudence—what is law? what is justice?—and to recognize that answers posed to these questions have both descriptive and prescriptive (or normative) aspects. Jurisprudence, in other words, tells us not so much what law and justice are as what each thinker hopes or believes they are, or ought to be. It will become clear that the answers suggested by Posner, White, and West to these questions are grounded in assumptions about language that vary in the degree to which they are explicitly articulated. Those assumptions become the next focus of my inquiry, where I again consider not only what each legal theory believes language is, or ought to be, but how a disjuncture between those descriptive and prescriptive language theories influences—a stronger word would be determines—the relationship each sees between law and justice and the potential for that relationship to thrive in the legal system we know.

It is to make the theoretical discussion concrete and visible that I then turn to the Reasonable Woman. Arguing that implicit requirements of reasonableness had constructed an imaginary 'reasonable woman' long before she was given that name, I return at last to *Carr*, and to Carr, to ask how the approaches to law and language of Posner, West, and White might attempt to find, recognize, or invent the Reasonable Woman in that case. That discussion brings us, finally, to the end of our 'rope'—to the limits and limitations of language for law seen as science, seen as literature, seen as rhetoric.

The Problem with Jurisprudence

It is significant that, where White has written *Justice as Translation* and West has written *Caring for Justice*, Posner has written *Problems of Jurisprudence*. Posner, in other words, does not attempt to provide any conception or metaphor for justice but instead to answer our first question—what is law?—by focusing on what he calls its consequences. We will see that 'consequences' take on a rather unique meaning in Posner's jurisprudence, so that his 'activity' or 'prediction' theory of law, rather than meshing with White's contention that both law and language are activities, clashes with it. Similarly, Posner's suspicion of what he calls the 'verbose and argumentative' would seem compatible with West's mistrust of law's 'verbose' or 'wordy' nature but instead leads to a jurisprudence that opposes hers. Before we can understand why such apparently compatible approaches to law and language lead to disparate results, we must first briefly review the legal theory of each as it is expressed or implied in these major works.

White might object to the label 'theory,' given his 'profoundly anti-theoretical' position in *Heracles' Bow* (123). What White objects to there is the use of theory as a 'program,' an invariable framework or structure (one thinks immediately of Posner's use of economics) imposed upon the material of law. As I use the word in this section I intend to depart from that usage and even temporarily from Aristotle's conception of *theoria* as a quasi-science of observation, so that by 'theory' I mean a hypothesis about the nature of justice and of law's relationship to it. White's hypothesis, then, is that justice can be usefully and validly understood as a kind of translation, a hypothesis first expressed in *Justice as Translation* but consistent with the conception of law present in his prior work. White points out that 'translation' is simply the Latin version of the Greek word, metaphor, and thus itself may be translated as 'to carry across' (*Justice as Translation* 235). Though White does not summarize it in this way, such carrying across takes place in two primary sites, that of the legal text and that of the person who creates the text, the translator. The legal text is thus a 'third' text (263), a carrying-over of the perspectives of at least two other texts that it is obliged faithfully to represent. In *Justice as Translation* White calls this faithfulness 'fidelity' (246); in the earlier *Heracles' Bow* the same function was performed by 'contraries comprehended' (114). Both are standards by which a judicial opinion may be ethically judged—the opinion is excellent, or ethical, to the extent it succeeds in incorporating into itself what is most valid and valuable in the texts that precede it (*Heracles' Bow* 116). The translator who must bring such fidelity about is by consequence almost obliged to be a 'third' person, one who can inhabit two or more worlds—perhaps not simultaneously but in sequence; he or she moves from immersion in one world to immersion in another (*Justice as Translation* 260). It is through this process of circulation among worlds that the translator may achieve a critical self-consciousness that allows some evaluation of the materials from which the text will eventually be created. Though he concedes there is 'no point outside culture' (252) White believes that we can 'act and speak with momentary, if qualified, confidence' within more than one world, that 'we should move from immersion in our world and its languages to a place critical of them, on the margin, and then return' (260).

There are numerous possible objections to White's hypothesis, including Stanley Fish's contention that such critical self-consciousness is literally impossible (*There's No Such Thing as Free Speech* 347-8). West has also objected to White's assumption on several grounds, including the 'transcendence' he posits for language (*Caring for Justice* 185). Yet her own hypothesis that justice and care are 'each *necessary conditions of the other*' (24, emphasis in original) seems to demand a similar kind of 'bilingual' capacity. *Caring for Justice* also marks a change, or evolution, in West's thought from the earlier *Narrative, Authority and*

Law when her legal theory seemed far more compatible with White's, differing primarily in her emphasis on the feminist implications of literary analysis in law. West has not abandoned literary analysis entirely, conceding in a full chapter in *Caring for Justice* that feminist and literary perspectives on law have significant 'common concerns' (180). Nevertheless, she cautions feminist activists to be 'wary' of White's attractive egalitarian and communitarian impulses; literary analysis can tend to take feminist attention away from the 'task at hand' given that the canon, both literary and legal, is ill equipped to enable or even hear the stories and voices of women (187). Where White's descriptive theory is fairly confident that justice is a process of translation, West falls back on a prescriptive theory that justice, which she claims is frequently seen as the antithesis of care, ought to be synthesized with it. This synthesis would then not replace but supplement important elements of justice with their counterparts in care—the emphasis of justice on consistency with that of care on nurturance, of integrity with compassion, and of impartiality with commitment to particular persons (38). Justice thus conceived would no longer be blindfolded but would exercise a protective gaze that, in West's ultimate analysis, would enable law to recognize harms suffered disproportionately by women as harms subject to protection and compensation (8).

No theory of justice is impervious to critique, of course, and West's conclusion that uncaring justice is as deficient as unjust care has been questioned on a number of bases, including its foundation in a presumed essentialism. But for Posner, the problem with West's jurisprudence is not its potential essentialism but that the granting of 'substantive' justice—the recognition of the plight of an individual litigant that is the equivalent of West's 'particular' justice—is likely to be shortsighted in its lack of attention to the consequences for 'unknown others who may be affected' by a judicial decision down the road (*Problems of Jurisprudence* 412). No more useful for Posner is White's suggestion that an ethically good judicial opinion will incorporate what is best from each of the opposing parties to a legal dispute, a strategy that works against the opinion's imperative to present itself 'as powerful, as confident, as certainly right' (211). Posner does not neglect the question of justice entirely, but devotes a chapter in *Problems of Jurisprudence* to a discussion of various formulations of it, especially Aristotle's understanding of 'corrective' justice in Book V of the *Nicomachean Ethics*. We have already seen that Posner's holding in *Carr* is consistent with the description of justice Aristotle provides there, so it is not surprising to find him concluding that corrective justice—a means whereby an ill-gotten gain, or some equivalent, is taken from the offending party and returned to the injured party—has 'significant domains of application' in the common law, though he believes its contributions may be limited (458). Because neither the jurisprudence of White nor that of West is entirely adequate for Posner, he draws on an ethic that differs radically from either fidelity or care. Posner's ethical principle is wealth maximization, the imperative for judges to decide cases in a manner that will 'enlarge the social pie'—increase the resources of society as a whole—without regard to the 'individual slices' allocated to any given person (388). Wealth maximization is made fully ethical for

Posner by the backing provided by the Pareto Principle, which holds that the best transactions are those that increase social wealth without making any one individual worse off. It is the 'insurance' of the Pareto Principle that provides compensation for those who might otherwise lose their personal hold on resources as society's overall wealth increases (390). As is characteristic of much economic analysis of law, Posner's theory holds that the distributive justice Aristotle treats along with corrective justice in Book V of the *Ethics*—decisions as to the proper size of any given piece of the pie—is off-limits to the judicial branch, the responsibility of the legislator rather than of the judge (388).

It may be for this reason that in his introduction to *The Problems of Jurisprudence* Posner tells us that he is a pragmatist. His is a 'functional, policy-saturated, nonlegalistic, naturalistic, and skeptical, but decidedly not cynical, conception of the legal process' (26) that can all be reduced to that one word, pragmatism. But what, outside of its manifestation in the legal process Posner envisions, does that word mean? Posner realizes the word is inadequate for the task to which he sets it, in part because the pragmatic tradition in philosophy is so diverse. As he attempts to whittle its meaning down to one viable for his own project Posner makes the claim that so-called 'legal' reasoning is actually 'practical reason' in its 'Aristotelian' sense (*Problems of Jurisprudence* 71). This claim, with which I (like Fish) am inclined to agree, is somewhat breathtaking, coming as it does from the foremost advocate of a (quasi-) scientific approach to law through economics and in the face of Aristotle's insistence on fairly clear distinctions between 'science' (*epistemé*) and *phronesis*, of which 'practical reason' is one translation.

There are certainly vestiges of Aristotelian *phronesis* in Posner's description of practical reason, including his initial claim that its methods are '[s]et against the methods of exact inquiry' (71). Aristotle's voice also echoes, albeit somewhat faintly, in Posner's recognition of the importance of 'authority' to legal ('practical') reasoning (78), to the role played by legal cases as vicarious 'experience' (89), the facilitation of legal interpretation by its place in a more or less homogeneous community (101), and even in the 'test of time' that, while Posner says it is of more importance in judging aesthetic works, still carries some validity in legal reasoning because 'what most people think is probably true' (112). In other words, what Posner recognizes about practical reason is that it is embedded in experience in a community marked by fairly reliable agreement as to values and standards of judgment as represented by those in whom it vests authority. But Posner gives practical reason an unusual twist; recognizing the 'means-end rationality' that Aristotle said was characteristic of *phronesis*, he does not explain it away or soften it, as Martha C. Nussbaum and Joseph Dunne both attempted to do (*Fragility of Goodness* 297; *Back to the Rough Ground* 269); noting that it is 'sometimes [called] "deliberation"...by philosophers' Posner himself calls it 'cost-benefit analysis' (105). Thus his embrace of practical reason is pragmatic in what we may recognize as distinctly modern and common-sense meanings of the term; recognizing its inevitability in law's indeterminate climate, and its appropriateness as a method by which 'people who are not credulous [may] form beliefs about matters that can't be verified by logic or exact observation' (72) Posner finds the methods of 'practical reason' simultaneously inadequate and indispensable. Plausibly collapsing reasoning from analogous cases into a method for weighing authority, and finding in the 'test of time' a 'market analogy' that is valid because 'competition can be depended upon to bring about the socially desired price' if certain invalid competitive practices (such as fraud) are forbidden (118-9), Posner unearths and values those aspects of practical reason that can be given an economic cast. Though he later recognizes a form of practical reason that he concedes may be more strictly 'Aristotelian' than his own, Posner understands such 'prudentialism,' drawn from an alternative translation of *phronesis*, as caution and conservatism. Such 'resistance to change' is unlikely to appeal to those with 'a preference for free markets,' he says, an attitude that is generally conceived as conservative but which Posner claims is actually 'libertarian' (442-3).

So Posner is not only a pragmatist; he is also a libertarian, a stance Nussbaum recognizes in the theory of sexuality he provides in *Sex and Reason*. Defining the attitude in that work as one that 'defends the rights of individuals to regulate their sexual conduct by their own choice except where it can be shown to cause harm or infringe the rights of others' ('"Only Grey Matter"?' 1697), Nussbaum characterizes Posner's position as 'strongly libertarian,' a 'hands-off' attitude that 'refuses to pass judgment on practices that many people deem immoral...because of the high worth it ascribes to personal liberty of choice' (1699). West modifies this assessment, describing Posner's position as only 'moderately libertarian' because its argument that we should not attempt 'to steer or control purely private, consensual sexual behavior' is paired with a conclusion that we also 'can and should do little else to create a social world more tolerant and accepting' ('Sex, Reason, and a Taste for the Absurd' 2413). The hands-off attitude, then, leads Posner to suggest 'modest and, for the most part, uncontroversial legal reform' (2414) that eventually leads to 'an astoundingly crisp endorsement of the status quo' (2427).

And if West muddies the waters just a bit, it is Fish, operating in his typical mode, who really stirs things up. Posner's attitude is not really pragmatism, he says, but 'almost pragmatism,' spoiling a fairly accurate pragmatist account of how law works (the descriptive project that says 'law is...') by building upon it a pragmatist program (a prescriptive project that attempts to determine what law ought to do). This attempt to describe 'what follows from the [pragmatist] account' is, says Fish, flawed because it is both foundationalist and essentialist, two attributes that pragmatism, as pragmatism, rejects (*There's No Such Thing as Free Speech* 209). Posner's Achilles' heel, according to Fish, is ultimately his empiricism. Posner suggests, for example, that a pragmatist legal agenda would identify goals for legislation, measure the success of the legislation in achieving those goals, and then amend or repeal the legislation if the goals are not met so that law 'really would be a method of social engineering,' what we are to assume is a wholly desirable result (*Problems of Jurisprudence* 122). Posner believes, says Fish, that 'the point of an enterprise is to get at the empirical truth about something,' and that said enterprise in law 'is to get the empirical facts right'

(*There's No Such Thing as Free Speech* 222-3). Posner 'should be immune to the lure of [such] empiricist essentialism,' Fish concludes, 'but he is not' (211). It is the empiricist bias, the desire to 'dismiss the myth of objectivity as it is embodied in high sounding but empty legal concepts' only to 'replace it with the myth of the '"actual facts" or "exact discourse" or "actual experience" or a "rational scientific account"' (210) that leads Posner to believe that the effects of a piece of legislation may be accurately separated from other possible influences, assessed by some quantifiable measure, and adjusted until they create a previously agreed-upon effect.

Posner's 'pragmatism' thus differs markedly from the emphasis on 'practice' that forms the basis of White's jurisprudence. Whatever Posner's claims for the pedigree of his pragmatism in Aristotle, it is White's understanding of law's nature that owes more to *phronesis* as Aristotle developed the idea. Starting with the claim that law is an activity ('doing' rather than 'observing' or 'making,' in Aristotle's terms), White connects that activity to elements crucial to Aristotle's understanding of *phronesis*, to human communities and the values they create, promote, or disable. For Thomas D. Eisele, White's major achievement is thus his ability to '[make] room for humans in a way traditional jurisprudence does not' (377). A critical element of that humanness is White's emphasis on language as the medium for law's activity, indeed for language as an activity itself, as (relying on Wittgenstein) a 'way of acting in the world' (*Justice as Translation* xiii). Though few take issue directly with that emphasis, what has evoked criticism and protest is the means by which White says law acts through language, a means he has called variously 'literary' or 'rhetorical,' and both of which seem, finally, to be methods of what he calls 'art' (*Justice as Translation* 18). West, in particular, takes exception to this characterization of law and its method; claiming that understanding law as art does a disservice, potentially to artists but most certainly to lawyers, she argues that 'artists don't aim for justice' and that, whatever the nature of justice may be, it is certainly 'not captured by an aesthetic ideal' (*Caring for Justice* 188). But for White 'art' is not pure aesthetic; instead, it is 'a means by which speakers act on their inheritance,' a 'reconstitution of language' that has ethical and political meaning (*Justice as Translation* 18, 216). Thus art is 'in every field,' says White, 'a way of addressing the limits as well as the resources of one's material' (265).

In both *Heracles' Bow* and *Justice as Translation* White calls a similar function 'constitutive rhetoric' (34; xiv), a term that does little to win over those who object to the less politically charged 'art.' Indeed, Robert Cover complains that in raising rhetoric 'to the pinnacle of jurisprudence' ('Violence and the Word' 1602 fn2) White neglects the coercive power of law. West is also suspicious of White's claims for rhetoric, questioning his contention that it may be something other than 'obfuscation, masks, legitimation, and disingenuity' (*Caring for Justice* 187). Ultimately, in trying to imagine what rhetoric might be, West echoes her nemesis Posner, who can acknowledge that White has demonstrated the role of 'rhetorical power' in law only by opposing rhetoric to strict logic (*Problems of Jurisprudence* 395). Conceiving rhetoric as a 'residual set of methods of reasoning and persuasion' that are employed for lack of a better option (when information or agreement are readily available) Posner concludes that Aristotle was wrong about rhetoric, that it comes into play not under conditions of radical uncertainty but 'when the facts are known and the question is how to bring an audience to understand and be moved by them' (*Overcoming Law* 544, 528-9). The conclusion Posner reaches based on these assumptions is that the Law and Literature movement can ultimately contribute to the 'understanding and improvement' of judicial opinions only in a very limited sense, to the imperative for 'judges and law clerks [to] pay more attention to the style of their opinions' and thereby improve their writing (*Law and Literature: A Misunderstood Relation* 297). West's similar conclusion is that rhetorical awareness might be able to 'cure law of its anti-humanist penchant for stilted, deadened, wooden prose;' going a bit beyond Posner she concedes that it might even lead to 'a more humanistic understanding of law's commands' (184). But rhetoric can do little else, in West's conception of it, not only because of its 'aesthetic' nature but also because of its connection, through literary 'high culture' (*Caring for Justice* 182) to a historically exclusionary community represented by the canon of literary and legal texts upon which White (like Posner) draws. This criticism is one to which White is vulnerable and which has been voiced even by supporters like Eisele, who cautions that we should not 'under-emphasize' the debt of law's materials to their inheritance (357).

Cover takes this criticism further than most, agreeing that 'law is all those things that White claims' but arguing that White neglects the fact that 'it is those things in the context of the organized social practice of violence' ('Violence and the Word' 1602 fn2). Cover thus calls into question, in advance of its formulation, White's eventual understanding of law and justice itself as 'translation,' an act that by 'putting two things together in such a way as to make a third, a new thing with a meaning of its own' (*Justice as Translation* 263) constitutes a potential act of violence to one or both of its components. In fact, White notices and comments on this possibility in the earlier *Heracles' Bow*, where he has made the New Critical claim that legal texts may be judged not just aesthetically but ethically on their success in 'comprehending contrarieties.' The danger of this requirement, he notes, is that in the enthusiasm evoked by the challenge to create a form that establishes a relationship between disparate texts or textual elements, 'one will avoid substantive questions about the elements comprehended in the form...and focus only on the relation that it gives them' (*Heracles' Bow* 121). In later assigning nearly the same task to 'translation,' White insists that the purpose is 'not to merge the two elements, or to blur the distinctions between them, but to sharpen the sense we have of each' (*Justice as Translation* 263); nevertheless, he recognizes that translation is 'the art of facing the impossible, of confronting unbridgeable discontinuities between texts, between languages, and between people' (257).

This frank recognition of the limitations of his recommended ideal is what leads White to declare for translation the ethic of fidelity that attempts to 'do justice' to the texts it attempts to bridge. Posner finds the translation analogy flawed because it is both too timid—'literal translation is not,' he says, 'an oxymoron' (*Law and Literature* 252)—and too bold. Conceding that translations may on occasion be less than literal, Posner nevertheless limits acceptable reasons for 'changing text' to endeavors other than law where justifications for less than literal translations do not 'apply' (253). Others also question the validity of translation as a model for justice, but for different reasons. Both Fish and West see in White's claims an unjustified belief in the transcendent capabilities of language. White's claim that texts may be made to speak to and within the ethic of times other than those in which they were created, a fundamental property of his formulation of both translation and interpretation (*Justice as Translation* 255) will not hold, says West, because for her the content of legal language may be 'utterly compromised by its genesis' (*Caring for Justice* 186). For Fish the problem lies elsewhere, in White's belief in what Fish calls 'anti-foundationalist theory hope,' the belief that 'by becoming aware of the rhetoricity of our foundations we gain a [nonrhetorical] perspective on them that we didn't have before' (*There's No Such Thing as Free Speech* 172, brackets in original). This hope is a 'full-fledged romance,' Fish tells us, in White's work; certainly, White's description of the translator as an individual who lives 'in the space between two languages,' a place presumably 'critical of them,' (*Justice as Translation* 260) makes a claim for 'critical self-consciousness' that, often advocated by White (20), is at least as often the target of Fish (*Doing What Comes Naturally* 437). Yet it is this space on the margins between worlds and languages that is absolutely essential to White's faith and hope for law and legal practice, a space in which justice itself is done.

While West differs substantially from both Posner and White, she also has interests and assumptions in common with each—including her analytical use of a rather settled canon of literary texts. With White she shares an interest in the lessons literature holds for law, though she is more interested in its narrative content than in its joint nature with law as a 'literary' activity. With Posner she shares a suspicion of the role language plays in law and an assumption that it should be limited in some way. When she takes issue with White it is on the basis of his commitment to traditional canons and the uselessness she assumes of 'aesthetic' analysis, an assumption she shares with Posner; when she takes issue with Posner it is on the basis of his positions on substantive legal issues. It was her use of Kafka to critique Posner's economic jurisprudence that first drew his attention to the Law and Literature movement; his initial and continuing response to that critique has been a sustained effort to discredit West's method, and by extension that of much of the Law and Literature movement at large. He therefore has not troubled to discuss her legal theory in much detail. Calling her both a 'utopian fantasist,' a label he explains she readily accepts (*Law and Literature* 198), and a 'romantic' on the order of Wordsworth and Blake (204), Posner notes and dismisses without argument or discussion what he sees as the basic elements of her jurisprudence. She 'dislikes capitalists,' he says (188) and may even believe that 'economists have so unrealistic a conception of human nature that even Kafka is more realistic' (190). She likes Freud's legal theory 'to the extent it sees the role of law as protecting the weak from the strong,' but dislikes the traces of social Darwinism in economic theory, believing (wrongly, he implies) that using competition to allocate resources favors the strong (205). Her project for making 'empathic nurturing the organizing principle of society' is apparently typical of 'utopian dreamers [who] believe in the perfectability of human nature and society' but she is 'wasting her time,' he says, 'trying to show Kafka's fiction has a radical message; she must have put it there herself' (205, 217).

However sketchy his description of West's legal theory, and however unargued his rejection of it, Posner's attention to West far exceeds that of White. The colloquy between Posner and West is referenced only in a footnote to White's discussion of a point on which he agrees substantially with West, that the economic model of voluntary choice 'does not adequately describe most human behavior' (*Justice as Translation* 64, 275 fn11). We therefore need to turn elsewhere to find a substantive discussion of her position and its implications—for my purposes to Steven B. Katz's response to West's published reservations about the 'law-as-literature movement' appearing three years after her 'Kafkaesque' critique of Posner's economic legal theory. Though genuinely 'friendly,' as he proclaims in the title of his article, to West's project and her insights, he notes the strong resemblance of her position on law's 'imperativism'—its nature as power rather than as 'interpretation,' as much Law and Literature scholarship holds—to a legal positivism that he finds likely to be inadequate for the moral empowerment West wishes to further (189). West is correct in noticing the tendency of Law and Literature to place meaning 'in the hands of communities,' thus potentially depriving those 'who have never had a real voice in the community' of a contribution to its debates, says Katz (188). But, like the positivism that insists on the separability of law and morality, West's imperativism locates the moral voice outside the bounds of the professional community; she therefore relies on an external critique that the community, Katz suggests, cannot hear in any meaningful way. 'What can an imperativist say,' he asks, 'when she must argue [a case] before the Supreme Court' (189)?

West does not answer this question directly, but by the time of her second book, *Caring for Justice*, she has both weakened her claims for Law and Literature and argues, in a brief passage, for the value not of imperativism but of positivism itself. While the 'anti-positivist invitation to focus on the ethics and aesthetics of the spoken legal word' she attributes to Law and Literature 'might humanize legal interpretation, and might push it in a more progressive direction,' West believes a 'realistic, hardheaded, Holmesian, "bad man" positivism may be the better jurisprudential sensibility of legal reformers' (187). What we need to understand, she says, is not the 'cultural heritage' but the 'political impact' of laws in order to know 'who is hurt, and how much, by the effect of law on the lives of its subjects. Positivism,' she concludes, 'contains an important grain of truth for feminist reformers' in its contribution to such knowledge (187). She has thus moved away from the position espoused in the earlier *Narrative, Authority and Law*, that while the nature of law is only 'partly revealed by [its] content—by its history and political and economic underpinnings' a significant part of its nature—its focus on future possibility—is best conducted and revealed through 'stories,' through its narrative method (346). By the time of *Caring for Justice*, West has turned to relational feminism and to the work of Carol Gilligan in moral psychology to develop a legal theory that is hospitable to and advances the 'empathic nurturing' that Posner found so inadequate in her earlier work.

Here West takes issue with the traditional assumption of traditional jurisprudence—that the aim of adjudication is 'to do justice.' The nature and direction of that aim, she notes, is dependent upon one's understanding of justice, which has been defined by such diverse values as efficiency (by Law and Economics), legal rights (by legal liberals), or even aesthetic integrity (by Law and Literature) (22). Her vehicle for questioning the primacy of justice as the aim of adjudication is the ethic of care, but before she can use that ethic to supplement or revise the ethic of justice, she must deal with the latter ethic as it is articulated in Gilligan's work. This articulation in a work that is widely and almost routinely cited throughout the literature of feminist jurisprudence presents a particularly vexing problem for legal theory. Very early on Gilligan clearly identifies the ethic of justice with the concepts of separation, rights, and power that she has already identified with male moral reasoning (xxii). Her sources for this definition appear to be a trio of male scholars, namely Sigmund Freud, Jean Piaget, and her own former professor Lawrence Kohlberg, whose studies of moral maturity (based entirely on the experiences of male subjects) her own work is intended to question and extend. From Kohlberg she derives the idea that justice requires not only fairness but a recognition of individual rights and responsibilities; justice in this 'principled' sense is understood to be universal and rational (21), and individuals who have achieved this level of moral development realize that law itself is very different from 'justice' (27). This sense of justice itself she links to childhood through Piaget, who notes a more highly developed 'legal sense' in male than in female children, citing boys' fascination with the elaboration of rules and procedures for resolving conflicts in contrast to girls' greater tolerance of exceptions to rules and innovations on them (10).

Finally Gilligan quotes Freud's conclusion that women 'show less sense of justice than men,' not only because their judgments are (supposedly) more influenced by feelings of affection or hostility, but also, interestingly, because they 'are less ready to submit to the great exigencies of life' (7, quoting from Freud's 1925 essay, 'Some Psychical Consequences of the Anatomical Distinction Between the Sexes'). This composite definition leads to a number of paradoxes that Gilligan may not recognize and certainly does not discuss, including that women's sense of justice may be 'underdeveloped' simultaneously because of their supposed lack of interest in rules and because of their failure to recognize that the presumably ultimate set of rules, law, must be distinguished from justice. Further, their unwillingness to cave in the face of those rules and submit to life's 'exigencies' (might we call them injustices?) again leads women away from a highly developed 'sense of justice.' Gilligan does not dispute the definitions of justice upon which she draws because that is not her purpose; rather, she disputes the conclusion drawn by prior psychological theorists, especially Kohlberg, that the ethic of 'justice' thus defined is indicative of a higher level of moral development than the ethic of 'care' that females overwhelmingly expressed in her own studies. The limitation she is seeking to correct, the casting of a problem with psychological theory as a problem in women's development (7) thus lies in the psychological theory, not in the legal theory. However, the risk for legal theorizing of accepting Gilligan's articulation of justice is that of rendering women, at least those expressing an ethic of care, either incompetent or, worse, irrelevant in the legal justice system. West's solution is to synthesize the two ethics, but her insistence that each is essential to the other may not be enough to overcome that risk; however subject justice may be to extension and improvement through its synthesis with an ethic of care, justice itself remains as 'male' as caring is 'female.'

The problem with jurisprudence—whether that of White, West, or Posner—is that it is not capable of answering the ontological questions it asks. We do not, ultimately, 'know' what justice is, what law is, or what relationship they 'have.' Rather than a descriptive enterprise, jurisprudence is prescriptive, telling us more about what each scholar believes law or justice should be rather than what either ultimately is. How troubling that problem may be is, however, another question, and one that we can begin to ask, if not answer, by turning to the language theory in which legal theory is grounded.

What is Language? (And Why Ask?)

White, West, and Posner all share one fundamental assumption about language, though their assessments of the consequences of that assumption vary widely. All three recognize that language is an artificial construct and that, as such, has a complex relationship to 'reality,' however reality may be perceived. Where Oliver Wendell Holmes had urged lawyers to 'think things, not words,' (quoted in *Problems of Jurisprudence* 241 fn30) all three recognize the belief expressed by this adage is, in Posner's terms, a form of 'naïve realism' that cannot sufficiently ground a legal theory. But all three also recognize, to varying extents, that language is an essential ingredient in the mix between law and justice, an ingredient that must be accounted for even if it is simply to discount its significance to law's substantive outcomes.

For White, of course, language is absolutely essential to law and justice both—law is, he has said, 'in a full sense a language' (*Heracles' Bow* 78) so that the question becomes not to identify the role of language 'in' law but to understand, given its nature 'as' language, what law does or could do. The fact that language (and thus, law) is artificial does not mean it is unreal (103) but that its texts are performative (*Acts of Hope* 306), 'practices,' or 'gestures' (*Justice as Translation* 245, 248). Law is for White quite literally 'something we do with words' (*Heracles' Bow* 49). West, too, recognizes that the artificiality of language has consequences for law, though her assessment of those consequences varies across her work. At times, as when she criticizes the use of 'one verbal construct [literature] to criticize yet another' (*'Caring for Justice'* 198) she suggests that the verbal has no substantive effects. Especially in her claims that 'the legalists' embrace of verbosity' betrays a 'destructive hatred of natural forms of life' and that the 'patriarchal apparatus' of law is 'the attempt of men to use the power of the "word" to attain what they cannot naturally lay claim to,' West clearly contrasts the artificial construct of language with the natural, leading to the conclusion that interest in the actual results of law requires feminists to train their sights on legal reform (193, 187). But her very suspicion of the power of the word shows us that West is all too aware of the real consequences of this artificial construct. The problem with language, for West, is that 'precisely *because* it is so wordy law inevitably carries with it the potential for its own misuse' (192, emphasis in original). The 'unnatural' is not necessarily the 'unreal.'

We would therefore expect West to be suspicious of White's project to 'resurrect' the 'man of letters' (182) not only because he is a man but precisely because he is 'of letters.' Such is the case, of course, though West pins the fault on the legal and literary canon as well as on its composition from the materials of language itself. Where for White law's texts and declarations constitute 'acts of hope,' speech acts that, as a 'way of being and acting in the world [make] a claim for [their] own rightness' (*Acts of Hope* xi) West demurs; law's performances are acts of power and need to be examined as such by a focus on their effects, particularly on the harms suffered primarily by women (*Caring for Justice* 8). And though Posner might seem to suggest a perspective compatible with West's in his pragmatic argument to 'lead discussion away from issues semantic and metaphysical and toward issues factual and empirical' (*Problems of Jurisprudence* 387) that conclusion is seriously modified by Posner's response to the artificiality he also recognizes in language. For Posner the empiricist it is 'the words on this page' that are undeniably real; it is the reality of the concepts for which they stand that he questions (162). Law is forever (and vainly) in search of mental entities in which to ground its decisions, he says, including such abstractions as intent and premeditation (163). While its focus on such entities does not render its effects unreal, a consequence is that the answer to one jurisprudential question—'what is law?'—becomes for Posner another question: 'why ask?' (220). If White concedes that 'not everything can be said' in the language that is law (*Heracles' Bow* 241) and if West finds that reality so disturbing that she calls for 'greater attentiveness to actions and to silences...and a little less to "what we say"' (*Caring for Justice* 200), Posner remains undisturbed, neglecting to answer his question-in-response to the question about law because that question is for him clearly rhetorical—and while rhetoric, to quote Posner, 'counts for a lot in law' (*Law and Literature* 271, *Overcoming Law* 395), what it counts for may be both more and less than expected.

Posner's sense of 'the rhetorical' is far from the sense in which I have used that term and thus requires some explanation. From an early position in the first edition of *Law and Literature* that rhetoric was simply 'style' and that certain uses of language, especially scientific, were simply 'not rhetorical' ('A Relation Reargued' 1376) Posner moved simultaneously in two directions in later work. Conceding both the existence of a 'scientistic rhetoric' (*Overcoming Law* 526) and the proposition that rhetoric can be seen as a 'kind of reasoning' (and thus as something different from, if not more than, style), Posner reconceives rhetoric as even less, as a 'subset of stylistic devices that is used to persuade' (*Law and Literature* 255). Rhetoric is thus simultaneously superficial and substantive, an 'undisciplined' form of reasoning with the potential to mislead because it can cause us to believe the false or disbelieve the true (*Overcoming Law* 529). As 'words on the page' rhetoric is real; as (in economic terms) a belief cost that influences our actions for good or ill, rhetoric is again real. But both rhetoric and language are stand-ins for 'mental entities' like intent, premeditation, and freewill—even law itself, whose 'thingness' Posner denies (*Problems of Jurisprudence* 163-7, 226)—or the even more nebulous 'metaphysical entities' whose reality cannot be determined. In the deepest irony, the artifices of language and rhetoric are more real, because empirically visible, than the 'realities' for which they substitute, including the ultimate metaphysical entity, justice itself (163).

This view of rhetoric, style, and language more generally leads to consequences for Posner's legal theory, his 'struggle against metaphysical entities in law' (185) that are both interesting and substantive. Unable to divest legal language of 'rhetoric' altogether Posner attempts to restrict it to an exceptional instance, the judicial opinion that he claims differs from the statute, constitution, or contract in that it is a 'literary' or 'rhetorical' text ('A Relation Reargued' 1376; *Law and Literature* 5). From an early position that meaning and form are inseparable in literature, and that consequently 'style is organic to judicial writing' ('A Relation Reargued' 1375, 1387) Posner moves to argue against the 'fusion of content and style' that he says is characteristic of the Law and Literature movement (*Law and Literature* 256). But his extended later analysis proves his earlier point that 'to divorce style and content is not yet an attainable ideal' in 'the areas of law that matter,…the areas of disagreement' ('A Relation Reargued' 1387). His analysis of several 'classic' opinions authored by Oliver Wendell Holmes goes a long way to show that 'how the opinion says what it says is as important as what it says,' even that judicial writing style can 'affect content' ('A Relation Reargued' 1376; *Law and Literature* 294). The result of this genuine insight is not, however, that style becomes for Posner a substantive element of the judicial opinion, as does rhetoric for White. Instead, the content of the opinion must become effective by being affective, effectively persuading its readers by affectively appealing to an element other than its reasoning. In the case of Holmes, for example, Posner consistently finds 'dubious legal and moral reasoning' (*Law and Literature* 273). Nevertheless, he admires Holmes's decision in *Buck v. Bell*, which upheld the involuntary sterilization of a reputedly mentally incompetent woman through the Bartlett-familiarized statement that 'three generations of imbeciles are enough.' In Posner's view this opinion

> is beautiful prose—vivid, passionate, topped off by a brilliant aphorism—but it is dubious legal reasoning.… *Buck v. Bell* would be a poorly reasoned, brutal, and even vicious opinion even if Carrie Buck really had been an imbecile; but it is a first-class piece of rhetoric (*Law and Literature: A Misunderstood Relation* 288-289).

In a lengthier analysis of Holmes's dissent in *Lochner v. New York* Posner notes Holmes's deceptive use of the 'plain' style; the calm assurance with which he states his unsupported opinions and which substitutes for logical proof; his unfair metonymic use of Herbert Spencer's *Social Statics* as representative of the philosophy of laissez-faire economics; and so on (285). He concludes:

> [The dissent] is not logically organized, does not join issue sharply with the majority, is not scrupulous in its treatment of the majority opinion or of precedent, is not thoroughly researched, does not exploit the factual record, and is highly unfair to poor old Herbert Spencer.... It is not, in short, a 'good' judicial opinion. It is merely the greatest judicial opinion of the last hundred years.... It is a rhetorical masterpiece, and evidently rhetoric counts in law...(285-286 [footnote omitted]).

We should not be surprised, given this ode to the rather pernicious values he sees in rhetoric, that Posner comfortably concludes *Carr* with his own rhetorical masterpiece, a passage that Nussbaum praises in *Poetic Justice* for its use of metaphor and its effective expression of indignation 'in a tricolon of ascending condemnation' (110). 'No reasonable person,' he wrote there

> could imagine that General Motors was genuinely helpless, that it did all it reasonably could have done. The evidence is plain that it (or at least its gas turbine division) was unprepared to deal with problems of sexual harassment even when those problems were rubbed in its face, and also incapable of improvising a solution. Its efforts at investigation were lackluster, its disciplinary efforts nonexistent, its remedial efforts perfunctory. The U.S. Navy has been able to integrate women into the crews of warships; General Motors should have been able to integrate one woman into a tinsmith shop (1012).

I can't help but admire Posner's audacity here; had the opinion actually engaged in careful reasoning in this paragraph, had Posner incorporated what was valuable and valid from both GM and the U.S. Navy, Nussbaum might not have accepted what she called 'the parallel between the task faced (and accomplished) by the Navy and the task refused by GM' (*Poetic Justice* 110)—and remembered Tailhook, symbol of the Navy's flamboyant failure to integrate women into warships, instead. Where both White and West have concluded, with differing levels of regret, that there are some things the law just can't say, for Posner it is clear that not everything need be said.

So what is language? (And why ask?) Because law either is a language, or at the very least must do its work through language, the beliefs of Posner, West, and White about the nature of language determine their views of what law is capable of doing. And because the concern with what law can do brings into focus the relationship of law to justice, however it is conceived, the conflicts between their prescriptive and descriptive language theories creates the skepticism and suspicion that Posner and West bring to their assessment of the potential of law to 'do' justice, while the congruence between the prescriptive and descriptive theories of White fuels his optimism. The language theory Posner presents as purely descriptive in his early article about the political differences of Sir William Blackstone and Jeremy Bentham—that a 'traditional' language functions in the manner of the free market ('Blackstone and Bentham' 603)—is in fact prescriptive, and it is the conflict between the market ideal and the 'reality' he perceives that makes of Posner a 'pragmatist' and skeptic. If we cannot avoid language we can certainly attempt to bypass it with mathematical representations like the Hand negligence formula discussed in Chapter 3. On those occasions where words are clearly necessary and the 'entities' for which they stand are as nebulous and metaphysical as justice we can treat language like a market by imposing the 'belief cost' of rhetoric, a commodity whose value is likely to be high when 'facts' are not known or when an audience is unlikely to understand or be moved by them (*Overcoming Law* 514). In fact, Posner assures us that 'rhetoric,' like negligence, can be represented by a formula:

$$EU_j = (1-p)B_j - pL_j$$

Here the expected utility ('EU') of any particular idea ('j') equals the (positive or negative) value of the probability ('p') that the idea will work, multiplied by the benefit ('B') to be expected if it does work, minus the loss ('L') incurred if it doesn't (501). Or, more simply, we can't be expected to act on an idea unless we believe the benefit of our action will exceed its cost. In the context of the judicial opinion it is not, however, the judges employing rhetoric who must 'pay' for it; rather, those who are persuaded by the language of the opinion must literally 'buy' it.

The reader by now will have become alert to a number of intriguing ironies. One such is West's reliance on legal positivism—not to mention the quintessential hangover of the nineteenth-century man of letters himself, Oliver Wendell Holmes—to alloy the moral ethic of justice with that of care, thus attempting, at least, to bring a 'moral' outlook to bear on a 'legal' one. The irony only becomes more intriguing given the attention of the positivists from Jeremy Bentham onward to the significance of language in law. Bentham's attempts to reform law hinged in large part on the reform of its language—in Posner's words, he attempted to purify law of 'metaphor and ambiguity' ('Blackstone and Bentham' 598). Bentham's approach to language, at least, has been lauded by both legal positivists and anti-positivists—the former including H.L.A. Hart, who concluded that Bentham and his contemporary and theoretical colleague John Austin were 'not dry analysts fiddling with verbal distinctions while cities burned' but scholars who knew that 'a study of the meaning of the distinct vocabulary of the law was as vital to our understanding of the nature of law as historical or sociological studies' (601). Among the anti-positivists, Lon Fuller claimed that legal positivism was 'primarily an analysis of the usages of legal language' (87); conceding that the clear thinking it valued was impossible as long as the law was 'cluttered up with metaphysical entities' (73), Fuller nevertheless concluded that positivism's legal conclusions remained 'purely formal and verbal,' unable to deal with the 'content of law' (88).

Yet another irony is the congruence of Posner's language theory with Bentham's despite his characterization of the latter's attempts at language reform as an 'assault on traditional language [that] prefigured the totalitarian assault on language by Newspeak, Hitler, and the Soviet press' ('Blackstone and Bentham' 598). Given his position on 'rhetoric' and its masterful use by Holmes, Posner may well agree with what he says Bentham believed—that 'intellectual confusion [is] rooted in linguistic imprecision,' that 'figurative language [shields] people from recognizing the error of habitual belief' (595). But Bentham was a legislative reformer; as a judge, Posner's interest in legal outcomes is so specialized that he restricts himself to considering what he calls 'consequences' only *ex ante*, on what parties to a legal dispute may reasonably have expected the outcomes of their actions to be as they committed them. In other words, if a decision seems reasonably 'right' at the time it is made, it literally *is* right for Posner even if its outcomes *ex post* are not what were reasonably expected—even if they are diametrically opposed to those expectations (*Problems of Jurisprudence* 389-90). 'Consequences' in this sense are at least as nebulous and as subject to the vagaries of language (both contractual and judicial) as 'justice' itself. For Posner, then, as for West, the conflict between the prescriptive and descriptive theories they hold about language creates a dilemma that they recognize to varying degrees.

For White, the situation is slightly different. Well aware of the dilemma of language, he proposes a resolution that is itself based in language; we need to get past the objectification of theoretical writing that 'turns everything it can into a noun' to the highly verbal world of practice invoked by literary writing (*Heracles' Bow* 126-7). The inevitably different readings constructed by individual minds are thus 'not to be lamented but celebrated' (97). To see why that may be so, at least for White, we now turn to an entity perhaps mental, perhaps metaphysical, but certainly discursive—the Reasonable Woman herself.

In the Pursuit of Justice (and the Reasonable Woman)

Who—or what—is the Reasonable Woman? To move toward an answer to that question, I discuss in this section how varying perspectives on language might conceive her—and how that conception affects the potential we may see for law to do justice to and through her. Beginning with a summary of her brief history in a series of judicial opinions, I move to consider how she may be conceived by Posner, West, and White. Finding aspects of their jurisprudence that seem to provide significant means for characterizing her, I also discover a tendency in the thought of all three to defer consideration of legal outcomes in favor of discussions of the nature of law (West), language (White), or the empirically visible facts of the situations of litigants before they became such (Posner). Though outcomes are significant to all three they are defined in such variant ways as to render their hypothetical legal subjects—whether Economic Man, Literary Woman, or Contrary Comprehended—more useful for the analysis of existing outcomes than for the creation of alternatives, better for the characterization of Carr as one or all three than for the alteration of conditions in the Workplace-as-Tinshop—absent the 'costs' (in almost any sense of the term) of litigation.

Perhaps the first inkling that such a creature as the Reasonable Woman might exist occurred in a 1928 legal commentary noting simply that an exhaustive search of common law cases had yielded 'no single mention of a reasonable woman' amid countless traditional references to the Reasonable Man (Herbert, quoted in Adler and Peirce 807). Nearly sixty years later such a mention did occur, not in a common law case but in a 1984 *Harvard Law Review* 'Comment.' Taking tort law as its point of departure, this Comment described a potential new standard of review its author deemed appropriate for sexual harassment cases, a standard called 'objective' in the sense that it was presumed to draw upon the perspective of a reasonable victim or plaintiff rather than the 'subjective' perspective of any particular individual ('Sexual Harassment Claims...' 1458-1459). The Comment received some attention in the dissent to *Rabidue v. Osceola Refining Co.*, decided in 1986, but the Reasonable Woman was not adopted as the standard of review for any court until 1991, when her adoption by the Ninth Circuit in *Ellison v. Brady* created something of a stir. Relying on the dissent to *Rabidue*, the *Ellison* Court held that the Reasonable Woman standard was more appropriate than the by-then customary 'Reasonable Person' standard derived from tort law (itself a replacement of the older 'Reasonable Man' standard) to determine whether behavior directed toward women creates a hostile work environment.

By 1994 and *Harris v. Forklift Systems*, the Reasonable Woman had been sighted (and cited) in most of the Federal Court districts. Her appearance, however, was modest and somewhat careless as she occasionally masqueraded as the Reasonable Person or the Reasonable Person of the Same Gender as the Victim. The Employment Law Center (a coalition of employment rights advocates) notes in a brief to the Supreme Court as it was considering the case of Theresa Harris that though 'the language varies slightly from circuit to circuit, the analysis is conceptually identical' (no page number). Numerous such briefs requested the Supreme Court to review the lower court holdings in *Harris*, especially the reliance in those holdings on the earlier *Rabidue* majority that had required plaintiffs to show 'serious psychological damage' in order to win their sexual harassment claims. A number of those briefs connected that review to the perspective to be adopted by the court in order to determine whether the work environment was hostile or abusive, arguing sometimes for the Reasonable Person standard, sometimes for the Reasonable Woman standard—as the brief of the Employment Law Center explains, the Reasonable Woman of the *Ellison* court is 'substantively identical' to the Reasonable Person of the court in *Andrews v. City of Philadelphia* (n.pag.). But the Supreme Court chose to explicitly review only the psychological damage requirement while invoking without discussion a Reasonable Person standard, requiring what it called 'an objectively hostile or abusive work environment—an environment that a reasonable person would find hostile or abusive' (21) for a determination of harassment. While both Justices Sandra O'Connor, who wrote the majority opinion, and Ruth Bader Ginsburg, who wrote a concurring opinion, find the Reasonable Person standard sufficient to do the work required of it, it is Justice Antonin Scalia who objects. Commenting in his concurring opinion that the words 'abusive' and 'hostile' do not provide 'a very clear standard' for judgment he concludes, 'and I do not think clarity is at all increased by adding the adverb "objectively" or by appealing to a "reasonable person['s]" notion of what the vague word means' (24).

While Justice Scalia certainly does not suggest the adoption of the Reasonable Woman standard as a means to achieving the clarity he seeks, she had nevertheless made her debut before the nation's highest court. She appears in quotations from the District Court's finding that some of the behaviors directed at Harris 'would offend the reasonable woman,' (14) and its ultimate conclusion that those behaviors 'would not drive a reasonable person, even a reasonable female manager, to quit' her job (21). The Reasonable Woman has thus worked her way into the language, however quaint the implications of the contrast of a female manager to a reasonable person may be. It remains to be seen, however, just who this Reasonable Woman presumably is. As the Employment Law Center explains, the Reasonable Woman is 'a theoretical construct, not an empirical derivation' (no page number). As such, she exists in what White might call the legal imagination; as such, she has appeared, perhaps in disguise, whenever judges have attempted to determine whether the empirical reality of any given woman's response to her circumstances is 'reasonable' and thus justifies a finding of sexual harassment. Even when the standard of reasonableness is clearly male, as in the *Rabidue* case, the complainant must be reasonable *as a woman*; thus Vivienne Rabidue, described by her employers as 'abrasive, rude, antagonistic, extremely willful, uncooperative, and irascible,' was hardly as compliant as both her employer and the court may have assumed a Reasonable Woman would be. The court's conclusion regarding her character puts it simply—she was, it concluded, 'a troublesome employee' (615). A more Reasonable Woman may have submitted to what Freud had earlier called the great exigencies of life rather than objecting to work conditions that, the court noted, merely duplicated larger social conditions. The 'sexually oriented poster displays' and 'obscenities' directed at Rabidue, 'although annoying,' said the court, 'were not so startling as to have affected seriously the psyches of the plaintiff or other female employees...when considered in the context of a society that condones and publicly features and commercially exploits open displays of written and pictorial erotica at the newsstands, on prime-time television, at the cinema, and in other public places' (616).

Where the *Rabidue* case attributes to a Reasonable Woman an assumed imperviousness to sexually exploitative circumstances, other cases have assumed a sensitivity that, when absent, can lead to a presumption of unreasonableness. Thus when Charlotte Staton, an ambulance dispatcher, filed a suit that claimed the county sheriff had made frequent sexual advances and eventually raped her, the court concluded that her ability to work for ten shifts after the 'act of intercourse' (998) meant either that the 'act' had not occurred or that she had been unreasonably undisturbed by it. While the implication is the former, the court states the latter, finding that whatever the nature of the 'act,' it had not interfered with her work sufficiently to qualify as sexual harassment (*Staton* 997-998). It was in the much milder case of Kerry Ellison that the Appeals Court justices assumed a Reasonable Woman would, like Ellison, be 'shocked and frightened,' 'really upset,' by a male coworker who stared longingly at her, constantly asked for dates that she constantly refused, and eventually sent her long letters in an attempt to 'maintain the idea that he and Ellison had some type of relationship' (875). Finally, it is in the District Court in *Harris*, a finding upheld by the Appeals Court before being reversed and remanded by the Supreme Court, that the court subjects the determination of reasonableness to a sort of mathematical average, noting that Harris, as a manager, was more sensitive than the other women in her office, none of whom were offended by the owner's 'sex based derogatory conduct' and 'jokes' (5-6). It is against these clerical employees that the magistrate measures Harris and based on their example he assumes that 'a reasonable woman,' even a 'reasonable female manager' would not have been seriously psychologically affected by her boss's behavior. This would be so even if, as a manager, she were more sensitive than those other women 'who, it appears,' he mused, 'were conditioned to accept denigrating treatment' (17). Were we to ask the question—'what's a Reasonable Woman to do?'—we would be hard-pressed on the basis of these examples to provide a satisfactory or even consistent answer.

Perhaps not coincidentally, however, Posner's Seventh Circuit is among the minority of Federal Districts that have not adopted a Reasonable Woman (or Reasonable Person of the Same Gender) standard for sexual harassment cases. Though he refers on three occasions in *Carr* to a 'reasonable person,' in the first instance it is to decide the question of factual error at the trial court level; in the next instance it is to determine whether GM had been negligent (1012) and, in the third, whether Carr could have claimed to have been constructively discharged (1011), a claim that is not at issue in the appeal before him. Indeed, Posner seems to invoke no standard at all as he considers whether the environment in which Carr worked was hostile, eventually determining that it was simply on the basis of his assessment that 'Carr's violent resentment of the conduct of her male coworkers toward her [was] plain' (1011). Yet his finding in her favor implies that he saw her behavior as reasonable—her claim that she behaved as she did in order to fit in with the other tinners was, he says, plausible (1011). But perhaps, rather than invoking no particular 'reasonableness' standard, Posner silently invokes a 'rationality' standard in the economic sense, a standard that is satisfied by the apparent maximization of utility or satisfaction. In that sense all the major players in *Carr* appear completely rational, whether we (or the court) can condone their actions or not. The tinners maximized their control over Carr and their domain at low cost and with little effort and obvious pleasure; Carr used the means at her disposal, however inadequate, to maximize her 'fit' with her coworkers; GM exerted minimal efforts to achieve a limited peace; the female welder, most efficient of all, maximized her personal space with a convenient and effective tool. In fact, there is no way in Posner's economic analysis to accuse any actions as irrational absent a showing of mental incompetence—and even actions in accordance with delusions could be 'rational' in the economic sense of the term. Posner's job as a judge is therefore not to determine whether any parties are rational—they all are—but to determine whether their automatically rational actions are disturbing the balance of the market in which they take place. Upon a finding of such a disturbance, the role of the judge is to impose a penalty that will cause the party deemed responsible to recalculate its costs and benefits and thus change its actions. There is no need for a Reasonable Woman in *Carr*, in other words, because everyone is Economic Man.

The situation could be seen otherwise, of course. Carr, rather than Economic Man, could be a plausible Literary Woman as West describes the person assumed by literary analysis in *Narrative, Authority and Law*. Where Economic Man, says West, 'relentlessly chooses what he prefers, prefers what he wants, wants what he desires, and desires what will maximize his subjective well-being'—in short, is 'perfectly rational' (252-3)—Literary Woman does not always know what is best for her and does not invariably seek it (254). Friendship (or 'community') with the tinners, then, might not have been what was 'best' for Carr. And if Economic Man suffers from a debilitating empathic impotence (253), utterly unable to comprehend any subjectivity other than his own, Literary Woman's empathic ability is 'truly Herculean' (257). While her empathic capacity does not make her unfailingly altruistic—West notes that she is 'at times masochistic, automatic, submissive, selfish, oppressive, and perhaps sadistic' (255)—she does desire connections with others, even seeking and tenaciously maintaining some connections that are harmful (*Caring for Justice* 2). We do not know whether Carr's desire for connection with the tinners was masochistic, but she did tenaciously pursue those connections beyond a point that could have been called beneficial. Finally, Literary Woman, says West, offers a moral promise, an urge for community that is the basis for our urge toward justice (*Narrative, Authority and Law* 262). In her later work, finding a model of Literary Woman in Gilligan's *In a Different Voice*, West uses that moral promise as the basis for a synthesis of justice and care. It is difficult to see much useful moral promise in Carr's search for community with the tinners, a search that, when it failed in the tinshop, wound up in court. Posner might well say that she misjudged the relative costs and benefits of her actions, perhaps in the absence of reliable information. Had he seen her as Literary Woman rather than Economic Man, might he have rewarded the moral promise she represented rather than punishing GM's 'market abuse'? If the Reasonable Woman became Literary Woman, would she still be reasonable?

To complicate matters just slightly: if the Reasonable Woman as Literary Woman becomes thereby unreasonable, might we save her rationality, if not her sanity, by making of her a Contrary Comprehended? After all it is this, says White, that the law does all the time, especially in judicial opinions like *Carr* that resolve the differences among disputing parties—in White's terminology by 'putting two things together in such a way as to make a third, a new thing with a meaning of its own' (*Justice as Translation* 263). In this sense both the judicial opinion (according to White) and the Reasonable Woman (for the time being) can be seen as a 'poem [that] comprises, brings together in one place and within one form, voices or feelings or languages (or facts or ideas or attitudes or wishes) that are normally not placed together and among which severe tensions or contradictions can be found' (*Heracles' Bow* 114). To the extent the 'poem' is able to provide 'a common place' for things that are 'in their own terms implacably opposed' it can be said to succeed; when those oppositions 'cannot be comprehended into one larger thing, with a form of its own' it can be said to fail (115). The imperative to comprehend the contraries, says White, is 'if anything even more plainly essential to the judicial opinion' than to the poem; the opinion relies upon the opposing stories of opposed parties presented at a hearing that by its nature 'places these meanings in contrast.' The opinion can therefore be judged excellent to the extent it recognizes and includes what is valuable in those opposed meanings; among the ways it may be judged deficient is by failing to comprehend the contraries in a coherent form or to include or sufficiently emphasize particular elements of those contraries (116). But its 'appealing neutrality,' White recognizes, is also a potential point of weakness, the danger that we may forget about the individual contrarieties—of our assumptions regarding the nature of 'reasonableness' and of 'woman'—and focus only on the presumed effects of their enchanting union. It is this weakness to which the Reasonable Woman is especially vulnerable, as those contraries go undiscussed and justices require widely varying levels of sensitivity, emotionality, and rationality of a Woman often deemed analogous to a Person, itself generally analogous to a Man (Ehrenreich 1178). Was Carr, then, a Reasonable Woman, a poem, a bundle of contraries comprehended in a 'larger thing, with a form of its own'? And is that comprehension by definition a success or a failure? The answer is that it depends upon whether we deem reasonable a woman's desire to work in a male environment—an abusive environment—and to make herself over in response to that environment. Might it have been more reasonable for Carr to 'zap' the tinners with a metaphoric welding arc, to create a separate space for herself, instead?

It is, in fact, a metaphoric capacity to which West attributes the empathic moral promise of Literary Woman, to her ability to '[gain] access to the other's subjective life' (*Narrative, Authority and Law* 258-9). But metaphor is not something the Reasonable Woman has—it is what she is, whether we believe she is better conceived as Economic Man, Literary Woman, or Contrary Comprehended. What we need to ask, then, is whether a metaphor can bear the burden of justice. And it is precisely this question that is not asked by Posner, West, or White, all of whom veer—in some cases purposely—away from the discussion of legal outcomes. While West is the most focused of the three on such outcomes, her Literary Woman cannot be depended upon to know her own best interests; her care, then, seems to extend more to others than to herself. What we are to attend to instead are those things the metaphor known as Literary Woman cannot say—but how are we to do that? Posner's answer is to look to her expectations, to determine whether it was reasonable or rational for Carr to expect to fit in with what all parties to the case describe as a vulgar group of men. If that expectation seems reasonable to us her attempt to do so remains the 'right' decision even given its obviously disastrous results, because neither those results nor Posner's ultimate holding in Carr's case constitute 'consequences' in his thought. No matter, though—because the 'rational' expectation yields the 'right' answer, Posner can find GM's expectation of an effortless peace in the tinshop irrational and, therefore, 'wrong.' Ultimately he is able to hold GM negligent in its failure to develop a policy for dealing with sexual harassment issues before they occurred, 'foreseeable though they are,' as he writes, 'when a woman is introduced into a formerly all-male workplace' (*Carr* 1012).

This diversion from the outcomes of legal cases appears also in White who, though far more optimistic than West (and more interested than Posner) regarding law's ability to do justice, admits that 'a kind of high-culture blindness' can mislead us into believing that 'sooner or later everything that really counts will be brought within the poems or the judicial opinions that we read' (*Heracles' Bow* 120-1). And while he devotes considerable attention to the question of what happens to 'the voices we do not hear in the texts that we read' (121) White cannot identify any reliable way to include them. Language simply cannot be made determinative or reliable enough to be applied in a manner that White calls 'theoretical in character [and] mechanically rational (or bureaucratic) in operation' (125). What he ultimately concludes is more important than judicial outcomes, which he calls 'merely substantive' (118), is that we are entitled 'not to "like results" but to "like process" (or "due process")' (134). What matters more than the result is how it is 'given meaning by the text'—as Posner has put it, the manner of the opinion's expression is more important than its content. For White that imperative is more clearly ethical than it is for Posner, though; 'the most important message is the one the judge performs, not the one he states' (117). Justice therefore lies in the right and opportunity to state one's case. Justice is enacted through that right and that right is enacted through language. Law's literally verbal nature—its reliance on verbs 'or more precisely upon the relation between actor and action that the normal English sentence expects'—corrects the mistakes of what White calls 'theory' which, in making 'seriously wrong assumptions about language, about knowledge, and about the reader...objectifies the world by nominalizing it' (125-7). The literary approach to law, in counteracting the theoretical assumption that words, like containers, simply carry 'bits of meaning, or information' (125) creates not only ambiguity but also the possibility that justifies its celebration. Outcomes, while important, are thus less directly related to justice as White sees it than the right to engage in the process that is law's language.

But can we not attend to both law's language *and* the outcomes it produces? In the next section I will suggest that White is on the right track; a Contrary Comprehended, reformulated just slightly as a point of rhetorical *stasis*, can push us from simply reading the 'poem' that is Reasonable Woman to reconceiving her meter and verse. In particular, I will argue that this 'rhetorical figure' of Woman is the truer oxymoron—at least in the language of law—than the 'welcome harassment' Posner identifies as such in *Carr*. I will do so by turning once more to Aristotle's four causes and an interrogation of the efficiency, materiality, formality, and finality of law.

Limitations, Limits, and the Things We Value

Before I turn to the four causes and to the place of language, law, and justice within them, an admission of sorts is in order.

There's a saying whose origins I have not heard identified, but which surfaces in informal rhetorical discussions from time to time. I suspect it has been borrowed from the engineering profession, or from one of the construction crafts that, as we have seen, were 'arts' in roughly the same sense that Aristotle claimed for rhetoric itself. The saying goes roughly like this: if the only tool you have is a hammer, every problem you see will look like a nail. This adage is true, I contend, not only for those who believe or claim that language is (or should be) a tool, but for every approach to language. Thus, if for Posner every problem is at base economic, it is also true that my orientation toward language persuades me that legal problems are rhetorical problems, amenable to understanding and amelioration, if not outright correction, through rhetorical means. This position requires that I answer the obvious questions: what does 'rhetorical' mean and what, therefore, are 'rhetorical means'? I confess to enjoying the multi-layered puns in these questions, an enjoyment that points to one aspect of 'the rhetorical'—'the rhetorical' takes pleasure in the meaning, significance, and use of language. But that statement cannot serve as a definition of the rhetorical, smacking as it does of 'the literary' that I have claimed is insufficient for a more deeply and productively rhetorical perspective on law. So let me repeat the definitions of rhetoric that I provided in Chapter 1 before I move to use 'rhetorical means' to approach the skittish Reasonable Woman: 'the rhetorical' means a perspective on language that is conscious of itself *as such*; in my expanded definition, rhetoric is a conscious perspective on language that sees it as a means not of interpretation but of the production of a broad range of 'texts.' Rhetoric is therefore not synonymous with language; nor is it a particular kind of language, nor does it establish any fixed or determinate relationship with language that is uniform across all methods or perspectives that can plausibly be claimed as 'rhetorical.' And it is certainly not (with a nod to Fish) a perspective on language that, by becoming conscious of its own assumptions, can escape them. Rhetoric as I understand and use it here takes language as its subject matter, and insists thereby that this subject matter provides it with more than a method—language provides rhetoric with a substantive 'content,' a 'material' cause in Aristotle's terminology, that issues in substantial 'final' causes, in very real effects in human life and community.

Posner, White, and West therefore all engage in 'the rhetorical' from time to time and to varying degrees, to the extent that they consciously deal with the meaning and effects of language. In a more limited sense, of course, we might say that all humans are engaged in 'the rhetorical' whenever they 'use' language, or any other system of signs, to persuade, communicate, or exert some kind of control over their circumstances. As my definition above suggests, however, I intend to restrict 'the rhetorical' to a more limited sense so that we may examine how consciousness of oneself as a being who may use, abuse, or even be used (or abused) by language affects how one understands the relationship of law, through language, to justice. A short review of the four causes Aristotle identifies and discusses in the *Metaphysics* is therefore in order.

You will recall that those causes include the efficient (more literally, 'source of motion'), the material ('matter'), the formal ('pattern'), and the final ('end'). To begin with concrete examples both natural and artificial, we might say that the efficient cause of a tree is nature and of a house an architect or builder. Their material, formal, and final causes might be, respectively, sunlight, soil, water—and bricks; leaves, branches—and floor plans; shade, shelter—and shelter. Note that I have said 'might,' for the variations possible on these themes seem nearly endless. The final cause of the tree might well be the production of carbon dioxide or the prevention of soil erosion, while the final cause of the house might be the creation of a family 'unit.' There are even meaningful senses, invoked by Aristotle himself, in which the source of both tree and house could be 'tree' and 'house': that which has matter, he says, 'comes from that which has not,' from its 'form' or 'essence' (*Metaphysics* VII.VII.6). Though the variations are not entirely arbitrary, they are dependent on our perceptions and purposes in a sense that I believe is quite valid. Here I no doubt disagree with Aristotle, who becomes curmudgeonly as he discusses those, such as I, who believe 'that there is truth in appearances' (IV.V.7). Defining 'truth' as that which appears to the percipient, such people finally come to the position that 'nothing has happened or will happen unless someone has first formed an opinion about it' (IV.VI.8). While I enjoy Aristotle's exasperation, I maintain my ground; things do happen outside our opinions, but our 'opinions' (Aristotle has somewhat unfairly substituted *doxa* for *aisthesis*, perceptions) lead to 'appearances'—the *phainomena* that Nussbaum points out are grounded in 'things we say' (*Fragility of Goodness* 240)—that are determinative of the purposes and relationships we posit for things as natural as trees and as artificial as houses and language. Are the causes as few (or as many?) as four? (Heidegger also asks this question [6].) And if so, must these causes be the four Aristotle identified? I'll take the risk of infuriating Aristotle and Aristotelians and saying that it doesn't matter. What does matter is the heuristic value of the structure (the formal cause) and the relationships it allows us to envision, vary, and question.

So where might language, law, and justice fit into the causal structure Aristotle provides? As almost always, the rhetorical answer to the non-rhetorical question is that it depends, in this case upon one's beliefs about the nature of each element. Because language is my particular interest (the problem looks like a rhetorical nail to me) allow me to take out my rhetorical hammer and build a structure from which law and justice are temporarily absent, a structure that is particularly popular in discussions about law from both 'positivist' and 'realist' perspectives and in which language functions as a nearly literal 'tool.' In this rather simple 'tool-use' theory, language functions as the efficient cause, the source of motion that hammers the material 'data' of legal or physical realities into a recognizable form, a text with the end of speaking the truth, or as close as it can get to the truth, about the data. In the purest tool-use theory, the hand that wields the hammer—the speaker or writer—remains non-existent or at least covert, maintaining 'objectivity' through a refusal to consider its own subjectivity. A close correlate of this theory is what has been called variously the 'mirror' or 'windowpane' (following George Orwell's 'Politics and the English Language') theory. Here the writer or speaker appears, but simply as an observer (a 'theorist' in the classical sense) who must either peer through a window or at a mirror for the reality of legal or material data or their reflection; language, seen as a more or less dirty window or smudged mirror, is a formal structure with the goal of enabling not access but at least a valid perspective on truth. This goal may be disabled as well as enabled, however; careless speakers and writers don't wash windows.

We can plausibly fit Posner's thought into either one of these structures, depending upon the work, its purpose, or his mood. Consider the tool-use theory: the judge (or at least his subjectivity, which is my working definition of his reasoning processes) remains covert; wielding the tool of his language, he creates a formal structure that fashions out of the materials of reality a (temporary, unless and until overturned) legal truth. Or consider the windowpane theory: peering through the smudged window of the narrative claims of the parties to the dispute, the judge determines the reality, or what will count for it, of their situations and then frames a window onto his own thought in the 'truth' of the opinion that the language of his holding either presents to view or attempts to hide. In both of these theories, the perspective on truth is openly skeptical and pragmatic; legal language, unlike what the early Posner called a 'people's' language or a 'traditional language' does not function like a free market, is not 'an immensely complicated yet private and decentralized institution,' free of legislature and bureaucracy and of prescriptions regarding its form, structure, or vocabulary ('Blackstone and Bentham' 603). Such a language belongs only to individuals; when it comes to legal language numerous professional and community strictures apply. The tool and windowpane theories, both of which Posner holds, ironically rule justice out of bounds in the context of law. The parties to the dispute, through their accounts and available texts such as contracts or, as in *Carr*, unread policy statements and unwatched training videos, provide an imperfect glimpse into the realities of their situations. The judge then wields the hammer—or, if he is Oliver Wendell Holmes, a more delicate tool—to pound out (Holmes: carve out) a decision that succeeds to the extent it is believed, obeyed, and upheld, not to the extent it is either 'right' or 'good,' neither of which is determinable. Law is not an element in this structure; neither are rightness, goodness, or justice itself. They are all mental or metaphysical entities for which no place can be made when one sees through a mirror, darkly.

West expresses no real language theory in *Narrative, Authority and Law*, where her faith is placed not in language itself but in its formulation into the 'stories' that she believes go farther toward revealing its nature than what she calls its 'content,' its history, politics, and economics (346). And while she does not posit a fully articulated language theory in *Caring for Justice*, it is clear that she has begun to place the blame for law's inadequacy on its language, whether assembled into stories or considered more abstractly as an entity in itself. If because of its 'verbose' nature law carries with it 'inevitably the potential for its own misuse' (192), agency, roughly equivalent to the efficient cause, seems to reside either in language or, because of its use of language, law itself. At least we have gotten law into the structure; if agency resides in language then law provides either the material cause (what language talks about) or the formal (how it can talk about it). If agency resides in law itself, then language may be either the formal structure through which law manifests or the material from which legal texts may be fashioned. Either way the process is tainted, given West's implicit assumptions about form and matter; the form renders impossible authentic accounts from women of their experiences because the matter (the literary or legal canon) demands only traditionally patriarchal forms. Justice, even synthesized with care, remains silent. As Hart explained in 1958, 'the facts and phenomena to which we fit our words and apply our rules are as it were *dumb*' (607, emphasis in original). Where Hart suggests that the decision-maker must then 'take the responsibility of deciding that words do or do not cover some case in hand' West suggests that the judge listen to the silences.

But what if language were to be matter in its Aristotelian sense, in the sense in which White sometimes speaks of it, as 'the living material from which meaning is made' (*Heracles' Bow* 126)? With White's conception of language as neither the efficient nor formal cause, but as the material, we approach a more nearly classical rhetorical theory of language. If that is so, then a more significant agency must be acknowledged as residing in the efficient cause; the judge or other legal speaker and writer enters the structure accompanied by a frank acknowledgment of subjectivity with all its problems and promise. If we exclude law and justice, just for the moment, from this analysis of the materiality of language the formal cause may then become the structure provided by traditional or professional genres, what rhetorical theorist Carolyn R. Miller has called 'typified rhetorical action' (151). Governing not only the form that a final written or spoken product can take but also the perceptive and intellectual process by which significant and insignificant 'data' are identified, professional genres represent the investigation that created them as much as the decisions they report (Rude 178-80).

What, then, of the final cause? As Aristotle said of productive processes in general, the final cause exists outside the process itself. It cannot be the literal product—whether we are speaking of houses or texts—because the product has provided the governing structure and thus the formal cause. Speaking of houses and other traditional, concrete products Aristotle explained that the judge of their excellence would not be the 'experts' who produced them but those who used them; thus the value of a house would be the judgment of the householder to make (*Politics* III.VI.10) while the value (or 'effects') of a lecture or speech would depend upon its listeners (*Metaphysics* II.III.1). Understanding the final cause in this manner, we might then characterize the four causes, imported into law, like this: the efficient cause, the source of motion (and literal legal 'motions') might be a problem conceived by parties to the situation as 'legal' or amenable to legal solution; the material cause, language, provides the element in which the motion may be made manifest and intelligible to those empowered to decide the issue; the formal cause may be provided by law itself through its structure of rules, conventions, precedent, and argumentative traditions; the final cause, the 'use' of the legal outcome itself, is the 'justice' that it does, however justice itself may be defined or understood. Once again, however, I have said 'might.' We might just as easily, for example, identify the efficient cause as 'law' itself, a mental entity that, providing the hammer, encourages citizens in a litigious society such as Athens or ours to see problems as specifically 'legal' nails. If we construct the causal system in such a way as to identify law as the source of legal motion, do we need to remove it from its place as the formal cause as well? Did we say there had to be four causes, no more and no less, with no duplication? Of course we did not, and there are compelling reasons to place 'law' in both the efficient and formal slots in the causal structure. Further, Aristotle's complex discussion and not entirely consistent vocabulary excuse our taking such liberties.

You will recall from Chapter 4 that there is an interesting linguistic connection between efficient and formal causes, between tools and the limits they are able to both create and dismantle or transgress. The 'limit,' which can be rendered in the classical Greek as both *peirata* and *peras* and is called by Aristotle in the *Metaphysics* both *peras* and *telos*, creates what Detienne and Vernant have called 'an organization of space' (288) that is, says Aristotle, the 'reality or essence' of a thing; the 'limit of our knowledge' of the thing is thus for Aristotle, at least in the context of the *Metaphysics*, 'a limit of the thing' itself (*Metaphysics* V.XVII.2). It is through the formal cause, then, 'that we recognize everything' (*Metaphysics* IV.V.21). But by organizing its space the limit (*peras*) does not make only the thing itself visible; it also makes visible the *peirata*, perhaps the 'tools' that, as its source of motion, created the thing (Atwill *Rhetoric Reclaimed* 47) but perhaps also the 'tip or end' of the limit itself (Detienne and Vernant 293). If we conceive law as both the efficient and formal causes in our rhetorical theory of its language, it then becomes both *peras* and *peirata*, the source of legal motion, the form legal arguments must take, and the potential means by which such arguments—and through them, legal forms themselves—may be both forged and undone. Recall now the compatibility of any *techné* with 'failure,' a compatibility that Roochnik attributes to the 'limits determined by the nature of its subject matter' (50). To avoid confusion, let us remember that Roochnik is speaking here of the 'limitations' of the material rather than of the 'limits' of which we speak, tools and boundaries (and their unraveling). Aristotle, acknowledging that matter 'admits of variation from the usual,' saw that variability as the cause of what Tredennick translates as the 'accidental.' But here Aristotle uses not *tuché* (literally 'chance') but *sumbebékos*, the 'incidental' or 'coincidental;' thus it is by coincidence, and not by art, that a confectioner might produce a healthy food (*Metaphysics* VI.II.6-9). Matter, absent art, can indeed produce the unexpected; nevertheless it is through the variations that Aristotle understood not as failures but as voluntary error that art produces its results—because, as he explained, 'artists...know the cause' (I.I.11). Excellence in *techné* is a result of the 'artist's' ability to respond sensitively—and sometimes fortuitously—to the materials with which she must work. In art the 'end' is 'a limit (*peras*)'—not a limitation, but a tool (II.II.10).

With 'law' as both efficient and formal causes, as the source of motion for legal problems and the structure that dictates the form of their solutions, language can be seen as a material cause that exerts influence on and/or exercises resistance to the motion and the structure. Philosopher Carl Mitcham claims Aristotle saw language as a manipulable matter, 'as pure, lifeless extension, in itself ordered toward nothing, something to do with as one pleases' (133); it is this attitude that underlies Posner's statement that rhetoric is of a 'ready-made' character, that the rhetorician, no discoverer, 'works with the materials he is given' (*Overcoming Law* 528). But I suggest that to think rhetorically in any meaningful sense requires us to think of language as a material like any other in Aristotle's thought; such matter resists the imposition of form, requiring the artist to 'let the matter guide the way;' it is in this sense, Mitcham explains, that Aristotle says matter desires or reaches out for form (122, citing *Physics* 1.9.192). To return to our specific legal problem, the creation of the Reasonable Woman to address the issues surrounding sexual harassment, we can see the four causes simultaneously invoked and rejected by those who refer to sexual harassment as an invention of feminists (O'Beirne 20) who made of it a legal problem with a specifically legal solution. Insisting on the creation through the efficiency of the judicial process of a legal 'problem' that can then be solved through application of a formal legal structure, the Civil Rights Act, legal scholar and advocate Catherine A. MacKinnon both co-operated with the 'desire' of legal language to take on a recognizable form and stretched the boundaries of the form to incorporate into it a new form with a life of its own—the 'sexual harassment' that, while theoretically actionable since the inclusion of the word 'sex' in the Civil Rights Act in 1964, had been ignored.

I have said that White is on the right track in providing us with a possible identification of the Reasonable Woman as a Contrary Comprehended, what I prefer to see as a point of rhetorical *stasis*. I have also earlier, in Chapter 5, aligned the four questions of *stasis* with the four causes, seeing in the factual issue the cause of efficiency, the source of (legal) motion in an event admitted to have occurred—what I have been calling here the legal problem. Whatever the social, psychological, or emotional problems attributed to Carr by both the District and Appeals Courts (and it is interesting that no such 'problems' are attributed to the 'vulgar' tinners) the legal problem is the demonstrated fact that she was unable to perform the work required by her position as an apprentice in the tinshop. In the definitional and jurisdictional issues I have seen the formal cause, a determination of the event's 'type' in specific laws and legal venues, in the Civil Rights Act and the Federal Courts. It is only if the behavior of the tinners toward Carr can be defined as 'sexual harassment,' and if that determination is made by the appropriate authorities, that she can be entitled to a legal solution to the admittedly legal problem. Finally, the qualitative issue functions as the material cause, providing the means for evaluating the nature and extent of the act through the language that characterizes it. It is in this location that the arguments are concentrated in *Carr*, because the definition of sexual harassment carries qualitative assessments. And it is in the difficult process of making those qualitative assessments that the Reasonable Woman is conceived and born, the union of contrary elements that exemplifies the literal tension of *stasis*, the dynamic point at which opposing or contrary forces meet. Because of the association of reasonableness with custom and its consequent naturalization (Whitman 1349) and thus with a specifically male tradition (Ehrenreich 1178) for centuries prior to its association with the female (specifically, Kerry Ellison) in 1991, the Reasonable Woman becomes a legal oxymoron, an association of the male with the female that should be fertile ground. To the extent the contraries of reason (seen as male custom) and woman are comprehended and made coherent in a tidy unitary form, this ground lies fallow; to the extent the tension of their association is recognized and questioned, the 'error' of the union is rhetorically productive. It is for the same reason that the apparent tension between welcomeness and harassment, a tension Posner calls oxymoronic, is also fertile; through numerous judicial decisions including that of the Supreme Court in *Meritor Savings Bank v. Vinson* in 1986 (in a provision the Court has not reconsidered) 'harassment' can be legally shown to be 'welcome' by way of reference to such factors as a complainant's 'sexually provocative speech and dress' (69). 'Welcome harassment,' then, as the dissent argues in *Carr*, is not an oxymoron at all—at least not in the context of law.

It is in the final cause, or 'end' of the process, that the legal outcome is located and in which justice, however we understand it, resides. If the legal forms known as the Reasonable Woman and Welcome Harassment are seen solely as literary texts, the literary penchant urged by Posner and White is such that they will be rendered coherent through the vision of their limits strictly as boundaries that enclose the unitary whole. Among literary perspectives, it is the deconstructive tendency to look for fissures in the text (a tendency that Posner, White, West, and Nussbaum have all rejected) that may reveal that the coherence is an illusion. But if we seek not only to read texts but to create them, in the tension between the terms of these legal forms we may see not only the boundaries but the end of the rope that creates them, the *peirata* as well as the *peras*. As MacKinnon demonstrated with what was arguably a phantom, sexual harassment itself, careful—or perhaps just insistent—tugging on that limit will allow the union to unravel sufficiently to be seen as a union rather than as a single and 'coherent' entity. In other words, what if 'we,' understood as rhetorical advocates for women who find themselves in the workplace-as-tinshop, were to insist that the courts take responsibility for their creation of a reality known as 'welcome harassment?' What if Carr were to be seen not as the metonym she was in the tinshop—reduced to the walking female body part known as 'Cunt'—but as a reasonable conjunction of contrary elements and desires, one of which was to forge a place for herself in a community through adoption of its language? What if Posner were to find the theft of her language as serious as that of her more literal tools, to understand that the tinners' use of language was in fact a misuse of their 'tools' to violate the limits of her emotional and physical space? What if the Reasonable Woman were not simply a metaphor? What if she were real?

Certainly, the role of language in determining beliefs about the relationship of law to justice is real. Beliefs such as West's, that methods of legal reasoning and analysis should address legal reform and the silenced voices of legal subjects, assume that law exists in a necessary relationship to justice—whether law is to be relatively passive, merely carrying out the dictates of justice, or whether it is to take on an active, creative role in defining what justice itself is. The position of Posner that legal analysis should remain separate from evaluative questions maintains that law may be held conceptually distinct from justice or at least that the nature of the law-justice relationship is not a critical component of legal analysis—law's content may be held as analytically distinct from its method. Law's relationship to justice must be mediated through language; if law is a language, as White maintains, then law speaks and justice listens. In a more moderate version justice speaks and law listens; just as law is a tool of justice, so is language a tool of law. Law works with or through its language, a more or less capable tool in the more or less capable hands of legal speakers and writers who endeavor to bring about a justice that has been agreed upon (or not) previously and through other means. In the most conservative formulation of these relationships justice may or may not speak—law itself isn't listening. The necessity of language to legal analysis is unfortunate, and the best analysis sees through or gets around law's language which, like a windowpane or mirror, should provide a perspective on justice or a reflection of it with as little distortion as possible. Law, it seems, should do the same for justice.

Each such theory in its own way responds to the most potentially radical hypothesis, that law *is* language, whether the response takes the form of celebration or fear, of an attempt to tame law's language or an attempt to defeat it. The result of the positive response to the radical thesis is not, however, necessarily legal radicalism. For White, law's existing language enables statements that make claims for their own rightness (*Acts of Hope: Creating Authority in Literature, Law, and Politics* xi) and thus allows legal speakers to 'imagin[e] an ideal into partial reality' (Ibid 307). Law's declarations, then, are acts of hope and faith in the legal system we now have and its ability to respond to the ethical imperatives of justice. The closest of our three major figures to come to legal radicalism, West, sees law's language as an obstruction of justice that law must see through, get around, or avoid. Her answer to the language question is that law should, on occasion, not speak at all. Posner, by far the most conservative of the three despite his libertarianism, takes first the skeptical position—that unreliable language must be leveraged with the cost of rhetoric to achieve results that may or may not correspond to justice—and then the hyper-rational position, the assumption that the two contrary terms of an oxymoron—'welcome harassment'—are by reason of their very contradiction an existential impossibility and thus to be judicially dismissed.

The messages that workers, both men and women, receive from the environments in which they work are real, persistent, and persuasive. As the Employment Law Center's brief in *Harris v. Forklift Systems* said about the 'pornographic displays' in her workplace, '[the] message flows from the wall of the workplace into the heart of it' (no page number). We have the opportunity not simply to read those messages but to revise them or substitute others. Recent work in rhetorical theory encourages us to seize those opportunities through its investigation into the implications of Aristotle's identification of rhetoric as a *techné*. Janet M. Atwill notes that Aristotle clearly states the implications of his position in the *Rhetoric*: the end of that particular *techné* lies in its hearers (*Rhetoric Reclaimed* 87; *Rhetoric* I.III.1). In arts as diverse as those of architecture, shipbuilding, technical communication, and rhetoric Robert R. Johnson points to the ethical imperative built into *techné*'s external ends and concludes that the end of the user-centered theory he advocates 'is only complete when coupled with the end of social action' (156). Furthermore, as he notes, the link to social action is brought about by and through language, 'a force that, like fire, can be used for burning, but [that] can also burn those who use it' (18). When understood as power, as a function that can persuade and control, language 'is altered from a relatively neutral activity to an activity charged with opinion and controversy.' With its usefulness, then, comes a social responsibility that, '[s]ince the time of the ancient Greeks…has been the disciplinary domain of rhetoric,' a domain that is in 'intimate contact with the social, ethical, and moral dimensions of language' (19). We have already seen the emphasis on the ethical imperative of use in Roochnik's analysis of the ends of *techné* (31); that imperative is apparent in the term Aristotle uses to describe rhetoric and that is translated into English, somewhat inadequately, as 'useful.' Rhetoric is *chreisimos*, Aristotle says, and thus among the *chreimata*, or 'valuable things' that we need or use, including goods, property, or even money. As Atwill explains, '*chreimata* only denotes "things" in relation to their value either to individuals…or in a system of exchange' (138). Rhetoric is *chreisimos*—useful and valuable—because by definition it brings individuals into a system of social exchange.

Rhetoric thus understood can equip us to seize the opportunities and carry out our revisions not in the amoral, ready-made fashion envisioned by Posner but with an awareness of our ethical positions and goals and the ability to work toward them—not, perhaps, in straight-line fashion but through a process of trial and, yes, error. Perhaps in this context the error can somewhat paradoxically come first, as we question the limitations of legal and workplace discourse by straining against and with its limits. 'The things we say' are important—indeed, they are crucial—because they often dictate the things we do and both create and inspire the things we make. All three lead us inexorably from, and inevitably to, the things we value.

Appendix

Carr v. Allison Gas Turbine Division

MARY J. CARR, Plaintiff-Appellant, v. ALLISON GAS TURBINE DIVISION, GENERAL MOTORS CORPORATION, Defendant-Appellee.

No. 93-2338

UNITED STATES COURT OF APPEALS FOR THE SEVENTH CIRCUIT

32 F.3d 1007; 1994 U.S. App. LEXIS 19091; 65 Fair Empl. Prac. Cas. (BNA) 688; 65 Empl. Prac. Dec. (CCH) P43,211

February 22, 1994, Argued
July 26, 1994, Decided

PRIOR HISTORY:
Appeal from the United States District Court for the Southern District of Indiana, Indianapolis Division. No. 89 C 1107. Larry J. McKinney, Judge.

DISPOSITION:
REVERSED AND REMANDED.

COUNSEL:

For MARY J. CARR, Plaintiff - Appellant: Lester H. Cohen, John H. Haskin, HASKIN & ASSOCIATES, Indianapolis, IN, Brenda Franklin Rodeheffer, Indianapolis, IN.

For ALLISON GAS TURBINE DIVISION, GENERAL MOTORS CORPORATION, Defendant -
Appellee: Wendell R. Tucker, BAKER & DANIELS, Indianapolis, IN.

JUDGES:
Before POSNER, Chief Judge, and COFFEY and ROVNER, Circuit Judges.

OPINION BY:
POSNER

OPINION:

[*1008] POSNER, Chief Judge. Mary Carr brought suit under Title VII of the Civil Rights Act of 1964, 42 U.S.C. @@ 2000e et seq., against her former employer, a division of General Motors, charging sexual harassment and seeking backpay and other relief. After a bench trial, the district judge rendered judgment for General Motors. Apparently fearful that the clear-error standard which governs our review of findings of fact and applications of rules to fact imposes an insuperable burden on an appellant, Carr's lawyer strained to persuade us at oral argument that the district court's opinion is infected by legal error, and specifically by a failure to have anticipated a decision by the Supreme Court handed down after he wrote his opinion. Harris v. Forklift Systems, Inc., 126 L. Ed. 2d 295, 114 S. Ct. 367 (1993). Such an approach is needlessly defensive, for despite colorful language in some decisions, e.g., Parts & Electric Motors, Inc. v. Sterling Electric, Inc., 866 F.2d 228, 233 (7th Cir. 1988); United States v. Markling, 7 F.3d 1309, 1319 (7th Cir. 1993), it is not true that the clear-error standard imposes an insuperable burden on appellants. Santa Fe Pacific Corp. v. Central States, Southeast & Southwest Areas Pension Fund, 22 F.3d 725, 727-28 (7th Cir. 1994). It requires us appellate judges to distinguish between the situation in which we think that if we had been the trier of fact we would have decided the case differently and the situation in which we are firmly convinced that we would have done so. Concrete Pipe & Products of California, Inc. v. Construction Laborers Pension Trust, 124 L. Ed. 2d 539, 113 S. Ct. 2264, 2279-80 (1993); Anderson v. City of Bessemer City, 470 U.S. 564, 573-75, 84 L. Ed. 2d 518, 105 S. Ct. 1504 (1985). Our scrutiny of the district judge's findings of fact thus is deferential, but it is not abject. As the Supreme Court pointed out in the Concrete Pipe case, we need not, to overturn a finding under the clear-error standard, adjudge the finding 'so unlikely that no reasonable person would find it to be true.' 113 S. Ct. at 2280.

The district judge believed that in a case such as this in which the harassment is by coworkers rather than by supervisors, the principal questions to be answered are whether the plaintiff was in fact sexually harassed to a degree that could be said to affect adversely the conditions under which she worked, whether it was unwelcome harassment, and whether management knew or should have known about the harassment yet failed to take appropriate remedial action. The only exceptional entry in this catalog is the question about unwelcomeness. 'Welcome sexual harassment' is an oxymoron; if as we concluded in Reed v. Shepard, 939 F.2d 484, 486-87 (7th Cir. 1991), the employee demonstrates by word or deed that [*1009] the 'harassment' is welcome (the plaintiff in that case had instigated sexual pranks—for example, had given one of her male coworkers a softball warmer designed to resemble a scrotum), it is not harassment. So there really are only two questions in a case such as this. The first is whether the plaintiff was, because of her sex, subjected to such hostile, intimidating, or degrading behavior, verbal or nonverbal, as to affect adversely the conditions under which she worked; for Title VII is not directed against unpleasantness per se but only, so far as relates to this case, against discrimination in the conditions of employment.

Harris v. Forklift Systems, Inc., supra, 114 S. Ct. at 371; Meritor Savings Bank v. Vinson, 477 U.S. 57, 91 L. Ed. 2d 49, 106 S. Ct. 2399 (1986). The second question is whether, if so, the defendant's response or lack thereof to its employees' behavior was negligent. Saxton v. American Telephone & Telegraph Co., 10 F.3d 526, 535-36 (7th Cir. 1993); Juarez v. Ameritech Mobile Communications, Inc., 957 F.2d 317, 320-21 (7th Cir. 1992); Guess v. Bethlehem Steel Corp., 913 F.2d 463 (7th Cir. 1990). It would be unrealistic to expect management to be aware of every impropriety committed by every low-level employee. But if it knows or should have known that one of its female employees is being harassed, yet it responds ineffectually, it is culpable. The two questions, harassment of the employee and negligence of the employer, are linked as a practical matter because the greater the harassment—the more protracted or egregious, as distinct from isolated (as in Weiss v. Coca-Cola Bottling Co., 990 F.2d 333, 337 (7th Cir. 1993), and King v. Board of Regents, 898 F.2d 533, 537 (7th Cir. 1990)) or ambiguous, it is—the likelier is the employer to know about it or to be blameworthy for failing to discover it.

The district judge did not formulate the legal standard in precisely these terms but he was close enough that we cannot find any error of law. If there was any error it was in the application of the legal standard to the facts, facts that we must treat as largely undisputed because the district judge believed the testimony of Carr and her witnesses and disbelieved the defendant's testimony where it differed from the plaintiff's. Disputes over the application of an agreed legal standard to the facts are just as much subject to the clear-error standard as disputes over the facts themselves (see Daniels v. Essex Group, Inc., 937 F.2d 1264, 1269-70 (7th Cir. 1991), so holding with specific reference to discrimination), but we think there was clear error and point out that when the issue is whether the law was properly applied to the facts, questions of credibility, the resolution of which is rarely subject to effective appellate review, Anderson v. City of Bessemer City, supra, 470 U.S. at 575; Winchester Packaging, Inc. v. Mobil Chemical Co., 14 F.3d 316, 319 (7th Cir. 1994), drop out. Insofar as there are credibility issues in this case, the district judge resolved them, as we have said, in favor of Carr. We are not entitled to reopen those issues, though invited by GM, in its brief and at argument, to do so.

Carr was a drill operator in GM's gas turbine division when, in August 1984, she entered the skilled trades in the division as a tinsmith apprentice. She was the first woman to work in the tinsmith shop, and her male coworkers were unhappy about working with a woman. They made derogatory comments of a sexual character to her on a daily basis (such as, 'I won't work with any cunt'), continually referred to her in her presence by such terms as 'whore,' 'cunt,' and 'split tail,' painted 'cunt' on her toolbox, and played various sex-or gender-related pranks on her, such as painting her toolbox pink and (without her knowledge) cutting out the seat of her overalls. They festooned her tool box and work area with signs, pictures, and graffitti [sic] of an offensive sexual character, hid and stole her tools, hid her toolbox, hung nude pin-ups around the shop, and would strip to their underwear in front of her when changing into and out of their work clothes. One of them placed an obscene Valentine Day's card, addressed to 'Cunt,' on her toolbox.

The card shows a man carrying a naked woman upside down, and the text explains that the man has finally discovered why a woman has two holes—so that she can be carried like a six-pack. A worker named Beckham twice exhibited his penis. The first time, during an argument in which Carr told [*1010] him the exit door 'swings both ways,' meaning that he could leave just as easily as she could, he replied that he had something that 'swings,' and he demonstrated. The second time, another male worker bet Beckham $5 that he would not expose himself. He lost the bet, although it is unclear whether Carr was in front of Beckham or behind him. And it was Beckham who told Carr on another occasion that if he fell from a dangerous height in the shop she would have to give him 'mouth to dick' resuscitation. Carr's male coworkers urinated from the roof of the shop in her presence, and, in her hearing, one of them accused a black employee who was only intermittently hostile to Carr of being 'after that white pussy, that is why you want a woman here, you want some of that.' A number of racist remarks and practical jokes of a racial nature were directed against this, the only black employee among the tinsmiths. A frequent remark heard around the shop was, 'I'll never retire from this tinsmith position because it would make an opening for a nigger or a woman.' Another of Carr's male coworkers threw a burning cigarette at her.

At first she disregarded the harassment but beginning in 1985 and continuing until 1989, when she quit—constructively discharged, she contends, the situation having become unbearable—she complained about the harassment repeatedly to her immediate supervisor, Jim Routh. To no avail. He testified that even though some of the offensive statements were made in his presence, not being a woman himself he was not sure that the statements would be considered offensive by a woman. His perplexity was such that when he heard the statements he would just chuckle and bite down harder on his pipe.

The district judge rejected the company's argument that the words and conduct that we have described were mere vulgar pleasantries, what is euphemistically known as 'shop talk.' Workers, like other people, often are foul-mouthed (Beckham was clocked using the word 'fuck' between 50 and 60 times in a period of ten minutes), and while there are still people in this country, male as well as female, who are deeply offended by dirty words, employers are not under a legal duty enforceable by suits under Title VII to purify the language of the workplace. Rabidue v. Osceola Refining Co., 805 F.2d 611, 620-21 (6th Cir. 1986); Ebert v. Lamar Truck Plaza, 878 F.2d 338, 339 (10th Cir. 1989). Yet there are gradations even here, and the district judge was surely correct that the words and deeds of Mary Carr's male coworkers crossed the line that separates the merely vulgar and mildly offensive from the deeply offensive and sexually harassing. For one thing, the words and acts of which she complains were, unlike what may have been the situation in Sauers v. Salt Lake County, 1 F.3d 1122, 1127 (10th Cir. 1993), targeted on her, and it is a lot more uncomfortable to be the target of offensive words and conduct than to be merely an observer of them. Patricia J. Williams, The Alchemy of Race and Rights: Diary of a Law Professor 129 (1991). For another thing, defacing a person's property (even if it is hers just to use while at work) and mutilating her clothing (even if it is hers just to wear while at work) are more ominous, more aggressive affronts than mere words.

So the behavior of Carr's coworkers was harassing, yet the district judge concluded that it was not actionable, because it had been 'invited.' 'She was not merely the recipient of crude behavior and crude language—she also dished it out.' A female welder, who worked in proximity to the tinsmiths, considered Carr vulgar and unladylike, a 'tramp,' because she used the 'F word' and told dirty jokes. This woman further testified that she herself had no trouble with the men in the shop—though occasionally she did have to zap them with her welding arc to fend them off. Carr indeed used such terms as 'fuck head' and 'dick head,' once placed her hand on the thigh of a young male worker, and, when shown a pornographic picture and asked to point out the clitoris, obliged. Once when her tool bench was moved (apparently not with hostile intent), she got into a shouting match with her coworkers. General Motors' brief describes her as 'vulgar, confrontational, profane, lazy and vindictive.' The district judge said that 'she contributed just as much abusive language and crude behavior as did the male [*1011] tinners, and therefore was just as responsible for any hostile sexual environment that consequently arose.' 'The tinners' conduct, to the extent it may have constituted sexual harassment, was not unwelcome.'

Of course it was unwelcome. A plaintiff's words, deeds, and deportment can cast light on whether her coworkers' treatment of her was unwelcome and should have been perceived as such by them and their supervisors, Meritor Savings Bank v. Vinson, supra, 477 U.S. at 69, but we do not understand General Motors to be suggesting that Carr enjoyed or appeared to enjoy the campaign of harassment against her. In this regard the case is different from Reed v. Shepard, supra, on which General Motors relies, where the plaintiff had manifested 'enthusiastic receptiveness to sexually suggestive jokes and activities.' 939 F.2d at 491. Reed, a corrections officer, never complained about sexual harassment, and rather than resigning because the conditions of her employment became intolerable was fired for encouraging two inmates to beat a third. The district judge made no finding of 'enthusiastic receptiveness' in the present case, and could not have done so, since Carr's violent resentment of the conduct of her male coworkers toward her is plain. What the judge found, rather, was that Carr had provoked the misconduct of her coworkers. Had she been ladylike, he thought, like the welder, they would have left her alone—maybe; for remember that the welder had to use her welding arc to protect herself, and Carr was not so equipped.

Even if we ignore the question why 'unladylike' behavior should provoke not a vulgar response but a hostile, harassing response, and even if Carr's testimony that she talked and acted as she did in an effort to be 'one of the boys' is (despite its plausibility) discounted, her words and conduct cannot be compared to those of the men and used to justify their conduct and exonerate their employer. Karibian v. Columbia University, 14 F.3d 773, 778 (2d Cir. 1994); Burns v. McGregor Electronic Industries, Inc., 989 F.2d 959, 962 (8th Cir. 1993); Swentek v. USAIR, Inc., 830 F.2d 552, 557 (4th Cir. 1987). The asymmetry of positions must be considered. She was one woman; they were many men. Her use of terms like 'fuck head' could not be deeply threatening, or her placing a hand on the thigh of one of her macho coworkers intimidating; and it was not she who brought the pornographic picture to the 'anatomy lesson.' We have trouble imagining a situation in which male factory workers sexually harass a lone woman in self-defense as it were; yet that at root is General Motors' characterization of what happened here. It is incredible on the admitted facts.

The judge had alternative grounds to 'welcome harassment' for dismissing Carr's case. One is that even if she was harassed, it had no effect on the conditions of her employment. Carr had a very poor attendance record in the tinsmith shop, partly for physical and partly for psychiatric reasons, and while she attributed some of her psychiatric problems (mainly depression) to the sexual harassment she received from her coworkers, there plainly were other factors in play as well. She had a troubled life. Her foster son had been executed for murder, and one of the charming comments that Beckham (the coworker who had exposed himself to her) had made to her was that he would have been happy to pay the electrical bill for the execution. The judge concluded that Carr had 'suffered because she was in a vulnerable, emotionally fragile state, because she was having difficulty coping with her many personal, non-job problems, and because she missed so much work for non-harassment reasons, thereby severely damaging shop morale and efficiency.' These observations would be pertinent if Carr were seeking damages for mental anguish caused by sexual harassment, but she is not. All she need show is that her conditions of employment were adversely affected. If because she was a woman General Motors had turned down the heat at her work station in order to make her uncomfortable, that would be actionable sex discrimination, even if the discomfort inflicted was too mild to be described as 'suffering.' Harris v. Forklift Systems, Inc., supra, 114 S. Ct. at 370-71. To obtain a remedy for constructive discharge, all Carr had to show was that the discrimination to which she was subjected was sufficiently serious to cause a reasonable [*1012] person to quit. Townsend v. Indiana University, 995 F.2d 691, 693 (7th Cir. 1993). The judge did not reach the question whether Carr had been constructively discharged or the further question whether, even if so, she would have quit anyway (or been fired) for reasons unrelated to sex, in which event the employer would not be liable. EEOC v. Consolidated Service Systems, 989 F.2d 233, 236 (7th Cir. 1993); Visser v. Packer Engineering Associates, Inc., 924 F.2d 655, 658 (7th Cir. 1991) (en banc); cf. Bohen v. City of East Chicago, 799 F.2d 1180, 1183 (7th Cir. 1986). General Motors never made the second argument, so it has been waived.

The judge further ruled that 'even if Carr were to show that she was subjected to unwelcome harassment, and that she was adversely affected by it, her claim still would fail because she has not shown that [GM] neglected to take appropriate responsive action.' We said that the standard was negligence, and we think it plain that negligence was proved. Carr began complaining to Routh, her immediate supervisor, in 1985, and four years later nothing had been done to correct the situation. The judge elicited from Routh's supervisor an affirmative answer to the question, 'So you, more or less, left these gals alone to develop their own methods of coping on the job?' Nevertheless the judge's opinion depicts General Motors as the victim of a conspiracy of silence among the tinsmiths. They would have thwarted any investigation by Routh (not that one was made), preferring, said the judge, 'letting a foul-mouthed few set low standards of behavior to enforcing any collective standard that embraces at least some element of civility or decency.' We do not find the picture of mighty GM helpless in the face of the foul-mouthed tinsmiths remotely plausible, but will pass the point by since the district judge acknowledged that beginning in August 1988 'Carr did maintain legitimate, active complaints; however, Allison responded adequately to these.' The responses were limited to several meetings that the company arranged between Carr and her tormentors, at one of which she and Beckham were asked to apologize to each other. No disciplinary action was undertaken against any of Carr's coworkers; no one was even reprimanded for the harassment. General Motors was astonishingly unprepared to deal with problems of sexual harassment, foreseeable though they are when a woman is introduced into a formerly all-male workplace. Supervisor Routh testified that if he encountered a problem of sexual harassment he would have to ask the personnel department what to do. His supervisor's recipe for solving problems of sexual harassment was to recommend that the woman work harder than the men to prove she could do the job. The personnel director of the gas turbine division acknowledged that the distribution of policies and posters dealing with problems of sexual harassment was 'uncertain,' and he could not remember having read any of them himself until shortly before he testified. At one of the meetings with Carr, management agreed to order a videotape on sexual harassment to show to the workforce, but it was never shown, a failure that Routh's supervisor blamed on the personnel department.

It is difficult for an employer to sort out charges and countercharges of sexual harassment among feuding employees, but we are dealing here with a situation in which for years one of the nation's largest enterprises found itself helpless to respond effectively to an egregious campaign of sexual harassment directed at one woman. No reasonable person could imagine that General Motors was genuinely helpless, that it did all it reasonably could have done. The evidence is plain that it (or at least its gas turbine division) was unprepared to deal with problems of sexual harassment even when those problems were rubbed in its face, and also incapable of improvising a solution. Its efforts at investigation were lackluster, its disciplinary efforts nonexistent, its remedial efforts perfunctory. The U.S. Navy has been able to integrate women into the crews of warships; General Motors should have been able to integrate one woman into a tinsmith shop.

The judgment is reversed with instructions to enter judgment on liability for the plaintiff (since no other result would be consistent with the record, In re Marchiando, 13 F.3d 1111, 1114 (7th Cir. 1994)) and proceed to a [*1013] determination of the remedy to which she is entitled.

REVERSED AND REMANDED.

DISSENT BY:
COFFEY

DISSENT:

COFFEY, Circuit Judge, dissenting. Initially, I am compelled to state that the conduct of some of the General Motors employees in this case, including the plaintiff-appellant Mary Carr, is appalling, disgusting and has no place in the work environment. Nonetheless, I am unwilling to join in the majority opinion because I believe it overrules the precedent in our circuit concerning 'unwelcomed' sexual harassment, Reed v. Shepard, 939 F.2d 484, 491 (7th Cir. 1991) (a decision joined in by the author of today's majority opinion).

As an initial matter, let us keep in mind that the standard of review is whether the trial court committed clear error. The U.S. Supreme Court recently stated that the clear error standard is 'significantly deferential,' Concrete Pipe & Products v. Construction Laborers Pension Trust, 124 L. Ed. 2d 539, 113 S. Ct. 2264, 2280 (1993) (emphasis added), and requires a reviewing court to uphold the findings of the lower court unless there is a 'definite and firm conviction that a mistake has been committed.' Id. at 2279 (quoting United States v. United States Gypsum Co., 333 U.S. 364, 395, 92 L. Ed. 746, 68 S. Ct. 525 (1948)) (emphasis added). I remain convinced as this court has often stated, that the trial court is in the best position to resolve factual questions because it has 'the best opportunity to observe the verbal and nonverbal behavior of the witnesses focusing on the subject[s'] reactions and responses to the interrogatories, their facial expressions, attitudes, tone of voice, eye contact, posture and body movements, as well as confused or nervous speech patterns in contrast with merely looking at the cold pages of an appellate record.' United States v. Duarte, 1 F.3d 644, 651 (7th Cir. 1993) (citations omitted) (emphasis added), cert. denied, 126 L. Ed. 2d 688, 114 S. Ct. 724 (1994). Had I been the trier of fact, I may or may not have reached the same conclusion as the trial judge, but 'it is not the function of this court to reweigh the evidence or to substitute its judgment for that of the trier of fact.' Dugan v. United States, 18 F.3d 460, 463 (7th Cir. 1994) (quoting United States v. Wisniewski, 741 F.2d 138, 144 (7th Cir. 1984)) (emphasis added).

In Meritor Savings Bank v. Vinson, 477 U.S. 57, 68, 91 L. Ed. 2d 49, 106 S. Ct. 2399 (1986), a bank supervisor had regular sexual intercourse with a female bank employee often against her will. The U.S. Supreme Court stated that 'the correct inquiry is whether [the victim] by her conduct indicated that the alleged sexual advances were unwelcome, not whether her actual participation in sexual intercourse was voluntary.' Id. Relying on Meritor, we stated in Reed v. Shepard, 939 F.2d 484, 491 (7th Cir. 1991), a case that is indistinguishable from the case before us, that 'the gravamen of any sexual harassment claim is that the alleged sexual advances were 'unwelcome.'' Id. (quoting Meritor Sav. Bank, 477 U.S. at 68). In Reed, a discharged female civilian jailer sued the sheriff and the sheriff's department alleging, among other things, sexual harassment. The alleged harassing conduct in Reed was even more 'egregious' n1 than this case yet the court found for the defendants stating [*1014] much of the evidence at trial emphasized Reed's enthusiastic receptiveness to sexually suggestive jokes and activities. The record of this case reveals numerous instances indicating that Reed's preferred method of dealing with co-workers was with sexually explicit jokes, suggestions and offers.... From the foregoing, the district court is justified where it held: 'The Court finds that language and sexually explicit jokes were used around plaintiff because of her personality rather than her sex.'

Although Reed suggests that tolerating and contributing to the crudeness of the jail was necessary for her career, other female employees testified that the male jail employees did not behave in this manner around women who asked them not to. The trial court's conclusion that Reed welcomed the sexual hijinx [sic] of her co-workers is strongly supported by the evidence presented at trial. This showing that she welcomed the activity is fatal to her claim, particularly where Reed admits that the 'harassment' did not adversely affect her ability to do her job. We agree with the trial court's holding in this regard that, 'the defendants cannot be held liable for conditions created by [Reed's] own action and conduct. Reed, 939 F.2d at 491-92 (footnotes omitted). The defendants cite numerous other lower court opinions adopting this approach. See Perkins v. General Motors Corporation, 709 F. Supp. 1487, 1500 (W.D. Mo. 1989) ('Perkins was an active, encouraging participant in sexually explicit conversations and actions'), aff'd in relevant part, 911 F.2d 22 (8th Cir. 1990), cert. denied, 499 U.S. 920 (1991); Weinsheimer v. Rockwell Int'l. Corp., 754 F. Supp. 1559, 54 Fair Empl. Prac. Cas. (BNA) 828, 832 (M.D. Fla. 1990) ('plaintiff's willing and frequent involvement in the sexual innuendo prevalent in her work area indicates that she did not find the majority of such conduct truly 'unwelcome' or ' hostile''); Loftin-Boggs v. City of Meridian, 633 F. Supp. 1323, 1327 (S.D. Miss. 1986) ('plaintiff often made jokes about sex and participated in frequent discussions and bantering about sex'), aff'd, 824 F.2d 971 (5th Cir. 1987), cert. denied, 484 U.S. 1063, 98 L. Ed. 2d 986, 108 S. Ct. 1021 (1988); Gan v. Kepro Circuit Systems, 28 Fair Empl. Prac. Cas. (BNA) 639 (E.D. Mo. 1982) (plaintiff actively contributed to the distasteful working environment).

The majority makes an attempt to distinguish the instant case from Reed by stating Carr did not manifest 'enthusiastic receptiveness to sexually suggestive jokes and activities' as Reed had. Reed, 939 F.2d at 491. This distinction escapes me given the trial court's explicit finding on the issue of Carr's receptiveness to the crude conduct Carr invited and encouraged the bad language, crude jokes, and constant sexual references which abounded in the tin shop, so that the tinners' conduct, to the extent it may have constituted sexual harassment, was not unwelcome. See Reed, 939 F.2d at 491-92 (plaintiff's 'enthusiastic receptiveness to sexually suggestive jokes and activities' indicated that harassing conduct was not unwelcome). Mem. Op. at 32 (emphasis added). How can the majority claim that Carr is distinguishable from Reed in view of the fact that the district judge made a specific finding that Carr 'invited' the crude behavior and cited the very language in Reed that the majority claims distinguishes the two cases? In contrast to the trial court's findings, the majority insists that Reed was receptive to the crude behavior while Carr provoked the crudeness from her male co-workers. See ante at 7. Such a distinction is implausible given the lower court's clear and unambiguous holding, quoted above, which states Carr 'invited and encouraged the bad language, crude jokes, and constant sexual references' and cites to the very language in Reed dealing with 'enthusiastic receptiveness.' (Emphasis added).

The majority attempts to distinguish Reed on the grounds that she 'never complained about sexual harassment' and she was fired for her misconduct on the job, ante at 7, yet the court in Reed did not rely on her lack of complaint, rather the court based its decision on her participation in the sexual talk and pranks. See Reed, 939 F.2d at 491-92. Moreover, the fact that Reed was terminated [*1015] while Carr resigned is of no consequence for GM might very well have discharged Carr for her acute absenteeism. See infra at 16-17. In an attempt to second guess and downplay the trial court's unmistakable holding that Carr welcomed the conduct as Reed had, the majority insists that Carr, unlike Reed, manifested 'violent resentment' toward the male tinners conduct and thus did not welcome it. Ante at 7. From my review of this record, I have been unable to discover any evidence of Carr's 'violent resentment' of the crude conduct other than the two complaints she filed with management (several years after the alleged harassing acts and shortly before her resignation). What the record does reveal, as I discuss infra at 17-18, is evidence that Carr was every bit as foul-mouthed, crude and willing to partake in pranks of a sexual nature as the men in the shop as well as the fact that Carr owned up to her responsibility for adding to the poor relationship she had with the male tinners.

I choose not to recite the language she used because I do not believe that quoting vulgar language contributes to the development of the body of law. However, the record does reveal fifteen specific references to the plaintiff Carr's repeated use of crude/sexual language, crude behavior and obscene story-telling. Reed was decided by this court in August of 1991 and the present case was argued before the court in February of 1994. It certainly is a matter of concern, in the absence of any directive from the Supreme Court, that the majority has seen fit to change the Circuit's law on harassment, for how is industry to implement new rules and regulations when the standards are ever-changing? An example of the majority's sugar coating the facts is the mischaracterization of the district court's holding and the defendant's argument on the issue of 'unwelcomeness,' stating 'we have trouble even imagining a situation in which male factory workers sexually harass a lone woman in self-defense as it were; yet that at root is General Motors' characterization of what happened here. It is incredible on the admitted facts.' Ante at 8. The point is not that the male tinners were defending themselves from this 'lone woman,' but rather that within the tinsmith shop there was a great deal of good-natured bantering, intermingled with unnecessary, repulsive, crude, sexual talk and innuendo. If Carr received more than her share of verbal abuse, a point I find very questionable based upon the record before us, it might very well have been due to factors other than her being a woman. For example, the majority glosses over the fact that she had an abysmal work attendance record that caused a great deal of consternation, discontent and even anger among the tinners who in all probability believed General Motors was overlooking her all-too-frequent absences from the workplace because she was a woman. The district court found that in Carr's four-plus years on the job in the tinsmith shop she was absent over thirty percent of her scheduled work periods (she missed some 395 work days between 1984 and 1989). The trial judge clearly took note of the impact of her absenteeism, stating 'these missed days had a very negative impact on shop morale. Tinners work together and rely on each other (including apprentices) to get particular jobs done. Regular, uninterrupted attendance is therefore quite important to smooth shop operation and to morale as a whole. The truth of this statement is evidenced by Routh's alleged comment to Carr, made after one of her numerous complaints, that the tinners 'would treat you better if you'd come to work.' Mem. op. at 14-15. If General Motors is to be criticized, it is for not discharging an employee whose acute absenteeism syndrome was causing severe morale problems within the tinshop. At the same time, GM should be commended for going out of the way to accommodate Carr during her absences due to her alleged health and/or psychological problems stemming from her step-son's execution.

In addition to her absenteeism, the record, considered as a whole, offers ample support for the conclusion of the experienced trial judge that Mary Carr was a participant in [*1016] the ribald antics of the tinshop. n2 For years she actively participated in the vulgarities of life in the tinsmith's shop. She now claims that she was a victim of the uninvited antics but as in Reed, Carr's words and conduct belie her argument. The trial judge summarized her conduct as follows:

> 'The problem for Carr is that she was not merely the recipient of crude behavior and abusive language—she also dished it out.... In short, she contributed just as much abusive language and crude behavior as did the male tinners, and therefore was just as responsible for any hostile sexual environment that consequently arose.'

Mem. op. at 31 (emphasis added). When testifying about Carr's foul language, the other females who worked in the tinshop, Rebecca Hornocker and Karen Johnson, explained that Carr was often the instigator of the coarse sexual talk and antics. n3

As the court stated in Reed, the 'language and sexually explicit jokes were used around the plaintiff because of her personality rather than her sex.' Reed, 939 F.2d at 491-92. The trial record makes it eminently clear and I am thus forced to agree that Mary Carr actively participated in foul, vulgar shop talk with a rough crowd of tinners, thus 'the defendants cannot be held liable for conditions created by [the plaintiff's] own action and conduct.' Reed, 939 F.2d at 492 (quoting lower court opinion).

In regard to Carr's active participation in the crude sexual behavior at the plant, the majority fails to explain the lower court's finding that 'Right after the August 1988 meeting, Carr thanked management for its efforts on her behalf, and she admitted to [Don] Stoehr that her own behavior had brought the poor shop situation about. To the Court, this appears to be a clear recognition by Carr that she bore responsibility for her problems, and that she had been dealt with fairly by management. It does not seem to be the statement of a person who has complained continually for four years and gotten nowhere.' Mem. op. at 37-38 (emphasis added). Not only did Carr confess that 'her own behavior had brought the poor shop situation about,' but furthermore she admitted that GM had responded to her complaint fairly. Again, this factual finding by the trial court is entitled to great deference on review. See Concrete Pipe & Products, 113 S. Ct. at 2280 (stating that the clear-error standard is 'significantly deferential').

Finally, I am disturbed by the majority's apparent disregard for the district court's findings concerning General Motors' alleged failure to respond to Carr's complaints. The majority states 'we are dealing here with a situation in which for more than four years one of the nation's largest enterprises found itself helpless to respond effectively to an egregious campaign of sexual harassment directed at one woman. No reasonable person could imagine that General Motors was genuinely helpless, that it did all it reasonably could have done.' Ante at 10. I seriously question whether the majority's argument is supported by the record, for General Motors was not aware of the alleged harassment against Carr for 'more than four years.' From 1984 until 1988, Carr never once entered a formal complaint about the alleged abusive treatment. In August of 1988, and again in November of 1988, less than a year before she left General Motors after being employed there for twelve years, Carr registered her initial formal complaints and GM responded immediately. n4 As we discussed [*1017] above, after the August 1988 complaint, Carr expressed in a letter to Don Stoehr her appreciation with the way GM handled her complaint and that she (Carr) was in part responsible for the problems in the tinshop. n5 It is rather obvious that Carr was satisfied with GM's response to her complaint in 1988 (a year before she resigned), thus her present dissatisfaction with General Motors might well be a post-event creation to avoid dismissal of her sexual harassment claim. Whatever the reason for her present allegations of GM's ineffective response, I do not believe the trial court's findings are clearly erroneous.

CONCLUSION

Because I am of the opinion that today's holding is in conflict with Reed, I

DISSENT.

Footnotes

n1 The appellate court opinion quoted the district court's findings as follows:

'Plaintiff contends that she was handcuffed to the drunk tank and sally port doors, that she was subjected to suggestive remarks..., that conversations often centered around oral sex, that she was physically hit and punched in the kidneys, and that her head was grabbed and forcefully placed in members [sic] laps, and that she was the subject of lewd jokes and remarks. She testified that she had chairs pulled out from under her, a cattle prod with an electrical shock was placed between her legs, and that they frequently tickled her. She was placed in a laundry basket, handcuffed inside an elevator, handcuffed to the toilet and her face pushed into the water, and maced....' Reed, 939 F.2d at 486. When questioned why she tolerated such behavior, Reed responded not unlike Carr in the case before us, 'Because it was real important to me to be accepted. It was important for me to be a police officer and if that was the only way that I could be accepted, I would just put up with it and kept [sic] my mouth shut.' Id. at 492.

If Carr's allegations were true, I doubt she would have waited over three years to make them known.

n2 The majority seems to have put a different spin on the facts in favor of Carr. For example, the majority insists two exposures occurred during her five-year tenure at the tinshop, while the district court made a finding of only one exposure incident and even in that incident, 'several tinners' testified Carr was not in a position to see anything. Mem. Op. at 9 & 30. As to the second alleged exposure incident, the court stated that no one corroborated her story. Id. at 9.

n3 Hornocker considered Carr to be a 'tramp' because of her 'manner, her gestures, and the way she talked.' Karen Johnson heard Carr using profanity and vulgar language in the classroom setting. Referring to Carr, Johnson testified that 'I saw that there was only a limited amount of time we could spend together without me feeling uncomfortable....' (Emphasis added).

n4 It is interesting to note that she filed her EEOC complaint in July of 1989 shortly before she quit.

n5 The letter is not part of the record, but both Don Stoehr and Mary testified at trial that she had sent the letter expressing her appreciation with GM's response to her complaint.

Bibliography

Adler, Robert S. and Ellen R. Peirce. 'The Legal, Ethical, and Social Implications of the "Reasonable Woman" Standard in Sexual Harassment Cases.' *Fordham Law Review* 61 (1993): 773-827.
Andrews v. City of Philadelphia. 895 Fed. 2d. 1469. 3rd Circuit Ct. 1990.
Aristotle. *The Nicomachean Ethics*. Trans. David Ross. Rev. by J. L. Ackrill and J. O. Urmson. NY: Oxford U P, 1925.
---. *Nicomachean Ethics*. Trans. H. Rackham. The Loeb Classical Library. Cambridge, MS: Harvard U P, 1926.
---. *Art of Rhetoric*. Trans. J. H. Freese. Loeb Classical Library. Cambridge, MA: Harvard U P, 1926.
---. *Politics*. Trans. H. Rackham. The Loeb Classical Library. Cambridge, MS: Harvard U P, 1932.
---. *Metaphysics: Books I – IX*. Trans. Hugh Tredennick. The Loeb Classical Library. Cambridge, MS: Harvard U P, 1933.
---. *Art of Rhetoric*. Trans. W. Rhys Roberts. With *Poetics*. Trans. Ingram Bywater. NY: Modern Library, 1954.
---. *Aristotle: The Physics: Books I-IV*. Trans. Philip H. Wicksteed, Francis M. Cornford. Cambridge, MA: Harvard U P, 1986.
Atwill, Janet M. 'Instituting the Art of Rhetoric: Theory, Practice, and Productive Knowledge in Interpretations of Aristotle's *Rhetoric*.' *Rethinking the History of Rhetoric: Multidisciplinary Essays on the Rhetorical Tradition*. Ed. Takis Poulakos. Boulder: Westview Press, 1993. 91-117.
---. *Rhetoric Reclaimed: Aristotle and the Liberal Arts Tradition*. Ithaca, NY: Cornell U P, 1998.
Baron, Jane B. 'Language Matters.' *The John Marshall Law Review* 34 (2000): 163-180.
Bazerman, Charles. 'A Contention over the Term Rhetoric.' *Defining the New Rhetorics*. Ed. Theresa Enos and Stuart C. Brown. Newbury Park: Sage Publications, 1993. 3-7.
Biesecker, Barbara. 'Coming to Terms with Recent Attempts to Write Women into the History of Rhetoric.' *Philosophy and Rhetoric* 25 (1992): 140-59.
Bizzell, Patricia and Bruce Herzberg, eds. General Introduction. *The Rhetorical Tradition: Readings from Classical Times to the Present*. Boston: St. Martin's Press, 1990. 1-15.
---. Classical Rhetoric: Introduction. Bizzell and Herzberg 19-37.
---. Renaissance Rhetoric: Introduction. Bizzell and Herzberg 463-82.
---. Enlightenment Rhetoric: Introduction. Bizzell and Herzberg 637-69.
Blackstone, Sir William. *Commentaries on the Laws of England*. 2d ed. Oxford: Clarendon Press, 1766-1769.

Boorstin, Daniel J. *The Mysterious Science of the Law: An Essay on Blackstone's Commentaries*. Chicago: U of Chicago P, 1941.
Braet, Antoine. C. 'The Classical Doctrine of *Status* and the Rhetorical Theory of Argumentation.' *Philosophy and Rhetoric* 20 (1987): 79-93.
---. 'Aristotle's Almost Unnoticed Contribution to the Doctrine of Stasis.' *Mnemosyne* 52 (1999): 408-433.
Brenneman, Deborah S. 'From a Woman's Point of View: The Use of the Reasonable Woman Standard in Sexual Harassment Cases.' *Cincinnati Law Review* 60 (1992): 1281-1306.
Brock, Bernard L., Robert L. Scott and James W. Chesebro, eds. 'An Introduction to Rhetorical Criticism.' *Methods of Rhetorical Criticism*. Detroit: Wayne State University Press, 1990. 9-22.
Buckner, Carole J. 'Realizing *Grutter v. Bollinger*'s "Compelling Educational Benefits of Diversity": Transforming Aspirational Rhetoric into Experience.' *University of Missouri at Kansas City Law Review* 72 (2004): 877-947.
Burlington Industries v. Ellerth. 524 U.S. 732. U.S. Sup. Ct. 1998.
Buzzanell, Patrice M. 'Reframing the Glass Ceiling as a Socially Constructed Process: Implications for Understanding and Change.' *Communication Monographs* 62 (1995): 327-354.
Cahill, Mia. *The Social Construction of Sexual Harassment Law: The Role of the National, Organizational, and Individual Context*. Aldershot, England: Ashgate/Dartmouth, 2001.
Campbell, Karlyn Kohrs. 'The Rhetoric of Women's Liberation: An Oxymoron?' *Quarterly Journal of Speech* 75 (1973): 74-86.
---. 'Hearing Women's Voices'. *Communication Education* 40 (1991): 33-48.
---. 'Gender and Genre: Loci of Invention and Contradiction in the Earliest Speeches by U.S. Women.' *Quarterly Journal of Speech* 81 (1995): 479-96.
---. 'Inventing Women: From Amaterasu to Virginia Woolf.' *Women's Studies in Communication 21* (1998): 111-26.
--- and Kathleen Hall Jamieson. 'Inaugurating the Presidency.' Brock, Scott and Chesebro. 341-61.
Cardozo, Benjamin N. *Law and Literature and Other Essays and Addresses*. NY: Harcourt, Brace and Co., 1931.
Carr v. Allison Gas Turbine Division. 32 Fed. Rep. 3rd Ser. 1007. 7th Cir. Ct. of Appeals. 1994.
Caws, Peter. '*Praxis* and *Techne*.' *The History and Philosophy of Technology*. Ed. George Bugliarello. Urbana: U of Illinois P, 1979.
Chase, Anthony. 'The Birth of the Modern Law School.' *The American Journal of Legal History* 23 (1979): 329-348.
Cicero. 'Pro Archia Poeta' *Orationes Selectae. English & Latin*. Trans. N.H. Watts. Loeb Classical Library. Cambridge, MA: Harvard U P, 1979. 2-41.
---. *Brutus, Orator*. Trans. G. L. Hendrickson and H. M. Hubbell. Cambridge, MS: Oxford U P, 1987.
Clark, David S. 'The Medieval Origins of Modern Legal Education: Between Church and State.' *The American Journal of Comparative Law* 35 (1987): 653-719.

Cochran, Augustus B. *Sexual Harassment and the Law: The Mechelle Vinson Case*. Lawrence, KS: U P of Kansas, 2004.
Cohen, Neil P. 'Teaching Criminal Law: Curing the Disconnect.' *St. Louis Law Journal* 48 (2004): 1195-1203.
Cole, Eve Browning. *Philosophy and Feminist Criticism: An Introduction*. NY: Paragon House, 1993.
Cotter, Thomas F. 'Legal Pragmatism and the Law and Economics Movement.' *Georgetown Law Journal* 84 (1996): 2071-2141.
Cover, Robert. 'The Supreme Court 1982 Term—Foreword: Nomos and Narrative.' *Harvard Law Review* 97 (1983): 4-68.
---. 'The Bonds of Constitutional Interpretation: Of the Word, the Deed, and the Role.' *Georgia Law Review* 20 (1986): 815-33.
---. 'Violence and the Word.' *Yale Law Journal* 95 (1986): 1601-29.
Currie, Brainerd. 'The Materials of Law Study.' *Journal of Legal Education* 3 (1951): 331-383.
Dearin, Ray. 'The Fourth *Stasis* in Greek Rhetoric.' *Rhetoric and Communication*. Ed. Jane Blankenship and Hermann G. Stelzner. Urbana: U of Illinois P, 1976, 3-16.
Detienne, Marcel and Jean-Pierre Vernant. *Cunning Intelligence in Greek Culture and Society*. Trans. Janet Lloyd. Chicago: U of Chicago P, 1978.
Dieter, Otto Alvin Loeb. 'Stasis.' *Speech Monographs* 17 (1950): 345-69.
Dunne, Joseph. *Back to the Rough Ground: Practical Judgment and the Lure of Technique*. Notre Dame, IN: Notre Dame U P, 1993.
Ebert v. Lamar Truck Plaza. 715 Fed. Supp. 1496. U.S. Dist. Ct. (CO). 1987.
Ehrenreich, Nancy S. 'Pluralist Myths and Powerless Men: The Ideology of Reasonableness in Sexual Harassment Cases.' *The Yale Law Journal* 99 (1990): 1177-1234.
Eisele, Thomas D. 'The Activity of Being a Lawyer: The Imaginative Pursuit of Implications and Possibilities.' *Tennessee Law Review* 54 (1987): 345-89.
Ellison v. Brady. 924 Fed. Rep. 2d Ser. 8712. 9th Cir. Ct. of Appeals. 1991.
Employment Law Center. 'Brief Amici Curiae of the Employment Law Center, a Project of the Legal Aid Society of San Francisco, the California Women's Law Center, and Equal Rights Advocates, Inc. in Support of Petitioner.' *U. S. Briefs* (1992): 1158 (no page numbers).
Enos, Richard Leo. 'The Archaeology of Women in Rhetoric: Rhetorical Sequencing as a Research Method for Historical Scholarship.' *Rhetoric Society Quarterly* 32 (2002): 65-79.
Equal Employment Opportunity Commission. 'Guidelines on Discrimination because of Sex.' *Code of Federal Regulations* 29 (1 July 2000): 1604.11.
Fahnestock, Jeanne and Marie Secor. 'The Stases in Scientific and Literary Argument.' *Written Communication* 5 (1988): 427-43.
---. 'Rhetorical Analysis.' *Discourse Studies in Composition*. Ed. Ellen Barton and Gail Stygall. Cresskill, NJ: Hampton Press, 2002. 177-200.
Faludi, Susan. *Backlash: The Undeclared War against American Women*. NY: Doubleday, 1991.
Faragher v. City of Boca Raton. 524 U.S. 775. U.S. Sup. Ct. 1998.

Fish, Stanley. *Doing What Comes Naturally: Change, Rhetoric, and the Practice of Theory in Literary and Legal Studies*. Durham, NC: Duke U P, 1989.

---. *There's No Such Thing as Free Speech...And It's a Good Thing, Too*. NY: Oxford U P, 1994.

Fisher, Walter R. 'The Narrative Paradigm: An Elaboration.' Brock, Scott and Chesebro. 234-55.

Foss, Sonja K., Karen A. Foss and Robert Trapp, eds. *Contemporary Perspectives on Rhetoric*. 3rd Edition. Prospect Heights, IL: Waveland Press, 2001.

Foss, Sonja K. and Cindy L. Griffin. 'A Feminist Perspective on Rhetorical Theory: Toward a Clarification of Boundaries.' *Western Journal of Communication* 56 (1992): 330-349.

---. 'Beyond Persuasion: A Proposal for an Invitational Rhetoric.' *Communication Monographs* 62 (1995): 2-18.

Freeland, Cynthia A. Introduction. *Feminist Interpretations of Aristotle*. Ed. Freeland. University Park, PA: The Pennsylvania State U P, 1998. 1-15.

Fuller, Lon L. *The Law in Quest of Itself*. Boston: Beacon Press, 1940.

Gaonker, Dilip Parameshwar. Rev. of *Back to the Rough Ground: 'Phronesis' and 'Techne' in Modern Philosophy and in Aristotle*, by Joseph Dunne. *Quarterly Journal of Speech* 84 (1998): 506-9.

Garver, Eugene. *Aristotle's* Rhetoric: *An Art of Character*. Chicago: U of Chicago P, 1994.

Gemmette, Elizabeth Villiers. 'Law and Literature: An Unnecessarily Suspect Class in the Liberal Arts Component of the Law School Curriculum.' *Valparaiso University Law Review* 23 (1989): 267-340.

Gilbert, Jacqueline A. and Deniz S. Ones. 'Role of Informal Integration in Career Advancement: Investigations in Plural and Multicultural Organizations and Implications for Diversity Valuation.' *Sex Roles* 39 (1998): 685-704.

Gilligan, Carol. *In a Different Voice: Psychological Theory and Women's Development*. Cambridge: Harvard U P, 1982, 1993.

Glazebrook, Trish. 'From φυσισ to Nature, τεχνη to Technology: Heidegger on Aristotle, Galileo, and Newton.' *Southern Journal of Philosophy* 38 (2000): 95-118.

Glenn, Cheryl. *Rhetoric Retold: Regendering the Tradition from Antiquity Through the Renaissance*. Carbondale: Southern Illinois U P, 1997.

Goodrich, Peter. 'Antirrhesis: Polemical Structures of Common Law Thought.' *The Rhetoric of Law*. Ed. Austin Sarat and Thomas R. Kearns. Ann Arbor, MI: U of Michigan P, 1994. 57-102.

Goodwin, Michele Cammers. 'The Black Woman in the Attic: Law, Metaphor, and Madness in *Jane Eyre*.' *Rutgers Law Journal* 30 (1999): 597-682.

Gorgias. *Encomium of Helen*. Trans. George A. Kennedy. Bizzell and Herzberg. 40-42.

Gotoff, Harold C. *Cicero's Elegant Style: an Analysis of the Pro Archia*. Chicago: U of Illinois P, 1979.

Grant, Judith. *Fundamental Feminism: Contesting the Core Concepts of Feminist Theory*. NY: Routledge, 1993.

Grassi, Ernesto. *Renaissance Humanism*. Binghamton, NY: Center for Medieval & Early Renaissance Studies, State University of New York at Binghamton, 1988.

Grimaldi, William M. A. 'Rhetoric and Truth: A Note on Aristotle *Rhetoric* 1355a 21-24.' *Philosophy and Rhetoric* 11 (1978): 173-177.

Groenhout, Ruth. 'The Virtue of Care: Aristotelian Ethics and Contemporary Ethics of Care.' *Feminist Interpretations of Aristotle*. Ed. Cynthia A. Freeland. University Park, PA: The Pennsylvania State U P, 1998. 171-200.

Guthrie, W.K.C. *The Greek Philosophers from Thales to Aristotle*. NY: Harper & Row, 1950.

Hackney, James R., Jr. 'Law and Neoclassical Economics: Science, Politics, and the Reconfiguration of American Tort Law Theory.' *Law and History Review* 15 (1997): 275-336.

Halloran, S. Michael, and Merrill D. Whitburn. 'Ciceronian Rhetoric and the Rise of Science: the Plain Style Reconsidered.' *The Rhetorical Tradition and Modern Writing*. Ed. James J. Murphy. NY: MLA, 1982. 58-72.

Haney, David P. 'Aesthetics and Ethics in Gadamer, Levinas, and Romanticism: Problems of Phronesis and Techne.' *PMLA: Publications of the Modern Language Association* 114 (1999): 32-45.

Hansmann, Henry. 'The Current State of Law-and-Economics Scholarship.' *Journal of Legal Education* 33 (1983): 217-236.

Hardin v. S. C. Johnson, Inc. 167 Fed. 3rd 340. 7th Cir. Ct. of Appeals. 1999.

Harding, Sandra. *Whose Science? Whose Knowledge? Thinking from Women's Lives*. Ithaca, NY: Cornell U P, 1991.

Harno, Albert J. *Legal Education in the United States*. San Francisco: Bancroft Whitney Company, 1953.

Harris v. Forklift Systems, Inc. 976 Fed. Rep. 2d Ser. 733. 6th Cir. Ct. of Appeals. 1992.

Hart, H. L. A. 'Positivism and the Separation of Law and Morals.' *Harvard Law Review* 71 (1958): 593-629.

Hawkesworth, Mary E. 'From Objectivity to Objectification: Feminist Objections.' *Rethinking Objectivity*. Ed. Allan Megill. Durham: Duke U P, 1994. 151-78.

Heckman, James J. 'The Intellectual Roots of the Law and Economics Movement.' *Law and History Review* 15 (1997): 327-32.

Heidegger, Martin. *The Question Concerning Technology and Other Essays*. Trans. William Lovitt. NY: Harper & Row, 1977.

Heilbrun, Carolyn and Judith Resnik. 'Convergences: Law, Literature, and Feminism.' *Beyond Portia: Women, Law, and Literature in the United States*. Ed. Jacqueline St. Joan and Annette Bennington McElhiney. Boston: Northeastern U P, 1997. 11-52.

Henson v. City of Dundee. 682 Fed. Rep. 2d Ser. 897. 11th Cir. Ct. of Appeals. 1982.

Hirschman, Linda R. 'The Book of "A".' *Texas Law Review* 70 (1992): 971-1012.

Hirschmann, Nancy J. *Rethinking Obligation: A Feminist Method for Political Theory*. Ithaca: Cornell U P, 1992.

Hohman, Hanns. 'The Dynamics of Stasis: Classical Rhetorical Theory and Modern Legal Argumentation.' *American Journal of Jurisprudence* 34 (1989): 171-197.

Hultzén, Lee S. 'Status in Deliberative Analysis.' *The Rhetorical Idiom: Essays in Rhetoric, Oratory, Language and Drama.* Ed. Donald C. Bryant. Ithaca: Cornell U P, 1958. 97-123.

An Intermediate Greek-English Lexicon: Founded upon the Seventh Edition of Liddell and Scott's Greek-English Lexicon. Oxford: The Clarendon Press, 1995.

Jarratt, Susan C. 'The First Sophists and Feminism: Discourses of the "Other"'. *Hypatia* 5 (1990): 27-41.

---. 'Speaking to the Past: Feminist Historiography in Rhetoric.' *Pre/Text* 11 (1990): 189-209.

Johnson & Hiss v. ITT Industries. 41 Fed. Appx. 73. 9th Cir. Ct. of Appeals. 2002.

Johnson, Robert R. *User-Centered Technology: A Rhetorical Theory for Computers and Other Mundane Artifacts.* Albany, NY: SUNY Press, 1998.

Kalimtzis, Kostas. *Aristotle on Political Enmity and Disease: An Inquiry into Stasis.* Albany, NY: SUNY Press, 2000.

Katz, Steven B. 'The Ethic of Expediency: Classical Rhetoric, Technology, and the Holocaust.' *College English* 54 (1992): 255-75.

Kelman, Mark G. 'Misunderstanding Social Life: A Critique of the Core Premises of "Law and Economics."' *Journal of Legal Education* 33 (1983): 274-84.

Kennedy, George A. *Aristotle* On Rhetoric: *A Theory of Civic Discourse.* NY: Oxford U P, 1991.

Kerper, Janeen. 'Creative Problem Solving vs. the Case Method: A Marvelous Adventure in which Winnie-the-Pooh Meets Mrs. Palsgraf.' *California Western Law Review* 34 (1998): 351-74.

Kimball, Bruce A. 'The Langdell Problem: Historicizing the Century of Historiography, 1906-2000s.' *University of Illinois Law and History Review* 22 (2004): 277-337.

Kitch, Edmund W. 'The Intellectual Foundations of "Law and Economics."' *Journal of Legal Education* 33 (1983): 184-96.

Knox, Bernard. *The Oldest Dead White European Males and Other Reflections on the Classics.* NY: W.W. Norton & Company, 1993.

Kuhn, Thomas S. *The Structure of Scientific Revolutions.* 3rd ed. Chicago, IL: University of Chicago Press, 1996.

Krieger, Stefan H. 'Domain Knowledge and the Teaching of Creative Legal Problem Solving.' *Clinical Law Review* 11 (2004): 149-207.

Lemmings, David. 'Blackstone and Law Reform by Education: Preparation for the Bar and Lawyerly Culture in Eighteenth-Century England.' *Law and History Review* 16 (1998): 211-255.

Letwin, Shirley R. 'Law and the Unreasonable Woman.' *The National Review* November 1991: 34-36.

Levine, Linda and Kurt M. Saunders. 'Thinking Like a Rhetor.' *Journal of Legal Education* 43 (1993): 108-22.

Locke, John. *An Essay Concerning Human Understanding*. Ed. Alexander Campbell Fraser. Vol. 2. NY: Dover, 1959.
Lutz, Jean A. 'Writers in Organizations and How They Learn the Image: Theory, Research, and Implications.' *Worlds of Writing: Teaching and Learning in Discourse Communities of Work*. Ed. Carolyn B. Matalene. NY: Guilford, 1989. 113-35.
MacKinnon, Catharine A., Ed. *Sexual Harassment of Working Women: A Case of Sex Discrimination*. New Haven, CT: Yale U P, 1979.
---. *Directions in Sexual Harassment Law*. New Haven, CT: Yale U P, 2003.
Mann, Susan. 'The Universe and the Library: A Critique of James Boyd White as Writer and Reader.' *Stanford Law Review* 41 (1989): 959-1009.
Marshall, Anna-Maria. *Confronting Sexual Harassment: The Law and Politics of Everyday Life*. Aldershot, England: Ashgate/Dartmouth, 2005.
Mattingly, Carol. 'Telling Evidence: Rethinking What Counts in Rhetoric.' *Rhetoric Society Quarterly* 32 (2002): 99-108.
McManis, Charles R. 'The History of First Century American Legal Education: A Revisionist Perspective.' *Washington University Law Quarterly* 59 (1981): 597-659.
Mellinkoff, David. *The Language of the Law*. Boston: Little, Brown, 1963.
Meritor Savings Bank v. Vinson. 477 U.S. 57. Sup. Ct. 1986.
Michelman, Frank I. 'Reflections on Professional Education, Legal Scholarship, and the Law-and-Economics Movement.' *Journal of Legal Education* 33 (1983): 197-209.
Miller, Carolyn R. 'Technology as a Form of Consciousness: A Study of Contemporary Ethos.' *Central States Speech Journal* 29 (1978) 228-36.
---. 'A Humanistic Rationale for Technical Writing.' *College English* 40 (1979): 610-17.
---. 'Genre as Social Action.' *Quarterly Journal of Speech* 70 (1984): 151-67.
---. 'What's Practical about Technical Writing?' *Technical Writing: Theory and Practice*. Ed. Bertie E. Fearing and W. Keats Sparrow. NY: MLA, 1989. 14-24.
---. 'Rhetoric and the Community: The Problem of the One and the Many.' *Defining the New Rhetorics*. Ed. Theresa Enos and Stuart C. Brown. Newbury Park: Sage Publications, 1993. 79-94.
Minda, Gary. 'Law and Literature at Century's End.' *Cardozo Studies in Law and Literature* 9 (1997): 245-258.
Minton, Shira Pavis. 'Hawthorne and the Handmaid: An Examination of the Law's Use as a Tool of Oppression.' *Wisconsin Women's Law Journal* 13 (1998): 45-73.
Mitcham, Carl. *Thinking through Technology: The Path between Engineering and Philosophy*. Chicago: U of Chicago P, 1994.
More, Thomas, Sir. *Utopia*. Mineola, NY: Dover Publications, 1997.
Moskovitz, Myron. 'Beyond the Case Method: It's Time to Teach with Problems.' *Journal of Legal Education* 42 (1992): 241-70.
Nadeau, Ray. 'Classical Systems of Stases in Greek: Hermagoras to Hermogenes.' *Greek, Roman and Byzantine Studies* 2 (1959): 51-71.

Neel, Jasper. *Aristotle's Voice: Rhetoric, Theory, and Writing in America.* Carbondale, IL: Southern Illinois U P, 1994.

Nussbaum, Martha C. '"Only Grey Matter"? Richard Posner's Cost-Benefit Analysis of Sex.' *University of Chicago Law Review* 59 (1992): 1689-1734.

---. 'Aristotle, Feminism, and Needs for Functioning.' *Texas Law Review* 70 (1992): 1019-28.

---. 'Skepticism about Practical Reason in Literature and the Law.' *Harvard Law Review* 107 (1994): 714-44.

---. *Poetic Justice: The Literary Imagination and Public Life.* Boston: Beacon Press, 1995.

---. *The Fragility of Goodness: Luck and Ethics in Greek Tragedy and Philosophy.* Updated Ed. Cambridge: Cambridge U P, 2001.

---. 'The Costs of Tragedy: Some Moral Limits of Cost-Benefit Analysis.' *Cost-Benefit Analysis: Legal, Economic, and Philosophical Perspectives.* Ed. Matthew D. Alder and Eric A. Posner. Chicago: U of Chicago P, 2001. 169-200.

O'Beirne, Kate. 'The Big Creep.' *National Review* 50/14 (August 3, 1998): 20-1.

Orwell, George. *Shooting an Elephant and Other Essays.* NY: Harcourt, Brace & World, Inc., 1950.

Panetta, Edward M. and Marouf Hasian, Jr. 'Anti-Rhetoric as Rhetoric: The Law and Economics Movement.' *Communication Quarterly* 42 (1994): 57-74.

Pantazakos, Michael. '*Ad Humanitatem Pertinent*: A Personal Reflection on the History and Purpose of the Law and Literature Movement.' *Cardozo Studies in Law and Literature* 7 (1995): 31-71.

Papke, David R. 'Law and Literature: A Comment and Bibliography of Secondary Works.' *Law Library Journal* 73 1980: 421-437.

Pavone v. Brown. 1998 U.S. App. Lexis 30461. 7th Cir. Ct. of Appeals. 1998.

Plato. 'Gorgias.' *Plato: The Collected Dialogues including the Letters.* Ed. Edith Hamilton and Huntington Cairns. Trans. W. D. Woodhead. Princeton, NJ: Princeton U P, 1989.

Posner, Richard A. 'Killing or Wounding to Protect a Property Interest.' *Journal of Law and Economics* 14 (1971) 201-32.

---. 'Blackstone and Bentham.' *Journal of Legal Education* 19 (1976): 569-606.

---. 'Wealth Maximization and Judicial Decision-Making.' *International Review of Law and Economics* 4 (1984): 131-5.

---. 'The Ethical Significance of Free Choice: A Reply to Professor West.' *Harvard Law Review* 99 (1986): 1431-48.

---. 'Law and Literature: A Relation Reargued.' *Virginia Law Review* 72 (1986): 1351-92.

---. 'The Decline of Law as an Autonomous Discipline: 1962-1987.' *Harvard Law Review* 100 (1987): 761-780.

---. *Law and Literature: A Misunderstood Relation.* Cambridge, MA: Harvard U P, 1988.

---. *Problems of Jurisprudence.* Cambridge, MS: Harvard U P, 1990.

---. 'Ms. Aristotle.' *Texas Law Review* 70 (1992): 1013-17.

---. *Sex and Reason*. Cambridge, MS: Harvard U P, 1992.
---. *Overcoming Law*. Cambridge, MS: Harvard U P, 1995.
---. *Law and Literature*. Rev. Ed. Cambridge, MA: Harvard U P, 1998.
---. 'Cost-Benefit Analysis: Definition, Justification, and Comment on Conference Papers.' *Cost-Benefit Analysis: Legal, Economic, and Philosophical Perspectives*. Ed. Matthew D. Alder and Eric A. Posner. Chicago: U of Chicago P, 2001. 317-341.
Poster, Carol. '(Re)Positioning Pedagogy: A Feminist Historiography of Aristotle's *Rhetorica*.' *Feminist Interpretations of Aristotle*. Ed. Cynthia A. Freeland. University Park, PA: The Pennsylvania State U P, 1998. 327-49.
Proctor, PollyBeth. 'Toward Mythos and Mythology: Applying a Feminist Critique to Legal Education to Effectuate a Socialization of Both Sexes in Law School Classrooms.' *Cardozo Women's Law Journal* 10 (2004): 577-602.
Quintilian. *Institutes of Oratory*. Trans. John Shelby Watson. Bizzell and Herzberg. 297-363.
Rabidue v. Osceola Refining Co. 805 Fed. Rep. 2d Ser. 611. 6th Cir. Ct. of Appeals. 1986.
Ramus, Petrus. *Arguments in Rhetoric against Quintilian*. Trans. Carole Newlands. Intro. James J. Murphy. Dekalb, IL: Northern Illinois U P, 1986.
Ranney, Frances J. 'What's a Reasonable Woman to Do? The Judicial Rhetoric of Sexual Harassment.' *National Women's Studies Association Journal* (Summer 1997): 1-22.
---. 'Posner on Legal Texts: Law, Literature, (Economics), and "Welcome Harassment."' *College Literature* 25 (1998): 163-183.
Reed, Thomas J. 'Training the American Aristocracy—An Historical Examination of American Legal Education Models.' *Texas Southern University Law Review* 6 (1981): 317-79.
Resnik, Judith. 'Changing the Topic.' *Cardozo Studies in Law and Literature* 8 (1996): 339-62.
Robinson v. Jacksonville Shipyards, Inc. 760 Fed Supp. 1486. U.S. Dist. Ct. (Midd. Dist. FL). 1991.
Roochnik, David. *Of Art and Wisdom: Plato's Understanding of Techné*. University Park, PA: The Pennsylvania State U P, 1996.
Rude, Carolyn D. 'The Report for Decision Making: Genre and Inquiry.' *Journal of Business and Technical Communication* 9 (1995): 170-205.
Samuels, Warren J. and Nicholas Mercuro. 'Wealth Maximization and Judicial Decision-Making: The Issues Further Clarified.' *International Review of Law and Economics* 6 (1986): 133-7.
Sarat, Austin and Thomas R. Kearns, eds. *The Rhetoric of Law*. Ann Arbor, MI: U of Michigan P, 1994.
'Sexual Harassment Claims of Abusive Work Environment Under Title VII.' *Harvard Law Review* 97 (1984): 1449-67.
Spencer v. General Electric Co. 894 Fed. 2nd 651. 4th Cir. Ct. of Appeals. 1990.
Sprat, Thomas. *History of the Royal Society*. Ed. Jackson I. Cope and Harold Whitmore Jones. St. Louis, MO: Washington University Studies, 1958.

Staton v. Maries County. 868 Fed. Rep. 2nd ser. 996. 8th Cir. Ct. of Appeals. 1989.
Sullivan, Dale L. 'Political-Ethical Implications of Defining Technical Communication as a Practice.' *Journal of Advanced Composition* 10 (1990): 375-86.
Thompson, Wayne N. '*Stasis* in Aristotle's *Rhetoric*.' *Quarterly Journal of Speech* 58 (1972): 134-41.
Torres, Arturo N. and Karen E. Harwood. 'Moving Beyond Langdell II: An Annotated Bibliography of Current Methods for Law Teaching.' *Gonzaga Law Review* 35 (1994): 1-61.
Tredennick, Hugh. Introduction. *Metaphysics: Books I – IX*, by Aristotle. Trans. Hugh Tredennick. The Loeb Classical Library. Cambridge, MS: Harvard U P, 1933.
Viner, Jacob. 'The Intellectual History of Laissez Faire.' *Journal of Legal Education* 3 (1960): 45-69.
Wanchik v. Great Lakes Health Plan, Inc. 6 Fed. Appx 252. 6th Cir. Ct. of Appeals. 2001.
Ward, Cynthia V. 'A Kinder, Gentler Liberalism? Visions of Empathy in Feminist and Communitarian Literature.' *University of Chicago Law Review* 61 (1994): 929-55.
Warnick, Barbara. 'Judgment, Probability, and Aristotle's *Rhetoric*.' *Quarterly Journal of Speech* 9 (1989): 299-311.
Weaver, Richard. *Visions of Order*. Baton Rouge, LA: Louisiana State U P, 1964.
Weisberg, Richard H. 'Law, Literature, and Cardozo's Judicial Poetics.' *Cardozo Law Review* 1 (1979): 283-342.
West, Robin. *Narrative, Authority, and Law*. Ann Arbor: U of Michigan P, 1993.
---. 'Sex, Reason, and a Taste for the Absurd.' *Georgetown Law Journal* 81 (1993): 2413-56.
---. *Caring for Justice*. NY: New York U P, 1997.
Wetlaufer, Gerald B. 'Rhetoric and Its Denial in Legal Discourse.' *Virginia Law Review* 76 (1990): 1545-97.
White v. The Money Store. 1998 U.S. Appx. Lexis 5495. 7th Cir. Ct. of Appeals. 1998.
White, James Boyd. *The Legal Imagination*. Chicago: U of Chicago P, 1985.
---. *Heracles' Bow: Essays on the Rhetoric and Poetics of the Law*. Madison, WI: U of Wisconsin P, 1985.
---. 'What Can a Lawyer Learn from Literature?' *Harvard Law Review* 102 (1989): 2014-47.
---. *Justice as Translation: An Essay in Cultural and Legal Criticism*. Chicago: U of Chicago P, 1990.
---. 'Imagining the Law.' Sarat and Kearns. 29-55.
---. *Acts of Hope: Creating Authority in Literature, Law, and Politics*. Chicago: U of Chicago P, 1994.
---. 'The Rhythms of Hope and Disappointment in the Language of Judging.' *St Johns Law Review* 70 (1996): 45-50.

Whitman, James Q. 'Why Did the Revolutionary Lawyers Confuse Custom and Reason?' *The University of Chicago Law Review* 58 (1991): 1321-68.

Winner, Langdon. *Autonomous Technology: Technics-out-of-Control as a Theme in Political Thought*. Cambridge, MS: The MIT Press, 1977.

Wilson, Richard J. 'Training for Justice: The Global Reach of Clinical Legal Education.' Penn State International Law Review 22 (2004): 421-31.

Young, Richard E. 'Concepts of Art and the Teaching of Writing.' *The Rhetorical Tradition and Modern Writing*. Ed. James J. Murphy. NY: MLA, 1982. 130-42.

Index

achreistos 30, 51
activity 33, 81
    fancy as 92
    imagination as 92
    language as 83
    and *phronesis* 142
    as *praxis* or *energeia* 35-6
agency
    individual vs. institutional 37-8
    of language and law 161-2
    in *phronesis* 100
    in *techné* 50
agency costs 73
anxiety 2, 129, 134
Aristotle
    on appearances 61, 160
    on causes 48-51, 160-163
    on *epistemé* 23-5, 54, 58
    on error 133-4
    on ethical method 16-17
    feminism and 5-8
    on justice 77-8
    misogyny of 7
    on *poiesis* 43
    on *praxis* 32-5, 38-43, 85-6
    on professionals 40
    on relationship of rhetoric to ethics 17
    on rhetoric
        as *techné* 11, 20, 113-114
        as useful 8, 167
    on rhetorical method 13
    stasis in 119-20
    on structure of soul 19
    on style 113-114
    on *techné* 44-51
    on voluntary acts 39
art
    as aesthetic 109, 142
    connection to justice 142
    as distinct from aesthetics 142
    as distinct from nature 48
    end of 50, 163
    error in 108, 133-5
    excellence in 51
    and matter 163-4
    as non-literary 4
    as production 108
    rhetoric as 16, 47
    as rhetorical 4
    and social orders 115
    as *techné* 11, 22, 108, 110
artificial 49
    language as 147-9
    style as 114
Atwill, Janet M. 2, 9, 17, 20, 50, 132, 166, 167

belief costs 78, 130, 149, 151
Blackstone, Sir William 3, 25-7, 29, 31, 55
    and legal science 26
    on property 62-4
boundaries 50-51, 108, 132-4, 163-5
burden of proof 124, 126
Burlington Industries v. Ellerth 82

Campbell, Karlyn Kohrs 9-10, 14, 132
canons 143-4, 148
    and culture 87
    feminism and 15, 101-2, 132, 139, 162
    rhetorical 132
Cardozo, Benjamin 88-9
Carr v. Allison Gas Turbine Division 81, 82, 107, 133
    economic analysis of 69-73

literary analysis of 94-9
rhetorical analysis of 121-3
rhetorical re-production of 123-9
summary of 17-18, 68-9
case method 3-4, 27, 55-7
   as scientific 3, 28
chreimata 30, 78, 167
chreisimos, rhetoric as 51, 167
Cicero 2, 17, 100, 116, 120-121
   on literature 86-7
   on style 114-117
comprehending contraries 37, 130, 138, 143, 164-6
   in *Carr v. Allison Gas Turbine Division* 152, 156-7
   and *stasis* 158
concreteness 90-92
   in *Carr v. Allison Gas Turbine Division* 95-6
   as ethical 92
consciousness 5, 7, 43, 52, 65, 81, 93, 144, 159
   and empathy 102
   and language 43
   and rhetoric 11, 17
consciousness-raising 7, 10
cost-benefit analysis 65-6
   as practical reason 140
   and values 76
cost-justified accident 65
   in *Carr v. Allison Gas Turbine Division* 72
Cover, Robert 99, 142-3
craft values 90
   in *Carr v. Allison Gas Turbine Division* 94-5, 98
craftiness 108, 133
critical self-consciousness 103-5, 131, 134, 138, 144
culture 12-14, 27, 32, 35, 38, 100-101
   economics as 51
   and ethics 103
   as high culture 101, 143, 158
   and immersion 138

   and language 81-5
   and literature 87
   and *phronesis* 99
   and texts 105
cunning intelligence, *see metis*

data 3, 28, 30-2, 55, 57-62, 73, 79, 102, 160-161
   in Aristotle 61
deception 110-112, 129, 150
   and metaphor 113
   and metis 111
   and rhetoric 110
   and Sophists 112
   and style 113
   and *techné* 114
deliberation 20, 38-42, 47, 54, 85, 92, 106, 112, 116
   as cost-benefit analysis 140
   in *techné* 133
detachment 22, 29-32, 51-2, 85, 90
   as distinct from deliberation 39
   and economics 30
   and empathy 102
   and *epistemé* 25, 29
   and experience 46
   and judicious spectator 37
   and *phronesis* 42
   as value-free 73
Dunne, Joseph 20, 35, 41-2, 45, 140

Economic Man 29, 31, 97, 152, 155-7
   in *Carr v. Allison Gas Turbine Division* 155-6
efficiency 30, 58, 63, 65-6, 70
   in *Carr v. Allison Gas Turbine Division* 73
   as distinct from efficient cause 48
   and factual issue 120
   judge-made law and 59
   and justice 146
   of law 158, 164
   and maker 49

and wealth distribution 64
and wealth maximization 51
Ellison v. Brady 1, 118-9, 136, 153
   Reasonable Woman in 155, 165
empathy 41-2, 52, 93-4, 100, 102
   in *Carr v. Allison Gas Turbine Division* 96-8
   contribution of literature to 102
   and economics 74
   as inherent in novel 36
   and judicial spectator 37
   Posner on 93-4
empeiras 30-31, 39, 131
   definition of 131
   as distinct from empiricism 32
   as experience 30, 39
energeia 35-6, 39
epistemé 16, 19, 20-21, 23-5, 53-8
   in Aristotle 24-5
   circularity of 63, 131
   and data 60-61
   as distinct from *praxis* and *poiesis* 42-5, 48-50, 107
   and the divine 29, 58
   and error 51, 108, 133
   and experience 32, 46
   and first principles 58, 62
   and language 79
   Law and Economics as 22
   legal science as 57, 73
   in Plato 23-4
   as science 25
   as useless 30-1
epistemology, feminist 76
error 108-9, 133-5, 163
   and feminism 133
   and oxymoron 165
   and rhetoric 132-3
   in *techné* 51-2, 129, 133-4, 163
error of fact in *Carr v. Allison Gas Turbine Division* 97, 122, 128, 155
ethos 100

failure, *see also* error

of market 67
techné as compatible with 51-2, 133, 163
fancy 36, 85, 92
   in *Carr v. Allison Gas Turbine Division* 97
Faragher v. City of Boca Raton 82
feminism 4-6, 14
   and Aristotle 6-8
   and case method 5-6
   and epistemology 54, 76
   and legal positivism 145
   and literature 101-2, 139
   and rhetoric 132-3
   and science 54
feminist method 15-16
first principles 24, 26, 63
   and legal science 54-64
form
   as ethical 36, 92, 96, 143, 157
   genre as 162
   and limits 163
   and matter 49, 133, 162, 164
   and meaning 149
   stasis as 110, 117, 120-21
formal cause 160-164
   Civil Rights Act as 164
   as distinct from final cause 48
   genre as 162
   language as 162
   law as 162-3
   as limit 163
   product as 162
   in *stasis* 120
four causes, Aristotle's 48-9, 108, 160-166
   in *Carr v. Allison Gas Turbine Division* 164
   in law 162
   and sexual harassment 164
   in *stasis* 120-21
Fish, Stanley 2, 42, 53, 86, 129, 144
   on critical self-consciousness 138
   language theory of 103-5
   on pragmatism 141-2

Freud, Sigmund 93, 144, 146, 154
Frye, Northrop 14, 84, 90-91
    theory applied to *Carr v. Allison Gas Turbine Division* 97-8

genres 9, 14-15, 132
    as formal cause 135, 162
    and morality 92
Gilligan, Carol 93-4, 145-7, 156
good, the 32, 42
    definition of 37
    and deliberation 39, 106
    and *praxis* 35-7, 42
    and *techné* 44
good practice
    12, 39, 41, 156-7
good practices, *see* good reasons
good reasons 11-14
    circularity of 12
Gorgias 8, 13, 46, 112-113
Gotoff, Harold C. 113-116
Grassi, Ernesto 12, 17

habit, rhetoric as 46
habit of mind 2, 16, 20-24, 38-9, 51, 106
    metis as 111
    phronesis as 33, 43
    techné as 44-5, 48
    theoria as 54
Harris v. Forklift Systems, Inc. 82, 118, 153-5, 166
    and Reasonable Woman, 153
Heidegger, Martin 21-2, 109, 115
    on Aristotle's causes 48, 160
Henson v. City of Dundee 82, 122, 125
heuristic 15-18, 110-11, 117, 134
    as distinct from hermeneutic 15
    formal cause as 160
    Nicomachean Ethics as 23
    rhetoric as 15-16
    stasis as 17, 48, 108, 110, 120-21, 124
Hirschman, Linda R. 6-7

humanities, the 83-4, 100
    and feminism 101
    history of 33-4
    Law and Literature as 33
    and *phronesis* 86
    and Sophists 35

imagination 41, 91, 93
    as bounded 86, 99
    in *Carr v. Allison Gas Turbine Division* 96-9
    and fancy 92
    judicious spectator and 37
    legal 13, 92
    and Reasonable Woman 154
    rhetoric as 110
immersion 30, 103, 106, 138
    deliberation and 44, 85-6
    empeiras and 106
    Law and Economics and 51
    Law and Literature and 32, 52
    and legal science 30
    and *phronesis* 22, 38, 41-2
    and *poiesis* 52
In a Different Voice 93-4, 156
interpretation 4, 14-15, 61, 84-5, 99-100, 103, 140, 144-5
    in Law and Literature 123, 129-30
    literary vs. legal 99
    and practical wisdom 100
    and rhetoric 17, 22, 108, 159

Jarratt, Susan C. 6, 15, 132-3
Johnson, Robert R. 20, 134, 167
judicious spectator 37-8, 96, 102
    in *Carr v. Allison Gas Turbine Division* 96-7
jurisprudence 137-47
justice
    and adjudication 146
    Aristotle's theory of 77
    in *Carr v. Allison Gas Turbine Division* 77-8
    and distribution of wealth 64, 74

as emotive utterance 76
as final cause 163, 165
Carol Gilligan's theory of 93-4, 146-7
Law and Economics on 53, 64, 76-7, 79-80
male and female sense of 93-4
phronesis and 40
relationship to language 4, 102, 136-7, 147-52, 158
relationship to law 5, 138, 165-6

Kalimtzis, Kostas 120-21
Kennedy, George A. 19-20

Langdell, Christopher Columbus 3-4, 27-31, 51, 55, 58-61
and legal science 27
role in development of case method 56
Langdellian method, *see* case method
language
as activity 33, 40, 81, 137-8, 142
and Aristotle's four causes 160-161
in *Carr v. Allison Gas Turbine Division* 68, 77-8, 82, 95, 98, 129
as culture 38, 42, 83
and deliberation 85
and *epistemé* 79
as free market 78
and limits 109, 117, 131, 135
as material cause 52, 164
as matter 49, 115
and *metis* 111
remaking 131, 134
and rhetoric 11, 17, 55, 57, 116, 129-30, 159
and silence 85
and *stasis* 121
language beliefs
and instrumentalism 53, 79
relationship to legal theory 5-6, 18, 57, 86, 102-6, 136-7, 147-52, 158, 165-7
tool-use (windowpane) theory 78-9, 161
law
and Aristotle's four causes 162-3
as humanities 33
as imperative 38
as science 3-4
Law and Economics 4-5, 29
critiques of 74-6
and distribution of wealth 63-4, 76
as *epistemé* 21
and Frye's anatomy 91, 97
and justice 83, 146
language beliefs of 102
Posner's role in 53, 57
as pragmatism 22-3
as science 32
Law and Literature 5, 32, 82-4
as aesthetic 101
as art 32
contrast to Law and Economics 22, 32
as exemplar of humanities 33
and feminism 101
as impractical 36-7
as interpretive 129-30, 145
and language 102
on legal outcomes 40
as *phronesis* 33
as practice 85
as *praxis* 22-3
rhetoric and 129
as sophistic 34-5
as subversive 32
White's role in 88
legal art 4, 22
legal outcomes 26, 105-6, 110, 120, 147, 152, 157-8
as final cause 165
as justice 163
legal positivism 91, 145, 151-2

legal science 3-4, 21, 23, 25-30, 35, 54-7, 74, 77, 79
   as *epistemé* 30-31, 73, 80
   method of 58-61
liberal arts 20, 34-5
   rhetoric and 2
limits 50, 108, 130-132, 163
   boundaries as 50, 165
   language as source of 103, 135
   and limitations 163
   and materials 133
   and *metis* 111
   and *techné* 133-4
literary method 14, 32, 85
literary properties 89-91
Literary Woman 152, 157
   in *Carr v. Allison Gas Turbine Division* 156
literature
   as ethical 105
   as humanizing 36
   as representative of humanities 33
   value of 86-9
Locke, John 55
   on language 116
   on property 62-3

MacKinnon, Catherine A. 1, 18, 134, 164-5
making 142
   as calculative 54
   and deliberation 44
   and doing 49-50
   law as 54
man of letters 37, 89, 148, 151
material cause, *see also* matter 160
matter
   and form 48-50, 162
   language as 49, 162, 164
   in rhetoric 50, 113-114, 164
   and style 115
   subject matter
      in *epistemé* 58
      of law 60-61

   of rhetoric 112, 159
   of science 29
   and *techné* 133, 163
   words as 6, 86
Meritor Savings Bank v. Vinson 82, 118, 122, 125, 128, 165
metaphor 91-3
   Aristotle on 113
   in *Carr v. Allison Gas Turbine Division* 150
   and empathy 100, 157
   Literary Woman as 157
   Reasonable Woman as 157, 165
   stasis as 117
   techné as 111
metis 107-8, 111, 133
More, Thomas 116

New Criticism 14, 37, 84, 102, 143
Nicomachean Ethics as heuristic structure 22
Nussbaum, Martha C. 5, 32, 83
   on Adam Smith's judicious spectator 37
   on Aristotle 6-7, 40-42
   on *Carr v. Allison Gas Turbine Division* 96-7, 150
   on cost-benefit analysis 74-5
   on empathy 102
   on ethical value of literature 85, 92-3, 96, 100
   on fancy 36, 92
   language theory of 103
   literary theory of 91-2
   on *phainomena* 16, 61, 103, 160
   on Plato 23-4

Odysseus 111
oxymoron 122, 127-9, 143, 165

Pantazakos, Michael 33-5, 88
Pareto principle 70-71, 140
peirata and *peras* 50, 108, 117, 131, 163, 165
phainomena 16, 61, 79, 103, 160

phronesis 16, 17, 33
   as circular 22, 39-42, 50, 86, 106, 131
   and culture 38, 99
   as distinct from *techné* 20-21, 43-5
   as distinct from *theoria* 85
   and error 51
   and immersion 22
   as instrumental 40-41
   knowledge in 40
   Law and Literature as 33, 85
   and pragmatism 22
plain style 114, 116-117
Plato 6, 8, 20, 77, 109, 111-112, 120, 132
   on rhetoric 46, 113
   on *techné* 20-24
poiesis 2, 16, 19, 43, 48, 107-8
   as distinct from *epistemé* 49
   as distinct from *praxis* 19-20, 43-4
   and failure 52
   as making 49
   as production 21
   rhetoric as 86, 129
Posner, Richard
   on Aristotle and feminism 7
   on Blackstone 29
   on choice 59
   on cost-benefit analysis 66
   on craft values 90
   on data 59-61
   and detachment 31, 39, 51
   economic theory of sexual harassment 67
   on empathy 93-4
   on first principles 58, 62
   jurisprudence of 137, 139-42
   on Langdell 29
   language theory of 79, 102-3, 148-50, 152, 161
   as libertarian 141
   literary theory of 36-7, 89-90
   method of 59
   as pragmatist 141
   on property 62, 64
   on rhetoric 8, 130, 151, 164
   on sexual preference 75
   on value neutrality 39, 76
   on wealth maximization 65
   on welcome harassment 17-18, 122
power
   in *Carr v. Allison Gas Turbine Division* 70-71, 123
   and knowledge 76
   of language 105, 111, 148, 167
   law as 38, 99-100, 104, 142, 145, 148
   sexual 68, 77
   in *stasis* 120
practical reason 22, 24, 40-41, 61, 140-141
pragmatism 76, 140-142
   Law and Economics as 22-3
praxis 16, 19, 85-6
   connection to the good 35-6, 39
   as circular 39-42, 49-50, 131
   and culture 85
   as distinct from *energeia* 35-6
   as distinct from pragmatism 22-3
   and error 51, 108, 133
   literary analysis as 22, 84
Pro Archia 86-7, 114
production 4, 15-17, 19, 21, 45, 48, 52, 54, 86, 107-108
   rhetoric as 129, 134, 159
   techné as 21, 43
professionalism 4, 11, 28, 37-8, 79, 81, 83, 90, 104, 105-6, 112, 116, 122, 134, 145, 161-2
   Aristotle on 40
property 62-5
   Aristotle on 64
   Blackstone on 62-3
   in *Carr v. Allison Gas Turbine Division* 68, 72, 196-7
   Locke on 62
   Posner on 64

psyche 19-20

Rabidue v. Osceola Refining Co. 82, 118, 125, 127, 136, 153-4
Ramus, Peter 2, 55, 87, 116
rationality
 in *Carr* 70
 economic 29, 55, 57, 65, 70, 74, 155-6
 formula as 49
 justice as 146
 means-end 140
 narrative 13
 Reasonable Woman and 156-7
 sexual activity as 146
 wealth maximization as 64
Reasonable Man 1, 136, 153
Reasonable Person 72, 96, 98, 136, 150, 153-5
Reasonable Woman 1, 136-7, 152-8, 164
 in *Carr v. Allison Gas Turbine Division* 155-6
 in *Ellison v. Brady* 1, 155
 as form 165
 as legal standard 153
 as metaphor 157
 as oxymoron 165
 as point of *stasis* 164-5
 in *Rabidue v. Osceola Refining Co.* 154
 in *Staton v. Maries County* 154
reasonableness 79, 137, 154-5, 166
rhetoric
 as art 4
 as art of persuasion 10, 16
 as belief cost 130
 definitions of 10-11, 159-60
 as ethical 12-13, 167
 and ethics 8-9
 and feminism 7-10, 14-16, 132-3
 as heuristic rather than hermeneutic 15-16, 123-4
 history of 2-3
 and justice 8, 112, 113
 and language 5
 as mixture of productive and practical 20
 as *praxis* 21
 as productive 20, 123
 as property of literature 129
 relationship to law 2-3, 54-5, 110, 112
 relationship to truth and justice 9
 and style 110, 117
 as *techné* 17, 46-8, 113
 as useful 51-2, 167
Rhetoric, Aristotle's *Art of* 46-8, 113-114
rhetorical argument 87, 130
 as distinct from legal argument 122, 128-9
rhetorical criticism, *see* rhetorical method
rhetorical method 11-16
 and literary method 12, 16
Roochnik, David 20, 23, 109-110, 112, 134, 163, 167

sexual ends 66
 sociable 68-70
sexual harassment 18
 as altering employment conditions 82
 definitional *stasis* in 118, 125, 164
 economic theory of 66-7
 and intent 96
 legal standard in *Carr v. Allison Gas Turbine Division* 71-2
 as market abuse 67, 73
 qualitative *stasis* in 118-119, 123, 125-6
 Reasonable Person standard 96
 Reasonable Woman standard 153-5
 and unwelcomeness 68
 and welcome harassment 122
shop talk 82-3, 106, 123, 126, 128

Sophists
  Aristotle on 46, 113
  feminism and 6, 132
  as humanists 34-5
  and law 112
  and Law and Literature 35
  and *metis* 111
  as professionals 112
  as rhetoricians 35, 87, 111-112
  and *techné* 109, 111-112
soul, *see psyche*
Spencer v. General Electric Co. 82
stasis 17, 48, 108, 110-111, 164-5
  in Aristotle 119-21
  and Aristotle's four causes 120
  connection of political and rhetorical 121
  of definition 118, 123, 125
  as element of burden of proof 124
  of fact 122, 124
  of jurisdiction or translation 119, 122, 126
  as political disease 120
  of quality 118-19, 123, 125-6
  Reasonable Woman as point of 158, 164
  summary of 117-20
stochastic, *techné* as 111, 113
style 110
  Aristotle on 113
  Cardozo on 88
  Cicero on 114-115
  as political 114
  Posner on 84, 143, 148-9
  rhetoric as 2, 87, 89-90, 93, 109, 110, 116-117
  as *techné* 113-114
  as technology 115

techné 2, 11
  as art 108
  and boundaries 50, 108
  as craft 111
  as distinct from *epistemé* 23, 45-6
  as distinct from *phronesis* 44-5
  as distinct from technology 21, 49, 115
  end of 48
  and error 51, 136, 163
  as ethical 167
  and failure 163
  history of 109-12
  and limits 50, 133
  as making 49-50
  Plato on 20-24
  and separability of products 132, 134
  techné 1 and 2 110, 112-113
  and tools 131
  translation of 109
theoria 16, 21, 23, 39, 40, 85, 138
  as habit of mind of *epistemé* 24, 54
tool
  language as 5, 53, 78-9, 81, 137, 159-61, 166
  law as 166
  rhetoric as 9
tools 108
  boundaries and 106, 108, 163
  in *Carr v. Allison Gas Turbine Division* 68, 72, 78, 95, 133, 155, 165
  neutrality and 79
  techné and 131-3

unwelcome harassment 18, 122, 125, 127
unwelcomeness in *Carr* 71, 127
useless
  aesthetic as 144
  epistemé as 31, 47, 51, 54
  legal science as 58, 79
  theoria as 86
  as value-free 30, 51, 73

value neutrality 30-31, 42, 76

violence
  law as 100, 142-3
voluntary acts 39, 77
voluntary choice 36, 145
voluntary error 51, 132, 163
voluntary failure 52

wealth, distribution of 30, 53, 63-4, 74, 76
wealth maximization 30, 51, 59-60, 74-5, 77
  in *Carr v. Allison Gas Turbine Division* 69-72, 80
  as ethical 65-70, 139-40
Weaver, Richard 12
welcome harassment 17-18, 68-9, 77, 109, 122, 124-5, 127-9, 158, 165-6
West, Robin 5, 32, 83
  on art 130, 142
  on culture 101
  on empathy 102
  on Frye's anatomy 90-91
  jurisprudence of 138-9, 144-6
  language theory of 103, 148, 161-2, 166
  on Law and Economics 97
  on law as imperative 38, 99
  literary theory of 90-91
  on Literary Woman 156-7
  on positivism 151
  on preferences 75
White, James Boyd 5, 22, 32
  on activity 33
  on art 130, 142
  on comprehending contraries 37, 143, 157
  conflation of literary and rhetorical 130
  on culture 3, 42, 83, 158
  on economics 63
  on fidelity 138, 143
  jurisprudence of 142-4
  language theory of 79, 103, 147-8, 152, 162
  on law
    as language 6
    as humanities 36
    as power 38
    as rhetoric 64
  legal imagination 92, 98
  on legal outcomes 105
  literary theory of 92-3
  on rhetoric 13, 130
  on translation 103, 138
willingness to pay 65-6
  in *Carr v. Allison Gas Turbine Division* 71-3
workplace 67, 81-82, 108, 153, 165-6